Love, Honor
&
Cherish

Also by the author:

One Life to Live:
Thirty Years of Memories

Love, Honor & Cherish

The Greatest Wedding Moments from All My Children, General Hospital, and One Life to Live

Gary Warner

abc
daytime
press

HYPERION
New York

Library of Congress Cataloging-in-Publication Data

Warner, Gary
Love, honor and cherish: the greatest wedding moments from
All my children, General Hospital, and One life to live / by Gary Warner.—1st ed.
p. cm.
ISBN 0-7868-6368-4
1. Soap operas—United States. 2. Weddings on television. I. Title.
PN1992.8.S4W37 1998
791.45'6—dc21   98-4406
                                            CIP

Book design by Christine Weathersbee

First Edition

1 3 5 7 9 10 8 6 4 2

Acknowledgments

I applaud the talented writers who penned the romantic words which illuminate the cherished love stories featured in this book. Most especially, I offer boundless praise to Agnes Nixon, Lorraine Broderick, Megan McTavish, Wisner Washam, Claire Labine, Pat Falken Smith, Douglas Marland, Bob Guza, Peggy O'Shea, Gordon Russell, and Michael Malone.

I wish to acknowledge several key ABC Daytime executives—President Pat Fili-Krushel, Angela Shapiro, Marjorie Rodgers, Gail Silverman, Molly Fowler, Randi Subarsky, and Harriet Abraham, for their assistance in the completion of this book. In addition, I extend my appreciation to staff members Danielle Zeitlen, Rosalie Macaluso, Jennifer Kriegel, Sue Johnson, Michele Vicario, and Marilyn Orrico.

My special appreciation to the writers assistants at the ABC soaps. Ron Carlivati, Rodney Christopher, Dave Goldschmid, and Nathan Fissell, who helped me with their own expertise.

I heap endless praise upon ABC's photography department, most especially Ann Limongello, the resident on-set photographer and archivist, as well as Brent Peterson, Jill Yager, Peter Murray, Michelle Mustacchio, Ann Ferrell, Ida Mae Astute, and Maria Melin.

I never could have have made my deadlines without the support of my research assistants Donna Hornak and Andrea Rothstein, and my team of experts which included Robert Schork, Connie Passalacqua, and Nancy Mattia.

I extend my appreciation to Joanne Berg, Tim Lund, Ravi Chandran, Elizabeth Korte, Carolyn Hinsey and her fellow editors at *Soap Opera Digest*, Amie Baker, Sharon Spaeth, Stacy Balter, and Jane Elliot for their valuable assistance.

My gratitude to the publishing team at Hyperion. Editor (and new mom) Gretchen Young, her assistant Jennifer Morgan, and the superb design team of Claudyne Bedell and Christine Weathersbee.

Finally, I offer my fondest thanks to the many other individuals who lent their time, talents, and expertise to the making of this one-of-a-kind salute to the glorious state of soap opera matrimony. Enjoy.

CONTENTS

Fairy-tale Weddings

❧ ❧ ❧

And the Bride Wore . . .

Weddings That Weren't . . .

Traditions
∞ ∞ ∞

Wild Weddings — Marital Mayhem
∞ ∞ ∞

Loveless Weddings
∾ ∾ ∾

Vintage Weddings— Bride and Joy!
∾ ∾ ∾

One Life to Live   228

All My Children   245

∝ ∝ ∝

∞ ∞ ∞

Fairy-tale Weddings

On the soaps, love is written in the stars. Kismet doesn't strike often, but when it does, the consequences can be dramatic. The gods must have been smiling on the day destiny united these star-crossed lovers in holy matrimony . . .

General Hospital

Duke Lavery and Anna Devane

October 16, 1987

Those eyes. That face. Those lips! Police Chief Anna Devane got more than she bargained for when she inadvertently dropped her scarf during the annual policeman's charity ball. As she stood at the bar for a drink, up strolled a dashing, mysterious stranger to return her missing garment. When he opened his mouth to speak, Anna learned that in addition to his handsome looks and charm, he was a Scotsman to boot! Duke and Anna tangoed on the dance floor before admiring onlookers, and they experienced an electric, instant attraction toward each other. But little did Anna know that the sincerity of their attraction was one-sided. Duke Lavery, upstanding nightclub owner and dockworker's union executive—actually was working for "the organization"—the Port Charles mob.

Under orders from his superiors, Duke romanced the police chief to keep her preoccupied while the mob worked to take over the port city. By the time Duke realized that he was falling in love with Miss Devane for real, he was so thoroughly

It took several tries before Duke Lavery, attired in traditional Scottish garb (right down to the tassels on his socks) made it to the altar with his lady love Anna Devane (top). In 1986 he tangoed his way into the life of supercop Anna. At first, she doubted the sincerity of the mysterious Scotsman, who kept many secrets, including the fact that he was connected to the Port Charles mob.

and inextricably ensconced in the organization, he knew that merely walking away from it would quickly put his life—as well as Anna's and her daughter, Robin's—in jeopardy. Desperate, Duke turned to one of the organization's top brass, fellow Scotsman Angus McKay, and confessed his true feelings for Miss Devane. Angus promised Duke that he would be free to leave the organization in six weeks—and gave Duke his ring as a symbol of his promise.

Confident that his shady past would soon be behind him, a carefree Duke looked forward to his new life with the woman he loved. Meanwhile, Anna and her co-chief of police, Bert Ramsey, had been growing concerned about the increasing level of mob-related activity in Port Charles. Rumors and suspicions ran wild, especially where Duke was concerned. It didn't make matters any better that Duke was evasive when it came to divulging all the whos, whats, wheres, and whens of his past to his future wife. But despite the glaring number of "gaps" in her beau's past, Anna turned a blind eye to the truth, allowing instead her heart to give Duke the benefit of the doubt. But things took a turn for the worse when Anna's life was threatened on more than one occasion—most notably by a bombing of her home—by Damon, one of Duke's immediate superiors, who was hostile to Duke's desire to leave the organization. This prompted Anna's ex-husband, former police commissioner

and World Security Bureau (WSB) agent Robert Scorpio, to return to Port Charles to find out who tried to kill the mother of his child. With Scorpio now on the case, the mob started to run scared, and tensions escalated. Scorpio took an immediate dislike to Lavery and tried in vain to

Despite her engagement to Duke, Anna remained close to her ex-husband, Robert Scorpio, who was not in favor of her budding relationship with the shady Scotsman (top). Anna beamed with joy after finally marrying Duke in a traditional Scottish ceremony. Their union survived Anna's miscarriage, Duke's infidelity and mob involvement, Anna's kidnapping by the deranged Grant Putnam, and the interference of Anna's ex-husband, Robert Scorpio, and Duke's ex-girlfriend, Camellia. Duke and Anna invited all of Port Charles to attend the nuptials, which featured bagpipe players, Scottish dancers, a kilt-wearing bridegroom, and a bedazzling bride, who was given away by her ex-husband, Robert (bottom).

convince his "ex" to see Duke for who he really was. When Duke realized that the mob was not about to keep its promise to free him from its clutches, he prepared a package of evidence and arranged a meeting with Bert Ramsey, Anna's co-chief of police, preparing to turn himself in and turn state's evidence. Little did Duke know that Ramsey was none other than Mr. Big, the local head of Duke's organization!

Ramsey pulled his service revolver on Duke in an attempt to silence him, and Ramsey was shot with his own gun. A horrified Anna and Robert arrested Duke for shooting a man they thought was an honest cop. In a poignant scene in the interrogation room, all the cards were laid out on the table when Duke revealed his mob involvement to Anna—including the painful truth that the mob originally had ordered him to propose to Anna! A tearful Anna threw her engagement ring across the table. Scorpio checked into Duke's claims that Ramsey was actually a crooked cop and, to his horror, discovered that his old partner was indeed working for the mob. Scorpio engineered a complex plan to bring down the mob and nail Ramsey, and Duke offered to help. In the ensuing melée, two hit men then attempted to take out Scorpio, but Duke intervened and took a bullet meant for Robert. Duke survived but suffered temporary paralysis. For his heroic efforts, Duke received a reduced sentence, and Anna promised to stand by her man.

"I don't want you to think about the past," Duke told his lady love before being carted off to jail. "I don't want you to even think about the present. Just concentrate on the future. When I get paroled, you and I are going to get married. We'll take Robin and we'll go to Scotland."

But still more secrets from Duke's ominous past would soon threaten their happiness: namely sister Camellia McKay, Duke's former love! Camellia and Duke shared many secrets, including the fact that Angus was their father, making them half siblings! Eager finally to end the vendetta between his family and the rival Jerome family, Angus agreed to drink poison and kill himself in prison. Duke was soon paroled, and convinced Anna not to investigate

The lilting sound of Scottish bagpipes filled the autumn air as Duke and Anna became man and wife (above). The kilted groom proudly struck a pose with his handsome wedding party. From left: Jake Meyer, Sean Donely, Dr. Tom Hardy, Dr. Tony Jones, Dr. Patrick O'Connor (right).

A stylish wedding ceremony provided a fitting conclusion to Duke and Anna's courtship. They were a fabled couple in so many ways ... Anna Devane with her lilting English accent, long auburn hair, and graceful demeanor, brought a sense of elegance to Port Charles. She was a perfect match for Duke Lavery, with his Scottish brogue, chiseled features, and elegant sense of style.

Angus's death—or risk exposing the "secret of L'Orleans." As Duke and Anna prepared to walk down the aisle, troubled Camellia learned that she and Duke weren't really siblings after all—prompting her to attempt a reconciliation with him. When Duke rejected her advances, Camellia set out to break up Anna and Duke with the help of investigative reporter Mark Carlin, who went to press with the story headlined POLICE CHIEF TO MARRY MAN WHO COVERED UP MURDER. The murder was that of Evan Jerome, whom Camellia killed in self-defense after Evan attempted to rape her. Duke and Angus buried Evan in the garden and hid the murder to prevent a mob war. That was the secret of L'Orleans!

A horrified Anna stood at the altar at Duke's club on their wedding day as a gaggle of press barged in to confront the couple. That was enough for Anna—the wedding was off! The ensuing scandal forced Anna not to only give up the man she loved but also her job as police chief. It would take many, many months of work on Duke's part to regain Anna's trust and affection. The turning point came at Mount Rushmore, when Duke saved Anna's life during a dangerous WSB caper. Before long Duke and Anna reconciled. Duke slipped a diamond ring on Anna's finger. "This time it's forever," he whispered as they made new plans to wed—at last!

DUKE AND ANNA'S WEDDING VOWS

DUKE
Anna, I love Robin as sincerely as I love you. You're both my very special family. I'd like to quote some Scottish literature if I can get it out! Our love is a circle. It has no end. That is my solemn vow.

ANNA
For you, Duke, I'll stay within that circle. And I pledge you my eternal love. That is my solemn vow to you.

PRIEST
Now that Duke and Anna have given themselves to each other by solemn vows, joining of hands, and the giving and receiving of rings, I pronounce that they are man and wife, in the name of the Father, the Son, and the Holy Spirit. What God hath joined together, let no one put asunder. Amen. Now, Duke, you may kiss the bride.

DUKE
At last!

SHARE A ROMANTIC RENDEZVOUS IN THE SCOTTISH HIGHLANDS

Duke Lavery returned to his roots when he whisked his new bride, Anna, to Scotland for their 1987 honeymoon. Though the scenes were actually taped at the Disney Ranch in California, you can experience the windswept moors, soaring mountains, breathtaking coastline, and cozy inns on your own trip to the area known as the Scottish Highlands. The northern Highlands' stark landscape is particularly dramatic, often described as the last wilderness area of Europe. Inverness, considered the capital of the Highlands, is a particularly popular area, thanks in part to the Loch Ness "monster."

When to go: Mid-April to mid-October; the Scottish Highlands reach their peak in the fall.

What to do: Head to Cawdor Castle, a fourteenth-century structure featured in *Macbeth*; Culloden Moor, a famous battlefield (now re-created) where Bonnie Prince Charlie's army was defeated by George II's troops in 1746.

Romantic rendezvous: The road down the south side of Loch Ness offers splendid forest walks near Inverfarigaig and a spectacular waterfall at Foyers, along with impressive views over the loch.

Stepping out at night: There's nothing better than spending an evening at a local pub. Talk about atmosphere!

Duke and Anna in the Scottish Highlands

For more information: The British Tourist Authority has branches in Los Angeles, New York, Chicago, and Atlanta.

> *Our love is a circle. It has no end.*
> *That is my solemn vow.*
> *—Duke Lavery*

Robert Scorpio and Anna Lavery

June 28, 1991

Whoever said love is better the second time around certainly had Robert Scorpio and Anna Devane in mind. The dashing European duo first met when they were working as spies for the World Security Bureau (WSB). Partners on many a dangerous assignment, Robert and Anna grew closer to one another as they survived each hair-raising caper. But their love for one another faced a mighty obstacle: The WSB has a strict rule forbidding agents to marry. Undaunted by their employer's stern mandate, Robert and Anna secretly married in a romantic outdoor ceremony in Italy—and kept their marriage a secret from their superior, the cunning WSB Chief Sean Donely. Little did they know that their boss was onto their secret wedding—not to mention Anna's secret sideline: as a double agent for the enemy organization, the DVX!

Robert had no idea that his bride was a double agent working for the other side. Desperate to preserve both of his agents, Sean set them up by assigning Robert to

What could be more romantic than a wedding in June? Perhaps a wedding in which the bride and groom, forced apart in the past by betrayal, feel that this time fate has brought them back together. Despite heartbreak, doubt, and one prior divorce, Robert and Anna's love inevitably reunited them. Their designer friend Delfina planned every distinctive detail of Robert and Anna's wedding—a traditional English afternoon ceremony held in the Quartermaine Shakespearean Gardens (above). In honor of Anna's English heritage, her bridesmaids, Felicia Jones, Bobbie Jones, and Tiffany Hill Donely, were outfitted in an Edwardian Ascot look, reminiscent of My Fair Lady. Anna's cherished friends wore gowns fashioned from soft green netting over full petticoats (left).

The Quartermaine family's lush Shakespearean gardens were abloom with gorgeous flowers for the festivities. The tasteful garden area contained plants and flowers that were cultivated in English gardens during Shakespeare's time and also were mentioned in his plays. Poppies, pansies, violets, carnations, rosemary, daffodils, iris, roses, columbines, crocuses, and marigolds blazed with breathtaking color as Robert, attired in a gray morning suit, eagerly awaited the arrival of his bride (left). The bride wore a dusty rose tea gown made of Chantilly lace to the traditional English country afternoon wedding. Her hat, made of tulle and straw, presented a distinctly turn-of-the-century flair for this celebration of love (right).

"root out the mole" in their ranks—hoping that Robert's discovery of his wife's treachery would break up their marriage. Little did Robert know that the mole he was looking for was sharing his bed! Scorpio was dismayed to discover that his new wife was a fraud! However, his love for Anna prevented him from revealing her duplicity to Sean, who mistakenly executed an innocent agent. Anguished and bitter, Scorpio made Anna promise she would get a divorce and stay out of his life.

The glorious wedding day was not without its harrowing moments. Blinded by searing visions of her father's fatal shooting, Dominique Taub grabbed

a guard's pistol and prepared to fire! Believing she was protecting Anna, Dominique turned the gun on the baffled best man, Mac Scorpio. Fortunately, Mac soothed Dominique and coaxed her back to reality (left). After years of separation, Mac Scorpio mended fences with his brother, Robert, and proudly served as his best man (right).

A remorseful Anna willingly agreed, and the two went their separate ways, burying this secret in their past. Imagine Robert's surprise when, years later, Anna shows up on his doorstep in Port Charles with the five-year-old daughter he never knew he had! After Anna and Robert parted company, Anna learned she was pregnant, and raised the child, Robin, on her own—telling the girl she was "Love," a family friend. Anna first came to Port Charles seemingly to cause trouble for Robert, who now was happily married to Holly Sutton and was the town's police commissioner. Anna's beautiful face still bore the horrific scars from the explosion that had caused their marriage to "explode." But Robert soon learned that Anna's scars were fake—she had been wearing them all these years as penance for her sins. As Anna cast away her faux scars, she cast away much of her darker side as well, revealing her sensitive, caring nature. Robert and Anna swiftly resolved their past differences and forged a platonic friendship for the benefit of their daughter, Robin. Robert left Port Charles for a brief time to live in Australia with his wife, Holly, but returned to town soon after Holly perished in a tragic plane crash, resuming his old role as the town's top cop. While it was clear to all who knew them that Robert and Anna still loved each other very much, the

Sean Donely proudly escorted Anna down the aisle in the traditional wedding, which in its exquisite garden setting was strictly a high-fashion affair.

two remained the strictest of platonic friends for years, helping one another through their various personal tragedies and failed relationships—including Anna's second marriage to reformed mobster Duke and Robert's failed romances with a series of women.

When not consoling each other for their personal heartache, Robert and Anna teamed up time and again for new espionage capers with their old pal and boss, Sean—while still raising their daughter, Robin. These years of shared emotional experiences, tragedies, and triumphs had slowly weakened the defenses of the duo, but the stubborn ex-spies refused to admit their feelings for one another, causing Robert to lambaste Anna for being an "old hag" and "frump." Scorned by Robert's hurtful remarks, Anna set out to prove to her ex that she wasn't just a washed-up old maid. The night of

Robin's Valentine's Day dance recital Anna made her move, by sliding her leg up and down Robert's as they sat in the darkened recital hall. Turned on, Robert fell for Anna's bait hook, line, and sinker. Anna led Robert up to his apartment, where in a kinky round of foreplay, she tied a hot and bothered Robert to a pole. But it was Anna who had the last laugh, when she pulled the plug on her scheme, gave Robert a stern tongue-lashing for accusing her of being an old maid, and poured a pitcher of ice water over his shirtless body—and leaving him there, tied up for the night, to ponder what had happened!

Robert and Anna—two people who gave full meaning to the words "charming," "elegant," and "sophisticated"—tenderly reaffirmed their love and reunited with their daughter Robin, as a family. Robert and Anna's love theme, "All in Love is Fair," punctuated the memorable wedding to end all weddings.

Once their egos got out of the way, Robert and Anna finally consummated their reconciliation—right in the middle of an earthquake! "The earth really moved," said Anna, unaware that the aftershocks were real and not man-made. Years after they discovered their love in Italy, Robert and Anna were together again—and soon to be man and wife.

Wedding Styles

a formal wedding typically is attended by one hundred or more guests and may take place in a church, hotel, or restaurant. The daytime version takes place before 6:00 P.M. The bride wears either a long dress and train with a veil that complements the dress or a shorter dress with a detachable train and veil. The groom will look dapper in a gray stroller (or morning coat), vest, and striped trousers. The evening bride's outfit is similar to the daytime bride's except that her dress is definitely long. The groom goes classic in a black tuxedo.

ROBERT AND ANNA'S WEDDING VOWS
A Traditional English Country Afternoon Wedding Ceremony

MINISTER
Friends, we are gathered together in the sight of God to bless this joining of Robert Scorpio and Anna Devane. What makes this such a joyous occasion is that Robert and Anna today are reaffirming their love and reuniting themselves as a family. I ask you now in the presence of God and these people to declare your intention to enter into union with one another: Anna, will you have Robert to be your husband, to live together in holy marriage? Will you love him, comfort him, honor and keep him in sickness and in health, and, forsaking all others, be faithful to him as long as you both shall live?

ANNA
I will.

MINISTER
*Robert, will you take Anna to be your wife, to live together in holy marriage?
Will you love her, comfort her, honor and keep her in sickness and in health, and,
forsaking all others, be faithful to her as long as you both shall live?*

ROBERT
I will.

MINISTER
*Let us pray. Eternal God, creator and preserver of all life, giver of all grace:
Bless and sanctify with your Holy Spirit Robert and Anna, who come now to join in marriage.
Grant that they may give their vows to each other in the strength of your steadfast love.
Enable them to grow in love and peace with you and with one another all their days. . . . Amen.
You may join hands and exchange your vows.*

(Robert and Anna join hands and face each other.)

ROBERT
*I, Robert, take you, Anna, to be my wife, to have and to hold from this day forward,
for better for worse, for richer for poorer, in sickness and in health, to love and to cherish,
until death do us part. This is my solemn vow.*

ANNA
*I, Anna, take you, Robert, to be my husband, to have and to hold from this day forward,
for better for worse, for richer for poorer, in sickness and in health, to love and to cherish,
until death do us part. This is my solemn vow.*

MINISTER
You may exchange rings now. The rings, please.
(Whispers to Robert)
With this ring, I thee wed . . .

ROBERT
With this ring, I thee wed . . .
(He puts ring on her finger. Minister nods to Anna.)

ANNA
With this ring, I thee wed . . .

MINISTER
(Placing a hand on their joined hands)
I now pronounce you man and wife. Those who God has joined together, let no one put asunder.

(Robert and Anna kiss, music starts up, and they walk
down the aisle under a canopy of spears.)

SEAN DONELY'S TOAST

SEAN

*Unaccustomed as I am to public speaking, today I must make an exception.
That's because my best friend . . . my long-time buddy . . . a man that I cherish
and always will . . . got married today. To a lovely lady I've also known for a very
long time. To Robert and Anna . . . a long and happy life. This has been a long time
in coming. (to Robert) Let me tell you something, buddy, it was worth waiting for!*

MAC'S "BEST MAN" TOAST

MAC

*As Robert's brother, and best man, I want to propose a toast—to Anna.
You know better than anyone what you're getting into. I mean, I grew up with Robert.
He was not an easy boy to live with. So, folks, don't think—now that he's matured—
it'll be a romp in the surf. It's not that he's not easy. It's that he's . . . difficult.
Or to put it another way . . . he's impossible!*

ROBERT

With friends like these . . .

MAC

*Anna, however, seems to have a rather amazing effect on my brother.
Softened him up a bit . . . turned him into a guy that even a brother can love.
(Turns back to Robert)
And I do love you, Robert. You, too, Anna. Congratulations!*

Anna
Will the rest of our days be as exciting as this one?

Robert
All I know is life with you will never be dull.

Untraditional Sites

ABC soap couples have become man and wife in some rather inventive locales. The first time that Robert Scorpio married Anna Devane, they tied the knot in a group ceremony held in the center of a quaint Italian piazza. Adam Chandler and Gloria Marsh sealed their vows aboard a luxury yacht on the high seas. If you want a wedding that proves what a creative and totally original couple you and your fiancé are, consider exchanging I dos in an untraditional place. From the top of a mountain to the bottom of an ocean, ceremony and reception locales have expanded beyond churches, synagogues, and Morty's Banquet Hall.

When considering an unusual site, though, make sure it's appropriate for the style of wedding you want (informal, formal), the number of guests you're planning to invite, the style of menu you're considering (lunch buffet, seated dinner, afternoon tea), the time of year you intend to get married, and your budget. If the locale is outdoors, you'll also want to have a backup indoor location on reserve in case the weather turns inclement. Some atypical places to exchange vows:

- airplane
- aquarium
- art gallery
- baseball field
- farm
- glacier
- ice-skating rink
- lighthouse
- museum
- roller coaster
- riverboat
- ski slope
- theater
- train station
- vineyard
- zoo

Robert and Anna married in a group ceremony held in an Italian piazza.

Frisco Jones
and
Felicia Cummings
June 20, 1986

*F*ate has a strange way of bringing star-crossed lovers together. The day that rock-and-roll singer Andrew "Frisco" Jones caught a pesky thief sneaking into his bedroom proved to be a day of destiny. Little did he know that the boy he captured was actually a beautiful young lady named Felicia Cummings. She would soon become the "lady of his heart."

Descended from Mexican royalty, Felicia Cummings was an Aztec princess who was in hot pursuit of the key to her royal heritage—a missing family treasure. Frisco thought the ring he had purchased was a little piece of costume jew-

Mr. and Mrs. Andrew Jones (above). In one of many of Frisco and Felicia's dangerous adventures, they managed to uncover a money laundering operation being run out of a traveling three-ring circus. Disguised as circus workers, the lovers discovered that the operation was headed by corrupt Police Chief Ramsey. (left). Felicia fainted upon seeing her not-so-late husband Frisco, who returned from the dead on the day she married another man, Colton Shore (right).

elry, not realizing it was actually part of a priceless trove of Aztec treasure that Felicia wanted back. Even though Frisco scoffed at Felicia's outrageous story, he found her mesmerizing! Before long Frisco and Felicia crossed borders and journeyed to Mexico in hot pursuit of the hidden treasure. Though months would pass before the stolen treasure was found, Felicia managed to steal something even more precious during the fall of 1984. She stole Frisco's heart.

Fearing that his police work was too dangerous, Felicia called a halt to her June wedding to Frisco, telling him that she was not cut out to be the wife of a cop. She couldn't bear the thought of losing him. At the last second, he soothed her frayed nerves and talked her into going through with the ceremony. In a whirlwind series of events, the minister was pulled off the tennis court and rushed to Bobbie Jones's brownstone on Elm Street to pronounce Frisco and Felicia man and wife. Frisco, a rookie police officer, donned his new uniform for the occasion, while his beautiful Aztec princess bride wore a traditional Spanish gown with a mantilla.

Back home in Port Charles, Felicia and Frisco's newfound love flourished. However, Felicia was not at all happy to stand by and watch Frisco flirt—with danger. The Aztec treasure adventure had whetted his appetite for adventure. The rock star–turned–spy went undercover for the Port Charles Police Department, helping the authorities in solving several perplexing mysteries. In each case the intrepid Frisco received an assist from an unexpected source—Felicia. United against crime in Port Charles, they made a fabulous team! However, when Frisco expressed a desire to join the force, Felicia balked. Law enforcement was much too dangerous for her tastes.

Felicia accepted Frisco's tender proposal of marriage and quietly hoped he would reconsider his dream to become a cop.

In June 1986 the people of Port Charles readied themselves for the wedding of the year! However, the marriage of Frisco and Felicia was promptly called off by the bride after an incident in which Frisco was nearly shot and killed.

"I'm just not cut out to be a policeman's wife," cried Felicia as

The garden of Bobbie's brownstone provided the impromptu setting for the nuptials. Felicia had planned for the wedding to be held at the Quartermaine masion, but she called off the gala affair because Frisco felt the setting was "too pretentious."

she canceled the impending nuptials. At the last minute, the reluctant bride reconsidered and agreed to become Frisco's wife. Bobbie and Ruby rushed to restore the canceled preparations, rounded up the guests, and located the minister, who had already been told that the nuptials had been canceled. Now the wedding was on! Bobbie's brownstone on Elm Street served as the setting for the simple and sweet wedding. With family and friends sharing in their happiness, Frisco and Felicia joyously became man and wife.

But their elation was not to last. Frisco grew frustrated with walking a beat. He hungered for the kind of international intrigue that only the World Security Bureau could offer. Soon after joining the WSB, Frisco was called away on assignment. On his last day in Port Charles, Frisco bid farewell to his loving wife. In an emotional scene at the airport departure gate, he handed Felicia a locket in the shape of a heart. Inside he had inscribed the words that summed up his feelings about Felicia. It read simply "Lady of My Heart."

Wedding Styles

an informal wedding takes place during the day in a chapel, judge's study, or garden. The number of guests is limited to an intimate group. The bride wears a suit or dress with a veil or hat. The groom can wear either a suit or blazer with coordinating trousers.

FRISCO AND FELICIA'S WEDDING VOWS

MINISTER

The wedding band is a circle with no beginning and no end. It is the symbol of the love between a husband and wife that will last until the end of time. Within this circle of love, Andrew and Felicia will be blessed with a new awareness of each other as two people become one in the eyes of God and man. They will cleave one to the other and put each other first in all love and faithfulness, learning that to love is to set each other free to realize all your goals and dreams. Andrew, as you place this ring upon Felicia's finger, repeat after me: With this ring, I thee wed.

FRISCO

With this ring, I thee wed.

MINISTER

Felicia, as you put this ring upon Andrew's finger, repeat after me: With this ring, I thee wed.

FELICIA

With this ring, I thee wed.

MINISTER

By the authority vested in me, I pronounce Andrew Jones and Felicia Cummings husband and wife according to the ordinance of God and the laws of this state. Whom God hath joined together let no man put asunder. The Lord bless you and keep you and make his face to shine upon you and be gracious unto you and give you peace both now and in the life everlasting. Amen. You may kiss the bride. Ladies and gentlemen, I have the honor to present to you Mr. and Mrs. Jones!

FRISCO

Well, we did it! We're married!

Felicia and Frisco's Second Wedding

January 26, 1990

With a heartfelt promise to return, Frisco Jones had left Felicia behind in Port Charles when he flew off for his first WSB assignment. Soon after Felicia received the horrible news that her husband was missing and presumed dead. Overwhelmed with grief, she found consolation with Colton Shore, a handsome newcomer. As time passed, Felicia refused to accept the fact that her beloved Frisco was gone. Colton offered his friendship and, in time, his love. Together, they followed Frisco's trail, which apparently ended in a country field in Canada, where a small stone marked his grave.

Finally Felicia was able to come to grips with Frisco's death. Returning to Port Charles, she accepted Colton's proposal of marriage. As they married in Port Charles park, a silent stranger stood a short distance away, grimly observing Felicia as she recited her wedding vows. It was Frisco!

With his life in danger, Frisco retreated to the catacombs under Port Charles, while his heart yearned to make his presence known to the only woman he had ever loved. One day, while Felicia walked along the Port Charles waterfront, Frisco stepped out of the shadows and softly called her name. She turned around, took one look at his stunning visage, and fainted. Frisco tenderly scooped Felicia into his arms and carried her off to the catacombs.

Once the shock wore off, Felicia needed time alone—to think! Which man did she love? Or could she possibly love both of her husbands? After much thought, Felicia broke the news to Frisco.

"Colton is my husband now and I intend to stay with him." Felicia spoke the words with conviction, though in her heart she could not deny her feelings for Frisco.

With great sadness, Felicia and Frisco made plans to divorce. However, when the time came to dissolve their marriage officially, Frisco refused to sign the papers. Instead, he passionately professed his love! Torn by his heartfelt confession, Felicia decided to

The Donely penthouse was transformed into a winter wonderland of twinkling lights, flickering candles, and fragrant flowers. Felicia chose an elegant yet simple outfit for her second wedding. A white velvet bolero jacket embroidered with pearls on the collar and cuffs worn over a form-fitting dress gave the outfit the look of a suit (above). The bride and groom wrote their own special vows for the informal ceremony (opposite page). The happy lovers decided rather suddenly to be married in the Donely penthouse. Among the few attending the ceremony conducted by a minister were hosts Tiffany Hill and Sean Donely, Anna Devane, Robin Scorpio, Katherine Delafield, and Bobbie Jones (left).

postpone the divorce until later—much later. Only after a bout with amnesia did Felicia realize that Frisco was the only man she had ever wanted. At a Halloween costume party on Spoon Island, Felicia finally poured out her feelings, confessing her eternal love to the only man she ever truly loved—Frisco Jones. Colton, crushed and bitter, left town as Felicia and Frisco basked in the glow of their love.

On Christmas Eve, Frisco surprised Felicia with a very special gift—her old wedding ring, with new sparkling diamonds added to the setting. One symbolized their 1986 marriage. The other represented the future.

"Will you marry me?" Frisco asked on bended knee.

"I thought you'd never ask," Felicia joyfully responded.

The remarriage of Frisco and Felicia was a private, exclusive, and impromptu affair. The happy lovers decided rather suddenly to be married in the penthouse of Tiffany and Sean Donely. Unbeknownst to anyone, Frisco moved up the wedding to accommodate the WSB, who sent him on a top-secret spy mission following the nuptials.

FELICIA AND FRISCO'S WEDDING VOWS

January 20, 1990

FRISCO

Felicia, I realized something important during the time I was without you. Whatever hope I had, whatever strength I was able to summon up I got from you, from your love, which, in spite of our being apart, I felt every moment of every day. But I also knew that without getting back to you, without having you by my side, my life would be unbearable. I might be alive, but my life wouldn't be worth living without you. It was the memory of your goodness and your love that kept me going. It was the hope of being with you again, forever, that made me survive. From this day forward, I dedicate my life to loving and protecting you. Forever.

FELICIA

We've been apart too long. Separated both physically and, at times, emotionally. The physical separation was out of our control. The emotional was because of the lack of trust and terrible secrets we kept from one another. My pledge and my solemn promise to you is never to keep anything from you again. To be honest with you always even if it may be painful. Without truth, love and trust can never grow. I love you, Frisco. And I'll never do anything to betray your trust or risk losing you again.

MINISTER

By the authority vested in me by the sovereign state of New York and in front of God and these assembled witnesses, I do hereby pronounce you husband and wife.

One soul, two bodies, going our
separate ways, but still together.
—Felicia Jones

John "Jagger" Cates and Karen Wexler

March 30, 1994

*J*agger and Karen's romance was a testament to all that young love can overcome even the greatest of obstacles. John "Jagger" Cates first hit the Port Charles scene in a robbery of Kelly's Diner that went dangerously awry. When one of Jagger's partners in crime prepared to shoot the owner, Ruby Anderson, Jagger stepped in and took the bullet to save her life. At first, the naive boy didn't think enough of himself to speak up and save himself, and was going to be sent from General Hospital to jail. Hospital volunteer Karen Wexler observed him trying to escape off the roof of the hospital, but Jagger's fear of heights took hold. Karen pulled him to safety, saving his life. Talk about memorable first impressions!

Ruby later took pity on Jagger, and gave him both a job and a room at Kelly's. When Jagger accidentally cost Karen her job at a burger joint, he persuaded Ruby to hire Karen at Kelly's as well. There was certainly a chemistry between Jagger and Karen. But she'd begun dating wealthy pre-med student Jason Quartermaine and fought her attraction to hard-bodied Jagger. He nobly kept his distance. One sultry summer afternoon Jason invited Karen out for a ride on his family's cabin cruiser. Little did they know that Jagger was also aboard! As fate would have it, a violent storm caused the boat to sink, and all three of them washed up on a deserted island—

Mr. and Mrs. John "Jagger" Cates (above). Jagger, Karen, and Jason Quartermaine never suspected that their afternoon of fun on the high seas would lead to disaster! A sudden storm shipwrecked their boat on an island off the coast of Port Charles (right).

In 1993, dark and brooding Jagger Cates found himself in the middle of a sizzling lovers' triangle. His heart belonged to wholesome Karen Wexler, while his bed belonged to sexy Brenda Barrett.

and so did Jagger's ex-partners in crime, Cal and Joseph Atkins, who had broken out of prison! Cal attempted to rape Karen on the island, but Jagger saved her, as Cal plummeted to the shore below. Convinced he was dead, the three teens made a pact to keep what had happened a secret and were soon rescued.

Karen's mother, Rhonda, was overjoyed to see her daughter. Falsely suspecting Jagger of causing Karen's bruises, she had her boyfriend beat up Jagger. When the new school year started, saucy Brenda Barrett was immediately attracted to her new classmate, Jagger. She wanted him—badly. Stranded in a snowstorm, Karen and Jagger finally admitted their feelings for each other, and they agreed to stop seeing Jason and Brenda, respectively. When a scorned Brenda circulated nude photos of Karen at PC High, Jagger was expelled for defending Karen's honor with his fists.

At the Valentine's Day dance, Jagger surprised Karen when he showed up and professed his love to her. As Jagger and Karen fell deeper in love, she wanted to make love with him. But she froze whenever he got too intimate. Jagger told her he'd wait until she was ready. She began having disturbing flashbacks to sexual abuse she suffered at the hands of her mother's former boyfriend, Ray Conway. Karen's downward spiral continued as she started wearing trashy clothes, frequenting teen raves, and stripping for nightclub owner Sonny Corinthos! Karen felt unworthy of Jagger and broke up

As if he were memorizing each moment, Jagger followed Karen as she descended the stairs at Kelly's Diner, which was festively decorated for the long-awaited nuptials. The bride picked out the faces of the people who had come to mean so much to her as she slowly moved down the aisle. Reaching her husband-to-be, Karen's face shone with elation and desire and a barely suppressed nervous anticipation. The moment she had dreamed of had finally arrived.

It seemed fitting that Kelly's Diner should serve as the setting for Jagger and Karen's candlelit wedding ceremony. Two years earlier Jagger—then a brooding streetwise kid—was shot while stopping his friends from robbing the diner. Recovering from the wound at General Hospital, Jagger met volunteer Karen Wexler and sparks flew. Within days they were sharing meaningful glances. Although they quickly fell in love, Karen's memories of child molestation led to severe problems in their relationship. After finally coming to terms with her troubling past, Karen and Jagger were finally free to marry. Jagger Cates swept Karen Wexler off her feet on Valentine's Day, 1993. Their love remained strong until Karen became haunted by memories of a past in which she was molested by her mother's old boyfriend, Ray. The secret chewed away at Karen, causing her to scorn Jagger. Feeling worthless, Karen entered the underground world of rave parties and began to work as a stripper. After stumbling upon her shocking new life, Jagger did not turn his back. Instead, he helped Karen come to grips with the dark memories that plagued her. With Karen's delicate psyche on the mend, they finally were able to plan a life together. During the reception, their loved ones bid a bittersweet good-bye to the newlyweds. The following week Karen was to begin medical school at Northwestern University. She was proud that Jagger, having earned his Graduate Equivalency Diploma, was about to follow his own dream by enrolling in an Illinois police academy. From left: Jagger's brother—Stone Cates—Robin Scorpio, Jagger, Karen, Karen's mother, Rhonda Wexler (bottom, right).

with him. Little did Karen realize that her new friend, Sonny's assistant, Stone, was Jagger's long-missing brother! Thanks to Sonny, Karen was soon addicted to stripping, pills, and Sonny, as the two shared a bed. Karen's secret double life came to an end when Stone, Jagger, and Karen all crossed paths at once. Karen's friends and family were supportive of Karen as she worked to rebuild her life. When Karen was finally able to tell Jagger about her sexual abuse, she felt ready to make love to him.

"You're good. You're kind and you're gentle. And nothing that has happened can change what I know," Jagger said as he held the trembling girl in his arms.

"I don't deserve you," she responded. "Why didn't I tell you when I had the chance? Why did I have to wait until you didn't love me anymore?"

"I never stopped loving you, Karen."

Karen and Jagger became engaged with bright futures ahead of them: Sean Donely agreed to help Jagger become a cop, while Karen received a scholarship to become a doctor. After setting their wedding date, Jagger asked Stone to be his best man. Before their wedding day, Karen and Jagger were each handed a final obstacle to overcome: A suicidal patient at General Hospital almost plunged out of a window with Karen, and Jagger was involved in a motorcycle accident with Stone on his way to the wedding. But Jagger and Karen ultimately made it to the altar.

Canadian adult contemporary artist Daniel Lavoie surprised the bride and groom by singing a special love song, "Woman to Man," at the wedding (above). It was a day filled with love—and surprise gifts. Karen's mother, Rhonda, dropped a bombshell when she tearfully revealed to her daughter that Scott Baldwin was Karen's natural father. Then the Quartermaine family presented the bride and groom with a shiny new motorcycle so they could ride off into the sunset in style. After the reception, Karen and Jagger hopped on their new bike and drove off in a soft shower of rose petals and rice, the bride's veil streaming softly behind her.

KAREN AND JAGGER'S WEDDING VOWS

JAGGER

I, John, take you, Karen, to be my lawfully wedded wife. To have and to hold. From this day forward. For better, for worse. For richer, for poorer. In sickness and in health. To love and to cherish until we are parted in death. This is my solemn promise and pledge.

KAREN

I, Karen, take you, John, to be my lawfully wedded husband. To have and to hold. From this day forward. For better, for worse. For richer, for poorer. In sickness and in health. To love and to cherish until we are parted in death. This is my solemn promise and pledge."
(They exchange rings.)

JAGGER

(Holding the ring poised before her finger, looking in her eyes)

If I understood all mysteries and all knowledge, if I had the faith to move mountains, but had not love, I would be nothing. If I were to have success and fame, fortune and honor, but had not you, I would be nothing.

(He looks down at her hand, holding the ring above her finger) (In Italian)

Con questo anello, io ti sposa. Quest'oro e argento, is ti do. Con tutto quello chi io sone, io ti onoro. E dividero con te, tutto i miei beni terreni.

KAREN

When I was a child, I spoke as a child, I thought as a child, and I reasoned as a child. But together we have given up childish ways for we have seen through a glass, darkly and then face to face. Today I understand in part, but every day of our lives, I will understand more fully that faith, hope, and love abide. But the greatest of these is love. With this ring, I thee wed. This gold and silver I thee give. With all that I am, I thee honor and all my worldly goods with thee I share.

TIFFANY TO SEAN JUST AFTER THE WEDDING CEREMONY

TIFFANY

They look like they could conquer the world.

SEAN

If they hang on to what they have now, they might.

KAREN AND JAGGER'S PARTING WORDS

JAGGER

I look around at all of you and I know it doesn't get any better than the people in this town. You accepted me and took me into your lives way before I deserved it. . . . You stood by me and my wife and supported us through some pretty rough spots. . . . I want you to know we're taking every single one of you with us . . .
(He stops, emotional. Karen finishes for him.)

KAREN

. . . In our hearts.

Thank you for giving me a dream, something to believe in, for the rest of my life.
—Jagger Cates

Scott Baldwin and Laura Webber

July 6, 1979

Young love bloomed in full during the late 1970s, thanks to star-crossed adolescent lovers Scotty and Laura. Troubled teen Laura Webber found a new friend in young law student Scotty Baldwin. But love quickly blossomed when, en route to a rock concert, the kids were caught in a hurricane and found refuge in an abandoned storage shed. After the incident, Laura's disapproving mother, Lesley, became upset that Laura and Scotty's relationship went from platonic to romantic. Laura bullied Dr. Monica Quartermaine into prescribing her birth control pills, but Scotty took a more reasoned approach to their burgeoning love and was willing to cool it for Lesley's sake. Laura, however, refused and defiantly planned a series of deceits to keep her affair with Scotty alive behind her mother's back.

Scotty and Laura's wedding day was filled with white lace, orange blossoms, and heartfelt pledges of everlasting love. After enduring the death of David Hamilton and their troubled courtship, the bride and groom were certain that their love could survive any crisis.

Their road to happiness became a bumpy one, thanks to Laura and Lesley's house guest, David Hamilton, on whom Laura developed a crush. Rejected by Lesley, David moved in on Laura instead. Laura didn't fight her attraction to the handsome artist, and the two enjoyed a secret affair over a period of weeks. But David had an ulterior motive in charming Laura. He kept her notes and poems, feeling he could use them against Rick and Lesley at the proper time. When David's hidden agenda came to light, things came to a head, and David ended up dead!

Laura actually had killed David in self-defense but blocked out the memory of it because of the trauma. Lesley valiantly took the rap for the crime to protect her daughter. When Laura's memory returned, she panicked and skipped town on a bus to New York City. Although they had gone their separate ways, Scotty still carried a

"I'm so lucky! I'm the luckiest girl in the world!" thought Laura as she prepared to speak her vows to Scotty. She had waited so long to become his wife, and now her hopes were finally coming true.

torch for Laura and located her in New York. Laura returned to Port Charles and cleared her mother of the charges—while getting a suspended sentence herself. Scotty helped Laura through her probation by rekindling their romance.

But trouble lurked right around the corner in the shapely form of student nurse Bobbie Spencer, who had set her sights on the vulnerable Scotty Baldwin. Laura and Scotty's relationship became strained by money problems and the young law student's long hours of study. Ever the opportunist, Bobbie was there to pick up Scotty's spirits. But Bobbie and Scotty's budding relationship fizzled out when Scotty ultimately chose to devote more time to his true love Laura.

Scotty was the first person Bobbie ever slept with that she cared about, so she wasn't about to let him go without a fight! A scheming Bobbie set out to bust up Scotty and Laura's marriage for good—with the help of her badboy brother, Luke. For a time, it appeared as if Bobbie had won her war against Laura Webber by claiming to be pregnant with Scotty's child. Scotty reluctantly

On a sandy beach in southern California, the new Mr. and Mrs. Baldwin rejoiced in the glory of their new marriage.

agreed to marry Bobbie but not to sleep with her ever again! Fortunately, the wedding of Scotty and Bobbie would never happen. Just days before the nuptials were to take place, Lesley's secret sleuthing proved that Bobbie was never really pregnant. A relieved Scotty blasted Bobbie for her trickery, then raced back into Laura's open arms.

Scotty and Laura made glorious plans for a June wedding, never expecting that her father, Rick, feeling that Laura was still too young, would vehemently oppose the union. Laura was angered and upset by Rick's refusal to the marriage, often taking out her frustration on her fiancé. Despite Scotty's assurances to the contrary, a defeated Laura concluded their marriage would never happen and returned her ring. Scotty then dove into an alcoholic tailspin—only to be rescued by his father, Lee.

Bobbie hatched a last-ditch scheme to snare Scotty once and for all. She arranged for Scotty to be drugged and for the ring to be taken from his pocket. Bobbie then took

a semiconscious Scotty back to his apartment, slipped the ring onto her finger, and awaited Laura's appearance. When the doorbell rang at Scotty's apartment, Bobbie dimmed the lights, messed up her hair, and greeted a stunned Laura, who mistakingly believed that Scotty was sleeping with Bobbie. Laura hurried away and crashed her car during her hysterical retreat. Upon her recovery from surgery after the accident, Laura's prayers were answered when she received permission to marry. At last, Laura was free to make frenzied wedding plans. Scotty, meanwhile, feared he wouldn't pass his exams, but he did, graduating at the top of his class! With their respective persons, demons, and skeletons behind them, Scotty and Laura were at last free to take that long walk down the aisle.

Bobbie Spencer's obsessive love for Scotty Baldwin led her to plan some dirty schemes to destroy his relationship with Laura Webber.

SCOTTY AND LAURA'S WEDDING VOWS

MINISTER

Friends and family of the bride and groom. We are gathered here today to join this man and this woman in marriage, an estate kindled by love, rooted in joy, and honored each day by all men and women who pledge themselves to one another. Marriage is God's institution for the comfort and continuation of mankind. All of us here today pray that your marriage will be a source of abundant happiness and that you will enrich it by your tender devotion, your mindfulness in little things, and your patience and constancy with one another today and forever. Laura, your vows.

LAURA

How do I love thee? Let me try to count the ways for you, Scotty; the moment I saw you I knew we were close in spirit, and now I want to share everything I am and everything I will ever be with you. You have taught me the true meaning of the words "trust" and to share everything I am and everything I will ever be with you. I will be proud to bear your name and your children. I know you are wiser and more mature than I am, but with your help, I will grow. I vow to love you, and in being your partner for life, I will be fulfilled.

SCOTTY

Laura, to our marriage I will give the most important thing I own: my life. This has been a day we've both fought for, but I'm grateful now for all the difficulties we've gone through, because they've only brought us closer together and made us more certain of our love. I believe in my heart and mind that we were meant to be together, Laura, and I'm going to spend the rest of my life proving to you and to those who are close to us that our love and our marriage were meant to be. This is the happiest day of my life.

MINISTER

Laura, will you have this man to be your husband? Will you love him, comfort him, honor him and keep him, in sickness and in health, in poverty and in wealth, and forsaking all others keep only unto him, as long as you both shall live?

LAURA

I will.

MINISTER

Scotty, will you have this woman to be your wife? Will you love her, comfort her, honor and keep her, in sickness and in health, in poverty and in wealth, and forsaking all others keep only unto her, as long as you both shall live?

SCOTTY

I will.

MINISTER

And now Laura and Scotty will seal their vows by the gift of a ring to each other. Repeat after me . . . With this ring, I thee wed in token and pledge of my constant faith and abiding love.

LAURA

With this ring, I thee wed in token and pledge of my constant faith and abiding love.

SCOTTY

With this ring, I thee wed in token and pledge of my constant faith and abiding love.

MINISTER

Laura and Scotty . . . having chosen one another from the many men and women of the earth, and having pledged your vows to one another before this gathering, I hereby pronounce you husband and wife.

SHARE A ROMANTIC RENDEZVOUS IN HOLLYWOOD, CALIFORNIA

Glamour and grit get equal billing in Hollywood, an area of Los Angeles famous for being the entertainment capital of America. Even though the true center of film and TV production has moved to nearby San Fernando Valley, Hollywood still upholds its reputation. The sights in this funky town can justifiably be called cheesy, but who cares? They're fun! When you arrive, look up toward the hills and you'll see the famous "Hollywood" sign spelled out in fifty-foot letters—the greatest star of all.

When to go: Year round. Mild temperatures prevail.

What to do: Hollywood's gaudy version of the Orient takes center stage at Mann's Chinese Theater, where celebrity hand- and footprints are laid in cement. For more celebrity enshrinement, step over to the Hollywood Walk of Fame, four city blocks along Hollywood Boulevard where the sidewalks are inlaid with brass stars featuring the names of over 1,800 famous stars. So you haven't caught a glimpse of Brad Pitt or Madonna walking down the street? The next best thing is the Hollywood Wax Museum, home of more than 180 celebrity wax figures in scenes from their famous movies. The naughty lingerie at Frederick's of Hollywood is as well known as any movie star. Don't miss the store's small lingerie museum, which contains the real-life undergarments of past and present Hollywood legends. In nearby Burbank, a store called It's A Wrap sells used clothes (in great condition) from soap operas.

Romantic rendezvous: Rent a red convertible, put on dark sunglasses, and drive through posh neighborhoods like the Hollywood Hills, West Hollywood, and Beverly Hills for a look at where the wealthy live.

Stepping out at night: The Pantages Theater, a former movie palace built in 1930, hosts Broadway musicals and top-name performers. If you're into making the scene, head to Sunset Strip—nightclubs and bars galore—or Melrose Avenue, with chichi restaurants.

For more information: Contact the Los Angeles Convention and Visitors Bureau at 633 West 5th St., Suite 6000, Los Angeles, CA 90071; phone (800) CATCH-LA.

> *You have taught me the true meaning of the words "trust" and to share everything I am and everything I will ever be with you.* —Laura Webber

Ned Ashton and Lois Cerullo

June 1, 1995

Ned and Lois's romance hit all the right notes with viewers—despite the fact that their relationship got off to a rocky start with a game of musical beds featuring Ned and his *two* wives!

When buttoned-down businessman Ned Ashton went to Buffalo on ELQ business, he knocked a band called the Idle Rich that he heard perform at the hotel bar. The band's manager, Lois Cerullo, a feisty go-getter from Brooklyn with indescribably long, decorated fingernails, challenged Ned. Having sung in college, Ned hopped on stage and wailed with Lois's band. He tore the place down! Lois promised to make him a star—but she didn't know his name. "Eddie Maine," Ned lied, as she led him to her bed for an incredible night of passion.

Their first wedding took place in City Hall under false pretenses. Buttoned-up corporate shark Ned Ashton was keeping a secret from his bride, who knew him only as rock and roll heartthrob "Eddie Maine." Juggling identities became a full time job for Ned/Eddie. Lois eventually discovered the charade, and married him again in a very traditional Catholic ceremony (top). The bride and groom and their entourage hit some choppy waters on the way to the altar. After taking a train ride from Port Charles to Brooklyn, the wedding party and guests boarded the Quartermaine yacht for a pre-wedding cruise near Coney Island. But the yacht sprung a leak and almost sank! Everyone sang "Nearer My God, to Thee," as they bailed out the water-logged boat until they were rescued (right).

Ned and Lois danced their way into our hearts with their unconventional, fantasy-filled romance (left). In the summer of 1994, a dream came true for Brooklyn native Lois Cerullo when she took "Eddie Maine" to Coney Island, the historic amusement park that had always been dear to her heart. The lovers strolled the boardwalk, munched on cotton candy, and even rode the classic Cyclone roller coaster (below).

Ned enjoyed his singing alter ego. But Lois raised the stakes when she made plans to turn Eddie and his band into a major rock group. When Lois started spending more time in Port Charles, Ned took Brenda Barrett into his confidence. When Lois insisted on meeting someone from his life, he introduced her to Brenda. After all, Eddie had already met all of Lois's family in Brooklyn. Ned, meanwhile, faced a big problem when he was blackmailed by Katherine into marrying her. But first Ned proposed to the true love of his life—Lois.

"You're the most beautiful, amazing, incredible woman, and every day I wake up in total awe and disbelief that you've come into

my life," he said on bended knee. "I don't know what I did to deserve you. . . . I mean, I don't deserve you, but I sure do love you—more than I ever thought I was capable of, and I would be so honored if you would be my wife."

Lois agreed, and after they eloped, the honeymooners shared a wonderful day at Coney Island. For weeks after Ned hopped from bed to bed! His wild charade came to an end when Lois saw Katherine on TV. And by Katherine's side, she saw "Eddie?" Katherine decided to throw herself a birthday party at The Outback and demanded that her new family celebrate with her. But Katherine ended getting a "surprise"

Despite several last-minute snafus (including a last-gasp appeal from Lois's angry ex-boyfriend Danny Zacarowitz to dump her groom for him) Lois and Ned managed to make a mad dash to the church. The last-minute trek through the streets showcased the picturesque Brooklyn neighborhood that Lois called home.

After her own wedding gown was devoured by squirrels, Lois graciously accepted an offer from Lila Quartermaine to wear her heirloom gown to her nuptials. Before the wedding, the eager bride and groom posed on the steps of the Brooklyn church where they were pronounced man and wife (left). Lois looked every bit the fairy-tale princess as her father, Carmine, proudly walked her down the aisle. As the organ player began playing the bridal music, Ned held his breath. Suddenly, there she was—luminous and practically glowing from happiness (right).

party after all, when none other than Lois popped out of her giant birthday cake.

"Happy birthday to Mrs. Ned Ashton from the other Mrs. Ned Ashton!" Lois exclaimed.

Ned's double life was kaput—and so were his two marriages! It would be a long time—not until they were in Puerto Rico on business—before Lois's icy attitude toward Ned began to thaw. Ned vowed to not let up until he won back Lois.

"I guarantee you that life with me will be full of surprises," he laughingly assured her as they got back together. Once Lois finally came around, Ned waged a campaign to win approval from Lois's very disapproving mother and father, Gloria and Carmine. Gloria was the first to give Lois her blessing, but Carmine was a different matter altogether. Finally Lois managed to get her "Pops" to cave in to his little girl's wishes and offered his blessing for the nuptials. All that remained was for Lois and Ned's families to meet and plan the wedding extravaganza!

Ned and Lois were on pins and needles as the Quartermaines and Cerullos met for the first time. Despite some one-upmanship between Edward and Carmine, the families got along well—at least well enough to throw together a wedding. And what a wedding it was!

SHARE A ROMANTIC RENDEZVOUS IN NEW YORK CITY

A honeymoon in Manhattan, New York City's best-known borough, is for couples like Ned and Lois who savor constant stimulation, never-ending excitement, and lots of choices. Restaurants of every imaginable cuisine, over 150 museums, countless stores, and world-famous sights all manage to crowd together on this 13.4-mile-long island. For a city that never sleeps, New York has one of the freshest faces in the universe.

When to go: Year round, but especially from late April to early November, when the temperatures are warmest.

What to do: Start with a tour of the classic sights of New York—Ellis Island, the Statue of Liberty, the Empire State Building, and Rockefeller Center. Then after visiting some of the outstanding museums, such as the Metropolitan Museum of Art and the American Museum of Natural History, spend time in a few lesser-known but just as spectacular institutions, such as the American Crafts Museum, or the Museum of Television & Radio. The latter lets you choose from a library of 54,000 TV shows and individually screen your selection. Some say the biggest draw for visitors to the Big Apple is New Yorkers themselves. From Soho to midtown to the Upper West Side, sidewalks are filled with people from every age and ethnic and religious group rushing by. Stop to enjoy the show.

Romantic rendezvous: Take a carriage ride through Central Park, which is 840 acres of meadows, lakes, bridges, and fountains. If the weather's warm, set sail on a Circle Line cruise or the Staten Island Ferry to see the skyline of New York from a nautical perspective.

Stepping out at night: The Times Square area, which wears an infamous label as the neon land of peep shows, movie theaters, and ribald New Year's Eve revelry, recently has cleaned up its act. Concerts galore take place every night in every part of town, from

General Hospital hit the Big Apple for the much-heralded remarriage of Ned and Lois. With the imposing New York skyline in the background, the lovers proudly struck a pose atop the Brooklyn Bridge.

the New York Philharmonic symphony orchestra at Lincoln Center to top-notch performers at Radio City Music Hall, where the Rockettes kick up their heels. Or steal away to a cozy jazz club or cabaret for more intimate entertainment.

For more information: Head to the Times Square Information Booth at 229 West 42nd Street, New York, NY 10036; phone (800) 692-8474, or visit online at www.nycvisit.com.

WORDS OF LOVE
NED PROPOSES TO LOIS

NED

Lois Marie, I, Edward Laurence Ashton, do solemnly swear to love, honor, and protect you from this day forward. For better or worse. For richer or poorer. In sickness and in health. And to be faithful to you until death do us part. I vow never to lie to you knowingly, never to violate your trust, and I intend to spend the rest of my days proving my love in a dazzling variety of creative ways that will make your head spin. And if, as I hope to succeed in making you love me more than you did before, more than you ever dreamed possible, even then you won't love me one-tenth as much as I love you.

LOIS

You are a silver-tongued devil, aren't you?

NED

Every word was from my heart.

LOIS AND NED'S WEDDING VOWS
A Traditional Catholic Wedding Ceremony

PRIEST

On behalf of Ned and Lois I welcome all of you to participate in this very important day in their lives. Dear friends in Christ, as you know, you are about to enter into a union which is most sacred and most serious, a union which was established by God Himself. It is serious because it will bind you together for life in a relationship so close and so intimate that it will profoundly influence your whole future. That future, with its hopes and disappointments, its successes and failures, its pleasures and pains, its joys and sorrows, is hidden from your eyes. And so, not knowing what is before you, you take each other for better or worse, for richer or poorer, in sickness and health, until death. May then this love with which you join your hands and hearts today never fail, but grow deeper and stronger as the years go on. . . .

Edward Laurence Ashton, do you take Lois Marie Cerullo, here present, for your lawful wife according to the rite of our holy mother, the Church?

NED

I do.

PRIEST

Lois Marie Cerullo, do you take Edward Laurence Ashton, here present, for your lawful husband according to the rite of our holy mother, the Church?

LOIS
I do.

PRIEST
Join your right hands and say after me.

NED
*I, Edward Laurence Ashton, take you, Lois Marie Cerullo, for my lawful wife,
to have and to hold, from this day forward, for richer, for poorer,
in sickness and in health, till death do us part.*

LOIS
*I, Lois Marie Cerullo, take you, Edward Laurence Ashton, for my lawful husband,
to have and to hold, from this day forward, for better, for worse,
for richer, for poorer, in sickness and in health, until death do us part.*

PRIEST
By the authority of the church, I ratify and bless the bond of marriage you have contracted.
(Blesses them with holy water)
*In the name of the Father, and of the Son, and of the Holy Spirit, amen. I call upon all
of you here present to be witnesses of this holy union which I have now blessed. Man must
not separate what God has joined together.*

THE BLESSING OF THE RINGS
PRIEST
*Bless, O Lord, these rings, which we are blessing in Your name, so that they who wear
them, keeping faith with each other in unbroken loyalty, may ever remain at peace with
You according to Your will, and may live together always in mutual love.
Through Christ our Lord . . . Amen.*

(Sprinkles rings with holy water)

*Now that you have sealed a truly Christian marriage,
give these wedding rings to each other . . .*

(Ned takes Lois's ring from the priest, places it on her finger.)

NED
*Take and wear this ring as a sign of our love and fidelity. In the name of the Father
and of the Son, and of the Holy Spirit.*

LOIS
*Take and wear this ring as a sign of our love and fidelity. In the name of the Father,
and of the Son, and of the Holy Spirit.*

PRIEST
*May Almighty God bless you by the Word of His mouth,
and unite your hearts in the enduring bond of pure love.*

NED AND LOIS
Amen.

PRIEST
*May you be blessed with children, and may the love you
lavish on them be returned a hundredfold.*

NED AND LOIS
Amen.

PRIEST

May the peace of Christ dwell always in your hearts and in your home;
may you have true friends to stand by you, both in joy and in sorrow.
May you be ready with help and consolation for all those who come to you in need;
and may the blessings promised to the compassionate descend in abundance on your house.

NED AND LOIS

Amen.

PRIEST

May you be blessed in your work and enjoy its fruits. May cares never cause you distress,
nor the desire for earthly possessions lead you astray; but may your hearts' concern be
always for the treasures laid up for you in the life of heaven.

(Joins his hands. Gestures to congregation)

We all pray through our Lord Jesus Christ, his Son, who lives and reigns with Him
in the unity of the Holy Spirit, God, forever and ever.

CONGREGATION

Amen.

(Ned takes Lois in his arms for a big, first officially married kiss.)

BRENDA BARRETT'S "BEST PERSON" SPEECH

It's incumbent upon me to toast the happy couple.
I'm not very good at public speeches,
so I'll just say . . . Ned, Lois. The labor was long
and difficult, but looking at you now,
I can't remember the pain.
To a long and happy life together. . . .

Ladies and gentleman . . . I present to you Mr. and Mrs. Ned Ashton! The second time around proved to be the charm for soul mates Ned and Lois. The newlyweds sealed their special day with a kiss.

I am so honored to be the woman whom you've chosen to share your heart. Once upon a time I thought it was impossible to love anyone more than I loved "Eddie Maine," but I was wrong because I love Ned Ashton so much more. —Lois Cerullo

All My Children

Dr. Cliff Warner

and

Nina Cortlandt

September 3, 1980

Of all the soap opera weddings, Cliff and Nina's 1980 storybook spectacular may have been the most lavish. It was certainly one of the most memorable. Viewers followed every romantic twist and turn in this classic tale of a patient who fell instantly in love with her handsome doctor.

Dr. Cliff Warner and Nina Cortlandt were destined to spend their lives together from the moment they met. Just days after joining the staff of Pine Valley Hospital, Cliff was called upon to perform life-saving surgery on young Nina, who had been wheeled into the emergency room suffering from an attack of acute appendicitis. From the moment

Moments before the ceremony, Nina looked radiant as she gazed over the grounds of Cortlandt Manor. The bride-to-be shared a private moment as she counted her blessings on this, the most significant day in her young life.

their eyes met, it was love at first sight! Upon her recovery, Cliff paid regular house calls on his beautiful patient. Holding hands and gazing into each other's eyes, they recited the poetic words of Browning and Wordsworth, and the soap world watched as these innocent youngsters fell hopelessly, impetuously in love.

Nina's overbearing, overprotective father couldn't stand the sight of the idealistic Dr. Warner. Palmer Cortlandt let it be known that Cliff had neither the capital nor the social position necessary to marry his daughter. In truth, Palmer's love for Nina bordered on obsession. He didn't want any man to take his only daughter away from him.

Handsome Dr. Cliff Warner contracted a dose of lovesickness when he paid house calls on his prized patient, heiress Nina Cortlandt (left). Palmer Cortlandt's overbearing feelings for his teenage daughter, Nina, bordered on obsession. The cold-hearted millionaire cautioned Nina that her suitor, Dr. Cliff Warner, was an opportunist who wanted her fortune, not her love. Despite his wicked machinations, Palmer could not keep Nina and Cliff from proceeding with their plans to hold the most spectacular wedding ever in Pine Valley (below).

In one evil machination after another, Palmer succeeded in separating the sweethearts. First, he hired a private eye to find a skeleton in Cliff's closet—anything he could use to discredit the too-good-to-be-true doctor in Nina's starry eyes. Unable to find a scandal in Dr. Warner's pristine past, Palmer created one of his own. Mr. Cortlandt paid off Cliff's former girlfriend, Janice Rollins, to claim that he had fathered her illegitimate son, then abandoned her in Chicago just prior to moving to Pine Valley. Although the story was a fabrication, Nina believed the seemingly sincere Ms. Rollins and nearly moved to

California to get away from Cliff. Just in time, the Cortlandt family housekeeper, Myra Murdoch, discovered Palmer's scheme and forced him to end it. Without implicating Palmer, Janice confessed to Nina that her story about Cliff fathering her child was a lie.

Cliff and Nina were lovingly reunited, vowing never to let anything separate

Nina's wedding party included bridesmaids Peggy Warner (left) and Brooke English (right). Just days before the wedding, Nina asked her newest and dearest friend, Monique Jonville, to be her matron of honor. Two years would pass before Nina discovered the truth that Monique was actually her mother, Daisy Cortlandt, who had been banished from her daughter's life by her husband, Palmer, after being caught in an extramarital affair.

them again. Cliff asked Nina to become his wife, but the shy teenager had reservations because she was afraid she would never be able to give him a child. Nina informed Cliff that her mother, Daisy, who suffered from diabetes, went into a decline at Nina's birth and died from complications four years later.

Nina was so confused about whether to marry Cliff that she fervently wished her mother were alive to advise her. She confided her fears to Myra, who revealed that she had some experience with the occult. To Nina's amazement, Myra held an eerie seance in which Daisy returned to counsel her daughter.

"Mother!" Nina gasped, listening to Daisy's soothing words. In reality, the late Daisy Cortlandt was very much alive. Banished fifteen years earlier by her husband, Palmer, after he caught her in an extramarital affair, Daisy returned to Pine Valley in 1980. Using the name Monique Jonville, she befriended Nina and secretly worked behind the scenes to ensure a happy future for her precious daughter.

At the same time, Palmer searched for a way to break the couple up again. He came upon the perfect plan when Nina began having vision problems related to her diabetes. Her doctor revealed to Palmer that he had found evidence of retinal hemorrhaging. It was imperative that Nina see a specialist at once, because her condition could lead to diabetic retinopathy and possible blindness if not treated. Palmer, in the most diabolical manipulation of his life, lied to Nina, telling her she was going blind. He fully intended to see that she received treatment, but not until he ensured the breakup of her engagement to Cliff. Palmer proceeded to convince Nina that, as a blind woman, she would be a burden to her husband.

"You can never be a wife to Cliff. He has such a bright future, Nina. Would you want to saddle him with an invalid?"

Palmer's manipulative words sunk in.

The bridal party arrived via horse-drawn carriage for the early September wedding, held on the grounds of one of Pine Valley's most stately homes, Cortlandt Manor (above). "You're marrying the woman you love!" whispered Cliff's best man, Dr. Frank Grant, in an attempt to bolster the spirits of the groom-to-be, who learned just hours before the ceremony that nurse Sybil Thorne (with whom he had had a one-night liaison during a breakup with Nina) was pregnant with his child.

Devastated, Nina promised her father to call off the wedding and never to tell Cliff or anyone else the true reason. Nina returned her engagement ring to Cliff, who was so distraught at losing Nina that he turned to a nurse, Sybil Thorne, for comfort. Cliff was ripe for seduction. And Sybil knew how to catch the man she had longed for from afar. They made love.

In time, Dr. Joe Martin learned that Palmer had not told Nina the truth about her condition, and he threatened to tell Nina everything if Palmer did not cooperate. Defeated, Palmer informed Nina that there was hope for her eyesight after all. After successful laser surgery to restore her failing vision, Nina reconciled with Cliff and together they planned a Victorian-style wedding to be held on the grounds of Cortlandt Manor.

A defeated Palmer watches in silence as his dear daughter Nina married "that young upstart," Cliff Warner (above). "To my beautiful bride. And the beautiful life we are going to be sharing—from this day on," Cliff cooed to his new bride, Nina, as they celebrated their marriage with a champagne toast (left).

While Cliff packed for his honeymoon in Martha's Vineyard, Sybil paid him an unexpected visit, then informed him that she was pregnant with his child. Flabbergasted, Cliff had serious misgivings about keeping the truth from Nina, but feared she would call off the wedding if she found out. So, after confiding this devastating secret to his best man, Dr. Frank Grant, an anguished Cliff decided to keep the news from Nina, and the wedding went on as planned—and it was truly a day to remember.

DAISY TO PALMER AT THE CONCLUSION OF THE CEREMONY

This is a time for celebration! Although I must say, one would have imagined it a funeral rather than a wedding—if they'd gone by your agonized look when you had to give the bride away!

Getting Married at Waveny, New Canaan, Connecticut

Years ago you vowed that when you got married, you'd have a wedding like Nina Cortlandt and Cliff Warner's (the first one, that is). Leaving out the scheming father and pregnant Other Woman, your wish can come true. The young lovebirds exchanged heartfelt I dos at Waveny House, a majestic 1912 mansion in New Canaan, Connecticut, that was a stand-in for Cortlandt Manor. With an entranceway framed by stone pillars, the regal building sits on over 200 acres and overlooks the bucolic countryside. The site's bountiful gardens and grounds were designed by Frederick Law Olmstead, Jr., a renowned landscape artist. A popular spot for wedding photos is the newly renovated rose garden, a beautiful area with flowers, fountain, and brick pathway. The exquisite first floor has a grand hall, library, sitting room, dining room, billiard room, commercial kitchen, and patio overlooking the grounds. Since Waveny House does not have an on-site caterer, brides and grooms must hire a food provider for the event as well as rent china, flatware, stemware, and table linens. The site can accommodate up to 180 guests; there is no minimum. Weddings can be booked all year round; in warmer months, they can be held outdoors.

For more details and rates on renting Waveny House for your wedding, call the New Canaan Recreation Department at (203) 966-0502, or write 677 South Avenue, New Canaan, CT 06840.

Mr. and Mrs. Cliff Warner led their assembly of guests in a toast during their wedding reception, held on the great lawn of the Cortlandt Estate.

SHARE A ROMANTIC RENDEZVOUS IN MARTHA'S VINEYARD, MASSACHUSETTS

Cliff and Nina returned time and time again to Martha's Vineyard, the site of their first honeymoon. Classically beautiful with clear-water beaches, white clapboard houses and picket fences, pristine churches, and a sea of yachts bobbing in Nantucket Sound, the Vineyard is refreshingly all-American. Located in the Atlantic Ocean off the southeastern coast of Massachusetts and accessible only by ferry and air, this maritime marvel is also quintessential New England with great seafood restaurants, a friendly attitude, and true-blue nautical charm.

When to go: Late spring to fall. The weather is warmest in July and August, the island least crowded but still gorgeous in September and October.

What to do: On Martha's Vineyard, you can be as active or as laid back as you like. Swim, sail, wind-surf, kayak, fish, or simply lounge on the beach on a blanket for two. Tennis and golf players will thrill at the abundance of places to practice their swings. When it's time to explore the island, hop on a bike (there are miles of paved trails) and wheel past rolling green meadows and Victorian gingerbread homes.

Romantic rendezvous: Go raspberry or straw-berry picking, or collect seashells on the beach. Take an invigorating walk along the shore and look up at the dramatic cliffs (a national landmark) near the red-brick Gay Head Lighthouse—it's one of five lighthouses on the island. Later take a bottle of chilled champagne, two flutes, and settle on the beach at sunset, a natural wonder that's expecially spectacular on the island.

Stepping out at night: At night, one of the busiest parts of town is Edgartown, where the brick-lined sidewalks feature restaurants, bou-tiques, galleries, historic churches, and whaling captains' homes.

For more information: Contact the Martha's Vineyard Chamber of Commerce at P.O. Box 1698, Beach Road, Vineyard Haven, MA 02568-1698; phone (508) 693-0085; or visit online at www.mvy.com.

I am Mrs. Clifford Warner, and that has such a beautiful sound to it.
—Nina Cortlandt, 1980

Cliff and Nina's Third Wedding

December 22, 1986

After reuniting in rural Maine, Cliff and Nina opted to marry just weeks later in the bustling metropolis of New York City. Their friends and family journeyed from Pine Valley to witness the sophisticated nuptials, themed in black and white, and held at the exquisite Tavern on the Green.

New York City's elegant Tavern on the Green served as the romantic setting for Cliff and Nina's third wedding. It had taken months for the couple to realize that, despite their two divorces, they were still very much in love with each other. Nina's love affair with Benny Sago had driven Cliff to divorce Nina (just as he had after her previous affair with handsome Steve Jacoby had ended their first marriage). Nina, distraught over Cliff's rejection, left Pine Valley on a round-the-world cruise with her mother, Daisy.

With Nina gone, Cliff turned to psychiatrist Amy Stone for affection. Hoping to wipe out the pain of Nina's loss, Cliff quickly asked Amy to marry him. Nina returned from her cruise to hear the shocking news—Cliff was marrying another woman. As the wedding day drew close, Cliff finally faced the truth—he didn't love Amy. Realizing he still cared deeply for Nina, Cliff couldn't bear to go through with the marriage.

He broke the news to Amy gently. Deeply hurt, Amy fled into the street and was hit by a drunken driver. In the hospital Amy, just before passing away, urged Cliff to "go to Nina. Go to the woman you love."

Amy Stone's senseless death devastated Cliff. Riddled with guilt, he made a fateful decision to quit medicine and leave Pine Valley forever. Fearing she could lose the man she still loved with all her heart, Nina tried to talk some sense into Cliff, but he

Nina's parents, Palmer and Daisy, watched with pride as their daughter exchanged vows with the man she loved. When, during the ceremony, the Reverend Finney asked, "Who gives this woman to this man?" Palmer and his ex-wife Daisy stood and spoke in unison: "her mother and I do" (top). As the musicians played a very slow, romantic waltz, Cliff took Nina by the hand amid the approval of the wedding guests who formed a circle around them to watch the bride and groom dance (left).

bitterly ordered her out of the house that had been the scene of so many cherished moments during their first two marriages.

Determined to make some sense of his shattered life, Cliff fled to an isolated lodge on the rocky shores of Maine. Hoping for one more chance to win back Cliff's affections, the newly matured Nina headed to Maine to find him.

Arriving at the lodge, Nina discovered that Cliff and a guide had already left to go to a remote hunting shack. During a fierce snowstorm, the guide fell ill, and Cliff lit some flares in the snow, hoping to alert the local authorities to their desperate plight. Seeing the flares, Nina feared that Cliff was the one in trouble, and convinced the local forest ranger to let her accompany him to the shack. When they arrived, Nina was relieved to see that Cliff was alive, but any reunion between them was put off by Cliff's concern for his ailing guide. The man needed immediate medical attention, but the storm made it impossible for them to get him to a hospital. Nina convinced Cliff to operate, and in a heartfelt declaration, she pledged her love for him.

Little Bobby Warner enjoyed this part of his parents' wedding the most—the cake cutting!

"When I was younger, people would talk about love growing and I never understood it," she whispered as tears welled up in her eyes. "I couldn't imagine feeling more than I already felt. But I love you today, Cliff, more than I ever did."

Energized by Nina's emotional words, Cliff heroically saved the guide's life, then completed the surgery in a hospital. Through a mix-up, however, Nina believed that Cliff had left town without her. She boarded a train home, thoroughly depressed. Apparently, Cliff didn't want her after all. When Cliff realized that Nina had left, he hired a helicopter and flew off in pursuit of the moving train! Catching up as it pulled away from its next stop, Cliff hopped aboard and told an ecstatic Nina he loved her. Reunited at last, they left the train, rented a room at a romantic inn, and made passionate love.

Taking a break from their romantic interlude long enough to discuss their future, Cliff and Nina agreed to marry as soon as possible. They chose New York City to become man and wife for the *third* time.

As a horse-drawn carriage whisked Nina and Cliff along Central Park West, the bride-to-be gently reached for the gloved hand of her once-and-future husband.

"Are you sure you want to do this?" Nina asked Cliff as they approached the spectacular entrance to Tavern on the Green, its lights twinkling brightly against the early evening sky.

"I have never been more sure of anything in my life. I was just thinking that, when we leave the reception, we'll be together for the rest of our lives," answered Cliff, gazing wistfully into Nina's eyes before pulling her into an everlasting kiss.

BEST MAN'S TOAST

TOM CUDAHY

*Once upon a time, there was a handsome, dashing doctor who met
a beautiful young woman. They fell in love, got married, and lived happily
ever after. Obviously, I'm not talking about Nina and Cliff!*

(Laughter)

*With Nina and Cliff, things didn't go quite that smoothly. They got knocked
down a few times. They kept getting back up. They made some wrong turns.
They corrected their course. When I played football, the coaches would tell me
"no pain, no gain." Well, Nina and Cliff know all about that. They faced a lot
of obstacles. But to look at them today, with their son, Bobby, is a true inspiration.
They proved that if love is strong enough, it really will conquer all. And so,
I offer a toast to Nina and Cliff, a wonderful couple who finally
have the happy ending they deserve.*

GETTING MARRIED AT TAVERN ON THE GREEN, NEW YORK CITY

When Nina and Cliff Warner took a third go-round at marriage, they chose a stylish setting loaded with glitz and glass. Tavern on the Green, a popular restaurant that's a must-eat-at for visitors to New York City, is situated amid the spectacular greenery of Central Park. Weddings and receptions take place in different parts of the restaurant. Ceremonies are often held in the stunning Crystal Room, followed by cocktails in the Rafter's Room, a baronial hall with stained glass and colorful crystal chandeliers, and the adjoining Terrace Room, which has a glass pavilion, Waterford chandeliers, and a hand-carved plaster ceiling. For dinner and dancing, guests head back into the Crystal Room. Tavern on the Green's sumptuous flower-filled gardens strung with lanterns are also available for weddings. The continental menu is customized to the bride and groom's tastes. (Among the restaurant's signature dishes are rack of veal, grilled salmon, and filet of Black Angus beef. Its sumptuous buffets of shellfish, sushi, and desserts are also legendary.) The maximum number of guests is 300. Prices start at $100 per guest.

For more details on having your wedding at Tavern on the Green, call the banquet department at (212) 873-4111. The restaurant is located in Central Park at 67th Street in New York City.

The guests showered the bride and groom with a hail of rose petals as they departed Tavern on the Green. Returning to Pine Valley, they shared a glorious family Christmas with their son, Bobby.

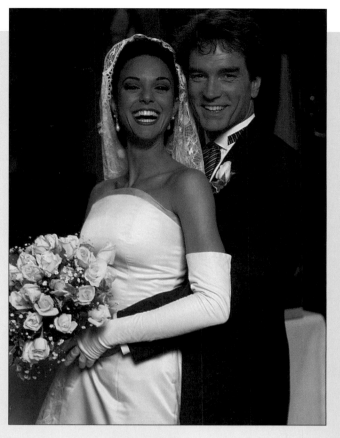

Edmund Grey
and
Dr. Maria Santos

March 11, 1994

Soul mates Edmund Grey and Maria Santos proved they could overcome any obstacle that dared to impede their strong and loving union. When Pulitzer Prize–winning journalist Edmund Grey met skilled surgeon Maria Santos in 1993, she brought a sense of order and calm, and eventually love, to his turbulent life.

Edmund had poured his heart into a complicated and ultimately ill-fated relationship with fellow journalist Brooke English, only to have his heart broken when she left him for Tad Martin. Brooke's rejection haunted Edmund, who fell into a depression. While drowning his sorrows at Pine Valley's country western bar, Edmund shared a flirtatious evening with the beautiful Maria Santos. Though he made it clear to Maria that he was romancing her on the rebound, she found herself falling for the charismatic writer. After many soulful conversations, they shared a night of passionate love that cemented their special relationship.

Despite his breakup with Brooke, Edmund continued to work side by side with his "ex" at *Tempo Magazine*. After foiling a senior citizen real estate scam, during which Edmund saved Brooke from being immersed in quicksand, the couple's sequestered feelings spilled out in a sizzling encounter. Kissing passion-

Surrounded by family and friends, Edmund and Maria pledged their love to one another. Maria was attended by her maid of honor, Dixie Cooney, while Edmund's half brother, Dimitri, served as best man.

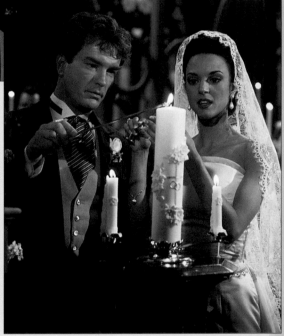

Bridesmaid Julia Santos and maid of honor Dixie Cooney wished the radiant bride their heartfelt best. In the story, Maria's white strapless dress was created by her mother, Isabel, to honor her oldest daughter on her special day (top). After the wedding, the entire Santos family gathered to welcome Edmund into their close-knit clan. (Left to right) Sister Julia, mother Isabel, father Hector, Maria, Edmund, sisters Rosa and Anita, and brother Mateo (then portrayed by Tito Ortiz) (center). During the ceremony, Edmund and Maria lit the unity candle, which represented the joining of their two separate souls as one. It was Maria's idea to incorporate this traditional element into the ceremony as part of her wish to show that she and Edmund were truly united as a couple (bottom).

ately, Edmund and Brooke admitted that they had never stopped loving each other. Still, after much anguish, Brooke chose to stay with Tad.

While still carrying a burning torch for Brooke, Edmund turned back to Maria, finally realizing that she was the one woman who made him incredibly happy. Out of the blue, he proposed marriage. Maria, flabbergasted, needed some convincing—and Edmund was up to the challenge.

"I'm through hanging on to the impossible," he told Maria, sweeping her into his arms. "Everything I ever wanted was right in front of me, but I couldn't see it. Now I see a gorgeous nose attached to one incredibly gorgeous woman."

"Are you out of your mind?" asked a wide-eyed Maria, who couldn't help but be charmed by her suitor's earnest approach. Still, before she could marry Edmund, Maria had to be certain that Brooke was a part of his past, not his future. Edmund had to settle for a "definite maybe" on the night of his gallant proposal, but he eventually convinced Maria to become his wife. However, the bride-to-be's insecurities intensified when Brooke's marriage to Tad fell apart, and Edmund flew to her side to help his for-

mer lover pick up the pieces of her shattered life. Maria, determined not to be Edmund's second choice, nearly walked out of his life—but Edmund was not about to let her get away. Forced to choose once and for all, Edmund told a teary Brooke that he could no longer give her the support she needed. Pledging his devotion to Maria, Edmund never looked back. His commitment to Maria was the biggest step he had ever taken in his life, but Edmund was certain that the time was right to make this wonderful woman his wife.

In the weeks before their wedding, Maria and Edmund met with Maria's pastor, who was genuinely touched by the couple's strong commitment to the responsibilities that lay before them.

In early March 1993 Edmund Grey and Dr. Maria Santos celebrated their union in a wonderful winter wedding witnessed by dear friends, family, and God. The exterior scenes were taped on location outside the Cathedral of the Incarnation, located in Garden City, New York. The historic church, built in 1885, provided an exquisite setting for the long-awaited nuptials. Impeccably attired in a handsome morning suit, Edmund arrived at the church to join his radiant bride-to-be, who was escorted to the nuptials by her father, Hector. The breathtaking wedding brought a fitting end to the passionate, whirlwind courtship of one of Pine Valley's most beautifully matched couples.

A year after their wedding, the residents of Pine Valley turned out again to witness Edmund and Maria marry for a second time as a testament to their everlasting love (bottom).

A floor-length mantilla gave this modern gown a traditional twist. Long white opera gloves provided a perfect accent for its strapless look. The ivory silk-satin gown featured a strapless, boned bodice and a fishtail skirt with train. A matching brocade riding coat (donned by Maria for her memorable carriage ride) added the finishing touch to this spectacular ensemble. The gown, estimated to cost $6,500, was custom made for Maria, though similar styles and fabrics are available at bridal boutiques. Designer Richard Schurkamp, All My Children's former bridal costume designer, was inspired by the 1950s designs of Christian Dior and Balenciaga.

There's a light that's shining in your eyes.
And I just keep staring at it;
and the more I look at it, the more I know.
Well, no matter what else happens tonight,
I can look at those eyes and lose myself in you
and run, not walk, into the future.
—Edmund Grey

Greg Nelson and
Jenny Gardner
February 14, 1984

Fate brought two of Pine Valley's sweetest kids, Jenny and Greg, together in the early 1980s. Jenny Gardner, raised in poverty by her flamboyantly tacky mother, Opal, had been in Pine Valley only a few months when she met Greg Nelson, the son of one of the town's leading families. Greg was equally captivated by Jenny, the girl from the "wrong side of the tracks." Had they not met in the autumn of 1981, Greg might have married his childhood girlfriend, Liza Colby, a purebred, snooty girl who worshiped clean-cut Greg. Greg loved Jenny. Bratty Liza was furious—and dangerous! She seized every opportunity to make Jenny feel unworthy of Greg. Still, even Liza's vicious mind games couldn't keep Greg and Jenny apart. In those first exciting months together, the two shared their innermost feelings and secrets.

"I've never felt like this about anyone before. We may not come from the same backgrounds, but we share important things, like feelings," Greg murmured.

"You sure know how to make me feel better when I'm upset."

"And you make me feel good, too. I really enjoy being with you, Jenny."

Greg Nelson, the all-American teenage son of one of Pine Valley's elite founding families, fell in love with Jenny Gardner, a shy girl from the wrong side of the tracks. Together, these two kindred souls shared the romance of a lifetime.

Concluding the ceremony, the Reverend Whitney made the marriage official: Jenny and Greg were man and wife at last! (left) Moments after the ceremony, Greg beamed as he stared into the eyes of his new bride. Wearing a gorgeous white gown, flowers in her flowing hair, and a contented smile, Jenny made a beautiful bride on her wedding day (right).

Greg's mother, Enid, was stricken by the mere thought that Greg would marry "beneath him." Teaming up with Liza, Enid manipulated the impressionable young Jenny into believing that she must break up with Greg—for his own good. Heartbroken, Jenny wrote Greg a "Dear John" letter.

Jenny's mother, Opal, could not understand why she broke up with Greg. They seemed so happy! Fabricating an excuse, Jenny told Opal she ended their relationship in order to pursue her modeling career, and went back to work at Foxy's to make money for her upcoming trip to New York. Greg and Jenny's mutual friend, Angie Hubbard, knew better. She understood that Jenny loved Greg, and she told him so. Before long Greg and Jenny were back together, which thrilled practically everyone—everyone except Enid Nelson and, of course, Liza Colby!

Liza couldn't wait to exact revenge on Jenny. She picked the night of the high school prom to destroy Jenny's life with the evil truth that her father, the dastardly Ray Gardner, was not dead as she thought and had told Greg, but in jail—locked away for raping Ruth Martin four years earlier. She taunted Jenny with that shocking revelation.

Stunned by the horrifying truth, Jenny fled immediately for New York. Back in Pine Valley, Greg pined away for his lost love, believing she was gone for good. Eventually she returned and, with renewed strength, she found the courage to confront Liza.

On Christmas Eve, while snuggling before a cozy fire at Myrtle's boardinghouse, Greg and Jenny exchanged gifts. She gave him a scarf that she had knit herself, while Greg surprised Jenny with an engagement ring. Jenny joyously accepted, and they

Romance has always been the main ingredient in the daytime soaps, so it was no wonder that All My Children chose Valentine's Day 1984 to marry daytime's most long-suffering lovers. The sweet ceremony, taped in the ABC studios in Manhattan, featured a montage of Greg and Jenny's most cherished moments. Viewers pulled for these tortured teens to get together, but family, friends, jealous lovers, and their own misguided pride worked to keep them apart for years. The montage of memories was presented to the tender tune, "Just You and I" (right). Jenny and Greg's closest friends, Angie and Jesse, shared a dance at the wedding reception, held at Pine Valley's finest restaurant, The Chateau. Later best man Jesse offered a toast to the newlyweds before they left for a honeymoon in Aspen (right).

planned to marry the following June. However, their plans changed suddenly when Greg was paralyzed while saving Jenny from a fall off a catwalk at Pine Valley University.

To spare Jenny the burden of living with a paralyzed man, Greg broke up with the girl he loved. He began months of grueling therapy and slowly began to regain the use of his legs. But spurred on by his mother, Enid, he kept the news of his possible recovery a secret from Jenny.

"Greg, I wouldn't rush into anything. There are no guarantees. The whole progress could stop at any point. Think how cruel it would be to Jenny to let her know now. You mustn't breathe a word of this to her."

"You're right. I'll wait until I can take her in my arms!" Greg declared as he began months of grueling therapy.

While modeling in New York, Jenny and her new beau, model Tony Barclay, were the talk of the town. Or so everyone believed! In actuality, Jenny and Tony's love affair was engineered by modeling agent Olga Svenson purely for business and public relations reasons. The charade worked so well that Olga suggested that they marry!

As her wedding day drew near, Jenny sent Greg a letter proclaiming her love. Enid, however, intercepted the letter and hid it from her son. Poor Greg believed he had lost Jenny forever until the day he discovered that hidden letter!

"She loves me! Jenny loves me!" Greg exclaimed as he read the tender note, barely able to contain his excitement. But this was Jenny and Tony's wedding day! In a flash, Greg raced to the church, hoping and praying he could stop the ceremony.

"*Jenny!*" Greg cried as he raced up the aisle and punched out Tony right smack in the middle of the wedding ceremony.

"Your letter, Jenny. The letter that you wrote me telling me how you felt, Jenny. I didn't get that letter until today!"

"What?"

"They kept it from me! My mother, Amanda, and that jerk that you almost married!"

"They kept it from you?"

"Yes! Yes! Jenny, look at me. Now that I've read the letter, and now that I know how you feel, you have to know that I feel exactly the same way. Jenny, I never stopped loving you!"

Finally, finally, with this incredible misunderstanding out in the open, Jenny and Greg could be together!

JESSE'S BEST MAN TOAST

"To Greg and Jenny. You're not just going on a trip to Colorado. You're starting a trip that's going to last the rest of your lives. And we all wish you a wonderful journey."

WORDS OF LOVE
GREG PROPOSES TO JENNY ON CHRISTMAS EVE, 1982

GREG

Merry Christmas, Jenny.

JENNY

Oh, Greg, what could it be?
(She begins to unwrap a small box he has given her.)

GREG

We've talked about it. And now I want to make it official.
(She opens the box to reveal a diamond ring.)

JENNY

I've never seen anything so beautiful in all my life.

GREG

Well, it's not that big a deal.

JENNY

It is a big deal.
(Choking back tears) *It's so lovely, Greg.*

GREG

You're lovely, Jenny. And I love you, with all my heart, and all my being.

JENNY

Oh, Greg, I love you.

GREG

Will you marry me, Jenny.

JENNY

(Her eyes shining as she looks up at him)
Yes. Yes, I will.

GREG

Oh, Jenny. My Jenny! I'm the happiest guy alive!

JENNY

And I'm the happiest girl.

GREG

(He slips the ring on her finger.)
I now pronounce us officially engaged.

JENNY

I can't believe this is happening.

GREG

Believe it. Because nothing's gonna stop us now.
(They kiss.)

We may not come from the same background, but we share important things like feelings. I knew right from the beginning that you were special. I've never felt this way about a girl before.
—Greg Nelson

Mateo Santos and Hayley Vaughan

May 23, 1997

Mateo Santos came into Hayley Vaughan's life when she most needed a friend. On the road to recovery after a bout with alcoholism and an endless string of bad relationships, Hayley believed that she had found a man she could trust and love. His name was Alec McIntyre—and she was dead wrong about him! This seemingly sincere businessman turned out to be even more insincere than Hayley's first husband, Will, who nearly raped her when she refused to make love with him. Alec's secret sins included embezzling huge amounts of cash from Hayley's cosmetics company and carrying on a sizzling affair with her alcoholic mother, Arlene.

Hayley's instincts told her that Alec was a creep, but still she agreed to marry him. However, on their wedding day in May 1995, Hayley panicked, aborting the impending nuptials. Still wearing her wedding dress, she fled to the beach where, distraught and confused, she encountered the man who would one day become her husband. On that fateful night Mateo sensed that something was terribly wrong with the beautiful blond woman in the wedding dress. He tenderly talked Hayley through the night, comforting her in her time of need. She returned home, and though Mateo's words of warning echoed in her head, she proceeded to go back to Alec anyway. Hayley was determined to make this relationship work!

The chance encounter had a profound impact on Mateo. He felt an instant attraction to the vivacious Hayley, one that seemed destined to lead to romance. Over the next weeks, they continued to be drawn to each other. One day fate brought Mateo and Hayley together in a stalled elevator. When Hayley panicked, Mateo calmed her with a kiss that she could not resist! When power was restored and the elevator doors flew open, there stood Alec, aghast at seeing his wife-to-be in the arms of another man!

More than ever, Mateo wanted Hayley. But how could he even begin to think that he could woo the high and mighty Hayley Vaughan? Why, she was a powerful corporate mogul—and he was a lowly bus boy at the Valley Inn! The fact that they were from two different worlds did not deter Mateo. Even after Hayley and Alec were finally married, Mateo did not give up. He was resolute in his quest to make Hayley see that slimy Alec was a scoundrel.

Just weeks after marrying Alec, Hayley made the shocking discovery that he was embezzling funds from her company, Enchantment. Tracking down her deceitful husband at a sleazy motel room, Hayley walked in only to see Alec in bed with her alcoholic mother, Arlene. Worse, he was forcing a bottle of booze down her throat—in effect, poisoning her! Shocked, Hayley fled to the beach. In desperation, Hayley was sorely tempted to take a drink of vodka, but with steely courage, she boldly poured the contents into the sea.

Out of the blue, Mateo arrived on the scene after punching out Alec, who was promptly jailed for his crimes. Seeing her savior in a new light, Hayley raced into Mateo's open arms. He tenderly kissed her tears away, and they made passionate love under the stars.

Though she had seemingly found her knight in shining armor, Hayley was not ready to commit to Mateo. It took time before the scars of her failed marriage to Alec would heal. Wallowing in despair, Hayley blamed herself for her constant failures in matters of the heart. Mateo held out hope that she would eventually realize what he always knew in his heart—they belonged together!

Months passed, and Hayley continued to push Mateo away. It was only when they journeyed to Jamaica in search of Mateo's missing sister, Julia, and her fugitive fiancé, Noah, that the cold war between the star-crossed kids finally thawed. Away from Pine Valley, Hayley and Mateo finally found the freedom to express their deep love and affection for each other. Against a breathtaking backdrop of the Caribbean sea, passion reignited. Fans of this popular couple finally had the long-awaited reunion they had been craving!

The lovers made plans to marry, but another formidable obstacle would scotch their plans. Hayley and Mateo's relationship was threatened by the arrival of Matt's "old buddy," Tanner Jordan.

Hayley calls off her wedding to Mateo (right). After six years of tortured romances and two heartbreaking bad marriages, Hayley found her true love in ultra-good-guy Mateo Santos. In 1997 they nearly made it to the altar, but Mateo's so-called friend, Tanner Jordan, came to Pine Valley and successfully drove a wedge between Hayley and her husband-to-be when he convinced Hayley that they had made love in a cave! In actuality, devilish Tanner had drugged Hayley, then raped her. Tortured by guilt, Hayley tearfully called off the wedding at the last possible second.

The smooth-talking Australian set his sights on Hayley and secretly manipulated events to make his "pal" Mateo look bad in her eyes. In an unusual twist, Hayley found herself fantasizing about Tanner, making her an easy pawn in his dangerous game.

Tanner, a licensed pilot, went to great lengths to be alone with Hayley, even going as far as taking Hayley up in his plane, then faking an "emergency" landing. Stranded in a cave somewhere in the hills of Virginia, Tanner spiked Hayley's juice with a powerful "date rape" drug. When she awoke from her drug-induced blackout, Tanner foxily hinted to Hayley that they had made love!

Safely home in Pine Valley, Hayley was racked with guilt as she made final arrangements for her marriage to Mateo. What should have been the most glorious day of her life was ruined by Tanner's vicious mind games. Shaken and distressed, Hayley devastated Mateo when she called off their wedding just moments

before it was scheduled to begin, then tearfully confessed her infidelity.

Stung by Hayley's confession that she had slept with his best friend, Mateo harshly informed her that their relationship was over. Or was it?

Despite his pained words, Mateo's love for Hayley refused to die. Soon she would need her knight in shining armor more than ever, because Tanner buried

Hayley landed in the hospital, but Mateo was determined to make her his bride without delay. Hayley's father, Adam, teamed up with the groom to arrange everything as a surprise to Hayley. With Adam and his wife, Liza, as the only witnesses, and the bride propped up in bed and surrounded by flowers, one of Pine Valley's sweetest and most adorable couples became man and wife.

Hayley in the very same cave in the wilds of Virginia. Entombed under a mountain of rocks, she seemed certain to die. Mateo miraculously raced to the cave, vanquished Tanner, then rescued his lady love in the nick of time. Vowing never to let her go, Mateo rushed Hayley to the hospital. Together at last, the lovers didn't want to wait another minute to get married. Finally, Hayley and Mateo became become man and wife—with a Virginia hospital room serving as their makeshift chapel of joy!

FATHER

Keeping in mind the fragility of the bride and the circumstances, I'll keep this ceremony as brief as possible. The setting of this hospital, while not the sanctified space of a church, is still holy, for it is a place of great joy as well as sorrow, a place consecrated by miracles, pain, prayer, and revelations of the peace which we all seek. The exchange of vows between Hayley and Mateo are made sacred by His presence no matter the setting, so let us begin. In the name of the Father and the Son and the Holy Spirit. Almighty God, hear our prayers for Hayley and Mateo who wish to be united in the sacrament of marriage. Increase their faith in you and in each other, and through them bless your church. We ask this through our Lord Jesus Christ, your Son, who lives and reigns with you and the Holy Spirit, one God, forever and ever. Amen

ALL

Amen.

FATHER

We have come together here today in this hospital room so that the Lord may seal and strengthen your love in the presence of the Church's minister and these witnesses. Hayley and Mateo, have you decided freely and without reservation to give yourselves to each other in holy matrimony?

HAYLEY

Yes.

MATEO

Yes.

FATHER

Will you love and honor each other as husband and wife for the rest of your lives?

HAYLEY

(Very emotional)

Could I say something here?

FATHER

Of course.

HAYLEY

Thanks to you, Mateo, I'm here and more in love than I thought I could ever be. I know that God is on our side and always has been. I was in that cave and so close to leaving this earth, but He brought you to me to save me. And I know that one of the reasons I ended up in that cave was that I failed on the honesty thing. If there had never been a secret kept, if I had trusted you with every doubt and flicker of doubt I had, none of those terrible things would have happened. And so I want to pledge to you that from now on I will tell you everything that happens to me, everything I think, everything I feel. I don't want us ever to have a moment that's not 100 percent honest, open, and trusting. And I know in my heart and in my soul that we can do it. For the first time in my life, I really believe in me . . . really. And I believe and trust you, and I believe and trust in God. We're going to make it.

FATHER

Mateo?

MATEO

We will make it, Hayley. My faith in you was less than it should've been. I was quick to judge when I had no reason to be. I've always known you were loving and true; nothing should have shaken my faith in you. I've learned what happens when trust gets damaged, and I will never, never let it happen again. We've been to the edge, survived the valley of the shadow. I never connected with those words before, never had a frame of reference for them, but I know that a spirit stronger than anything I've ever experienced came and taught me to trust my heart and my soul instead of my mind and my fears, blessed me with the certainty that love is the strongest power in the universe. Till the day I die I will trust you, Hayley, and I will believe in you. I love you, I always will, and nothing will ever come between us.

FATHER

Will you love and honor each other as man and wife for the rest of your lives?

HAYLEY

I will.

MATEO

I will.

FATHER

Since it is your intention to enter into marriage, join your right hands, and declare your consent before God and His church. Mateo, do you take Hayley to be your wife? Do you promise to be true to her in good times and in bad, in sickness and in health, to love and honor her all the days of your life?

MATEO

I do.

FATHER

Hayley, do you take Mateo to be your husband? Do you promise to be true to him in good times and in bad, in sickness and in health, to love him and honor him all the days of your life?

HAYLEY

I do.

FATHER

You have declared your consent before God. May the Lord in His goodness strengthen your consent and fill you both with His blessings. What God has joined, men must not divide.

SHARE A ROMANTIC RENDEZVOUS IN JAMAICA

Like Hayley and Mateo, you will be seduced by Jamaica's 4,000 square miles of breathtaking landscape. Romantic couples will certainly fall in love with Ocho Rios, known for its exotic gardens, because it's a lavish playground that caters to romance. The resort area's spectacular scenery embraces cobalt-blue waters, amazing waterfalls, and towering green mountains. Add a laidback ambiance, lively night life, and a bevy of sports (diving, snorkeling, golf, tennis, horseback riding) and you've got a dream honeymoon spot.

When to go: Year round. Prices are highest and crowds largest from mid-December to mid-April. July to September is when hurricanes, though rare, threaten.

What to do: Take time out from enjoying one of Ocho Rios's fabulous beaches and head to Dunn's River Falls, a series of tiered waterfalls that dramatically cascade 600 feet down the mountains. Link hands and climb up the slippery rocks. Stop along the way to take a dip or stand under the falls and feel the warm water tumbling luxuriously down your back. The hibiscus are always in bloom at lush Shaw Park Gardens, a botanical wonderland made for a romantic stroll.

Romantic rendezvous: Sail away on a catamaran cruise at sunset as the tropical treats of Jamaica come into full view. Take a relaxing drive through Fern Gully, a former riverbed that now has over 500 varieties of fern, many of which can't be found anywhere else in the world.

Stepping out at night: If you like to party and dance, you can stay up all night at Ocho Rios. Whether it's the weekly nighttime beach party thrown by your resort (live music, food, lots of rum) or a local club with a reggae band, the night life is alive and well.

For more information: The Jamaica Tourist Board has branches in Los Angeles, New York, Chicago, and Miami; phone (800) 233-4582, or you can visit their Web site at www.jamaica-travel.com.

In 1996 passion reignited for estranged lovers Hayley and Mateo when they journeyed to Jamaica. Alone together in their tropical paradise, the pair made love under the stars.

WHEN IT COMES TO ROMANCE, *ALL MY CHILDREN*'S HAYLEY VAUGHAN HAD MORE THAN HER SHARE OF DISASTERS BEFORE FINDING WEDDED BLISS WITH MATEO SANTOS . . .

- 1991: BRIAN BODINE

When Hayley turned down her high school beau's tender proposal, he married illegal immigrant An-Li Chen to give her a green card.

- 1992: WILL CORTLANDT

Heartbroken over her breakup with Brian, a drunken Hayley eloped with wicked Will, but before she would allow him to consummate their marriage, he was unceremoniously murdered by Janet Green.

- 1993: CHARLIE BRENT

Charlie came back to Pine Valley and teamed up with Hayley to form a private investigative agency. The lovers split over Hayley's attraction to Alec McIntyre.

- 1995: ALEC MCINTYRE

Behind his fiancé Hayley's back, this ruthless businessman slept with her mother! Hayley married Alec but had the marriage annulled upon discovering her new husband's duplicity.

I've never been happier in my whole life. I'm going to make sure you're safe and protected and happy forever, Hayley. I promise.
—Mateo Santos

Noah Keefer
and
Julia Santos
June 7, 1996

From the day she arrived in Pine Valley, Julia Santos tried to catch the eye of every man who crossed her path. This gorgeous but flighty young woman grew up fast when a random tragedy nearly ended her life during the summer of 1994. Julia never believed she could feel beautiful again after her face was badly scarred by shards that fell from a chandelier when a tornado ripped through Pine Valley. Deeply depressed by the disfiguring wound that left a jagged scar across her cheek, Julia fled into the streets.

Finding shelter in a rundown tenement, Julia was befriended by a street-smart giant of a man named Noah Keefer. Noah took the fragile girl under his wing and gently wiped away her tears. The moment they locked eyes, sparks flew! At first, Julia let Noah believe she was a prostitute, and she was desperate to hit the streets again.

Splendidly decked out in a wool navy-blue military-style jacket, stretch breeches, and knee-high boots, Noah quipped to his friends that "I feel like the doorman at the Royal Plaza Hotel." But to Julia, he was the consummate Prince Charming. Gasps of admiration greeted the bride when she appeared on the Wildwind terrace. Julia looked like she stepped out of a storybook in her white ballroom gown and matching jeweled headband—complete with the requisite glass slippers (above). The moonlit terrace of the Wildwind mansion served as the lush setting for Noah and Julia's extravagant nuptials. The vast space was transformed into a fairy tale's enchanted forest as family and friends treated the bride and groom to a lavish Cinderella ceremony, complete with brilliant costumes, twinkling lights, bewigged footmen, and a string quartet playing the wedding's musical theme, "A Dream Is a Wish Your Heart Makes."

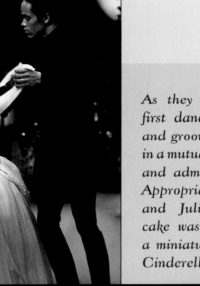

"Sex was the only thing I was ever good at," she uttered in despair. Noah forbade the feverish girl from leaving his company, suspecting that she was not telling him the truth.

As the weeks passed, their relationship ran the gamut from animosity to mutual respect to friendship to . . . *love?* During those dark days together, Noah brought light into Julia's life. Though they held each other spellbound, neither flighty Julia nor stubborn Noah was willing to admit that each was feeling something special and wonderful.

As they shared their first dance, the bride and groom locked eyes in a mutual look of love and admiration (left). Appropriately, Noah and Julia's wedding cake was crowned by a miniature replica of Cinderella's castle.

As the days passed, Noah became Julia's confidant, her savior, her protector. Just as Julia was regaining some semblance of self-esteem, tragedy struck again. On the squalid streets, Noah could not protect Julia from drug dealer Louis Greco, who raped her. In the horrible days after

the rape, Noah tried his best to soothe Julia. Though she refused help, Noah carried her to the bathroom and bathed her. Thankfully, Noah was there for Julia every step of the way when she realized she was pregnant with Louie's baby. This gentle giant stood by her when she bravely testified against her attacker. He supported Julia in her painful decision to have an abortion and gallantly lied to her parents that he was the father of her child so they wouldn't have to know that she had been raped. Julia held Noah's hand through another emotional ordeal—an AIDS test—which fortunately proved negative.

One night, in an burst of uncharacteristic emotion, Noah confessed his deep feelings. He poured out his heart, telling Julia how much he loved her. But despite her devotion to him, Julia was not ready to love anyone. Feeling ashamed and heartbroken, Noah began to believe that their racial differences were the real reason that Julia rejected his plea of love. She took great pains to make Noah realize that race (he was black and she was Hispanic) had nothing to do with her feelings. Although color was not the issue, Julia remained confused, forcing Noah to move on with his life. On the rebound, he fell into the waiting arms of Taylor Cannon, who tried every conceivable trick—even a phony pregnancy—to hang on to him.

As she regained her confidence and self-esteem, Julia finally felt ready to love her knight in shining armor. Free of roadblocks, they became engaged. As they basked in the glow of their impending marriage, Julia and Noah believed that their biggest problem was going to be winning her parents' approval. However, they soon encountered an even bigger obstacle when rapist Louie Greco wrangled an early release from prison. Seeking revenge, he began stalking Julia and her loved ones. Noah was fiercely determined not to let Greco run their lives.

"I'll kill you if you ever go near Julia again," Noah warned the cocky ex-con. But Louie, seemingly unafraid, just smiled. Noah meant every word of his stern warning. Weeks later, when Louie kidnapped Julia, Noah saved her and stopped himself from killing her attacker. When Louie pulled out a gun, Noah defended himself. In a struggle, Louie hit his head and died. However, when the police arrived, there was no gun to be found. Noah's spurned ex, Taylor, had witnessed the incident and could have cleared Noah of any wrongdoing. Instead, she pocketed the pistol!

Most newlyweds are showered with rice or birdseed as they take their leave. Noah and Julia were treated to a gentle shower of bubbles!

Noah and Julia tried to ignore the criminal investigation as they made final plans to marry. Noah treated Julia to a night of celebration and passion in New York before returning to Pine Valley for their wedding day. It was to be a white winter wedding for the star-crossed couple. During their wedding rehearsal, Noah gently spoke some heartfelt, impromptu vows.

"You are my lady, Julia. And my life. Be with me now and forever."

But once again, happiness eluded the tortured twosome. Based on Taylor's lies, Detective Derek Frye stunned the gathered guests by barging into the wedding ceremony to arrest Noah Keefer for murder.

A prison escape ensued, followed by Noah and Julia's harrowing stowaway journey to Jamaica, where they married themselves in a private, heartfelt ceremony. The path to freedom became clear when Taylor finally confessed to withholding the evidence to clear Noah's name. Noah was finally free—free to make Julia his wife in a well-deserved happy ending to an incredible love story.

With a wave of Aunt Grace's magic wand, and a pair of glass slippers provided by Erica Kane, Julia and Noah became Cinderella and Prince Charming in an enchanting fairy-tale wedding.

WORDS OF LOVE

Noah and Julia's Wedding Ceremony

Julia and Noah discovered how much their love meant to others when
friends and family caught the spirit of this spectacular couple and
"testified" in an impromptu celebration of love . . .

HAYLEY

*Thank you for giving me the first fairy tale I could actually believe. There is such a thing
as forever love. The kind that gets bigger with time. The kind you can wrap your heart in,
and know that your heart won't break. The rest of you may get jostled, but your heart
will remain intact. That's nothing less than magic. I marry you in the name of magic.*

JACK

*You trusted each other. You trusted your love.
You trusted the truth would out. I marry you in the name of trust.*

BROOKE

*Sometimes you have to hold your breath, climb the high wire—and jump
off without a safety net. Courage doesn't mean being afraid. It means feeling the fear—
and doing it anyway. Noah and Julia, I marry you in the name of courage.*

ADAM

*Rule number one of the Chandler code—dogged persistence is the root of success. If you want
something—and you know it's right—never give up, never give in. Thank you, Noah and Julia,
for proving what I've known all along. I marry you in the name of persistence.*

DIMITRI

*Noah, you and I have a lot of armor. It takes a special person to break through it. It's good to
be strong—pride's a fine thing—but too much of it—take it from me . . . . Never let your
pride keep you from Julia. Never let your pride tell your heart which way to turn. I marry
you in the name of surrender—letting go of whatever holds you back.*

ERICA

*Lies are a most destructive thing. You're not afraid of
the truth, Noah. You never blink. It's your greatest strength.
That's one of the reasons this marriage is blessed.
I marry you in the name of truth.*

MARIA

*My beautiful sister was obsessed with her looks,
because she was shaky about what was in here.*
(Indicates her heart)
*Julia was afraid of not measuring up—the curse of the middle
child. You changed that. You looked at Julia and saw more
than a lovely girl. You caught the Julia spark—and kept it
going, when the whole world conspired to put it out. You set
Julia free to be herself. The remarkable person she always was.
I marry you in the name of freedom.*

ANITA

*A lot of people worked really hard to keep you and
Noah apart. But you stood together, no matter what.
I marry you in the name of—of—*

MATEO

Unity!

After surviving many calamities
together, Julia and Noah pledged
their troth. The bride and groom
recited their own personal vows to
one another during the innovative
ceremony.

NOAH AND JULIA'S WEDDING VOWS

NOAH

*My whole life growing up I heard "There's a great big world out there, Noah.
You can own a piece of it if you try. Go someplace. Be somebody. Find what you want
and fight for it." Trouble is, I could never find it. I never found anything worth fighting for.
till you fell into my life, Julia Santos. Everybody needs a reason—you're mine. I promise,
in front of God and these people, I'm going to make you happy, J.
Over-the-moon happy. Happy for the rest of your life. With this ring,
I thee wed, forever and ever, world without end.*

JULIA

*My life didn't start till you, Noah. My sister's right. I always felt like something
was missing. I was scared all the time. Even when things went well—deep down
I thought I didn't have what it takes. I never felt safe—till I found you.
You made me strong, when the world was caving in. You made me whole,
for the first time ever. I love you more than I'll ever be able to say. I promise,
in front of God and all these friends and family, to spend the rest
of my life showing you how much. Te amo, Noah.
With this ring, I thee wed, forever and ever, world without end.*

DIMITRI'S TOAST

To Noah and Julia—love and laughter and happily ever after.

EDMUND'S TOAST

Here's to the husband, and here's to the wife—may they remain lovers for life.

OPAL'S MAGICAL MYTH

(To Rosa)

*Did you know if you take home a piece of wedding cake,
sleep with it under your pillow,
you'll dream of the man you're gonna marry?*

ROSA

Really??

OPAL

Cross my heart!

JULIA'S FAREWELL WISH

*Thank you all for the best wedding I ever dreamed of.
If my fairy godmother could grant another wish, I'd ask that everyone
in the world could begin their marriage surrounded by so much love.*

Julia

I'm afraid I'm going to wake up.

Noah

Not a chance. We're dreaming the same dream. This one is forever.

SHARE A ROMANTIC RENDEZVOUS
IN ORLANDO, FLORIDA

Wedding dreams do come true at the Wedding Pavilion in Walt Disney World near Orlando, Florida. Surrounded by palm trees on a private island, the glass-enclosed pavilion is an elegant setting for upscale weddings that can accommodate as many as three hundred guests. The pavilion consists of a nondenominational chapel with a center aisle and his and her dressing rooms for the bride, groom, and their attendants. There's also a full-scale salon on the premises called Franck's (a re-creation of the salon from the 1991 movie *Father of the Bride*) to help with all wedding necessities, from invitations to flowers. Couples can even invite a Disney character or two to attend the wedding (sorry, Mickey isn't allowed to give away the bride nor is Goofy permitted to stand up for the groom), and the bride can arrive in Cinderella's glass coach. Vows are said in full view of Cinderella's Castle, across the Seven Seas Lagoon at the Magic Kingdom. Once the I dos are said, the just-marrieds and their guests move on to a reception at one of the many Disney resorts. For more details on the Wedding Pavilion and Disney Fairy Tale Weddings, call 407-828-3400.

> I never found anything worth fighting for. Till you fell into my life, Julia Santos. Everybody needs a reason—you're mine.
> —Noah Keefer, 1996

Stuart Chandler
and
Cindy Parker
May 26, 1988

"What does 'love' feel like?" Stuart Chandler wondered aloud to his niece, Skye.

Just days earlier Stuart had met Cindy Parker, the mother of one of his art students, and he was captivated by her innocence and beauty. Skye recognized the symptoms. Stuart was glowing! There was no doubt that he had fallen in love with the young beautician. Why else would he show up at the Glamorama twice in a week to get his hair cut?

Skye told Stuart that some people express their love with gifts. What a great idea! Stuart bought an expensive present for Cindy, but he didn't dare give it to her in person. He dropped the gift off anonymously at Cindy's workplace, the Glamorama, then watched from afar and was crushed as she tossed the beautifully wrapped package in the trash. Only later did Stuart learn that Cindy believed the gift was sent to her by her ex-husband Fred, a drug addict. Thinking Fred was trying to win her back, she had disposed of the present without opening it. Stuart beamed with the knowledge that Cindy cared for him after all!

"He's a very special man," she confided to her friend, Angie Hubbard. Over long talks in the park, Cindy and Stuart were soon inseparable. She felt secure in Stuart's promise that he would always be there for her in good times and bad.

Stuart didn't dare confide his feelings to his twin brother, Adam, who had already accused the poor Mrs. Parker of being a fortune hunter. But Adam's foul disposition didn't stop Stuart from seeing the young woman who had captured his heart.

Bridesmaids Brooke English, Angie Hubbard, Donna Sago, and flower girl Laura Cudahy assisted Cindy on the morning of her wedding (left). "What if I blow it?" wondered Cindy's son, Scott, as he nervously prepared to give his mother away. When the Reverend Thompson asked, "Who gives this woman to be married to this man?" Scott paused for a moment, then shouted, "Me! I mean, I do!" (below)

"I love you, Cindy!" he blurted out one day.

"Oh, Stuart. It's too early to be talking about love," she told him gently in return, though it was apparent that feelings were stirring inside her.

In December, Cindy received terrible news when Angie told her that her ex-husband, Fred, had died of AIDS. Cindy steadied herself as she broke the sad news to Scotty, but later broke down in Angie's arms, knowing that she could be afflicted with the disease too. Her worst fears came true when tests soon revealed that she had contracted HIV, the virus that causes AIDS.

When Stuart gently promised Cindy he would be there for her, she hugged him for the first time. Allowing her feelings to show, she told Stuart that, next to Scott, he was the most important person in her life.

Hearing the news of Cindy's illness, Adam urged his brother to leave her immediately.

"She has AIDS! It's a dangerous disease," he admonished.

"I know what it is, Adam. And I know Cindy has it. But that's not a reason to break up with her."

"It's for your own good."

"What about Cindy? You don't walk out on a friend because they're sick. That's when they need you the most."

Cindy's illness only made Stuart realize how deeply he cared for her. Despite the challenge from his brother, Stuart asked Cindy to marry him. With tremendous joy and excitement, they made plans to tie the knot in Paris—the City of Light. However, it became apparent that they would have to marry in Pine Valley when Cindy's health began worsening. Together they demonstrated tremendous courage in the face of this terrible disease when some misguided Pine Valley residents feared AIDS to such a degree that they tried to drive Cindy out of town. Cindy was harassed and nearly killed in a fire set by a vigilante group. Cindy would have perished had it not been for the heroic efforts of Skye Chandler, who raced into the burning fire and rescued her. Only later did it become known that Skye had been a member of the AIDS-fearing vigilantes, and it was she who arranged the fire, only to have second thoughts at the last moment.

The mood was bittersweet when Stuart Chandler married Cindy Parker in the parlor of the Chandler Mansion on a gorgeous day in late May 1988. Adam was on hand for the occasion, having been swayed by Stuart's love and Cindy's tremendous courage. Though tragedy loomed, the bride and groom were filled with boundless excitement, as they faced their future together—united as man and wife.

WORDS OF LOVE

Stuart "Formally" Proposes to Cindy

March 16, 1988

(Stuart kneels on one knee in front of Cindy, opens ring box.)

STUART

Do you like it?

CINDY

Oh! It's beautiful!

STUART

You can have a diamond if you want—but they looked so cold to me.
This was like the beginning of a new morning.

CINDY

I love it.

STUART

I love you, Cindy. And I'm going to be a good husband.
I'm going to love you and take care of you forever.
(He slips the ring on her finger.)

WORDS OF LOVE

(Scott worries to Stuart about walking his mom down the aisle.)

SCOTT

I'm scared. What if I don't give her away right?

STUART

You're not giving her away. You're sharing her. With me.
And you can't not do it right.
Because there is no wrong way to share someone.

STUART AND CINDY'S WEDDING VOWS

STUART

Every morning when I wake up, I thank God for sending you to me. You're strong and brave, gentle and kind. You're also beautiful, inside and out. I never thought I'd be lucky enough to be standing here saying I do, but I do, Cindy. I love you with all of my heart. I love Scott, too, and I'm proud he'll be my son. Your family is my family and my family is yours. I want to be with you every minute I can. And I promise I'll love you forever, even longer than forever! That's how I feel. Amen.

REVEREND THOMPSON

Cindy?

CINDY

I've learned the hard way that life is uncertain. Bad things happen sometimes. So do good things. Like you, Stuart. Meeting you has changed my life. You have a wonderful gift to make people see themselves and things as they really are and still love what they see. And in sharing that with me, you have brought me a peace I didn't know I could have. I can face the uncertainties. With you holding my hand, I can face anything. My strength is your strength. My love is your love. Now and always. Amen.

STUART

(To Cindy)
Take this ring as a sign of our love, which will never die.
(He puts it on her finger. The Rev. Thompson
gives Stuart's ring to Cindy.)

CINDY

Take this ring as a sign of our love, which will last longer than forever.
(She puts it on his finger.)

REVEREND THOMPSON

Forasmuch as Stuart and Cindy have consented together in holy wedlock and have witnessed the same before God and this company . . . I pronounce that they are husband and wife together, in the name of the Father, and of the Son, and of the Holy Spirit. Those whom God hath joined together, let no man put asunder. Amen. You may kiss the bride.

Stuart and Cindy's path to the altar was littered with roadblocks, all of which they overcame in the months leading up to their much-anticipated wedding. Stuart beamed with pride after marrying Cindy in a beautifully tender ceremony in which they recited their own vows. Soon after the wedding, Cindy's worsening condition caused her to go in and out of Pine Valley Hospital. With Stuart's support, she bravely fought off the infections that ravaged her frail body, each time returning home to resume as normal a life as she possibly could under such difficult circumstances. Stuart adopted Cindy's son, Scott, and the new family enjoyed a precious few months together before Cindy's passing in February 1989.

> *Bad things happen sometimes. So do good things. Like you, Stuart. Meeting you has changed my life. — Cindy Chandler*

Tad Martin and Dixie Cooney

December 29, 1989

Mr. and Mrs. Tad Martin. "No matter how tough it gets along the way, if we hold on to two things, we'll do okay. Two things, Dixie. Humor and love."

Few soap couples arrive at the altar without traveling through an obstacle course laden with heartache. Tad and Dixie journeyed through their own personal hell—thanks to Adam Chandler!

In 1989 Adam Chandler married Brooke English, but their marriage suffered when she was unable to give him the son he so desperately wanted. Pretending he wanted to adopt a child was easy for Adam. Lying was a piece of cake. But producing a male heir required a strategy. And, of course, Adam had one. Her name was Dixie Cooney. Dixie left Cortlandt Manor and her Uncle Palmer to go to work for his hated neighbor, Adam Chandler. Dixie was hired as the nanny for Laura, Brooke's daughter. When Laura was killed by a drunken driver, Dixie stayed on as a servant in Adam and Brooke's employ. Like Brooke, Dixie was beautiful. Unlike Brooke, she was fertile.

Adam swept the hopelessly love-struck Dixie Cooney off her feet and seduced her in the Chandler boathouse. Just as Adam had hoped, Dixie became pregnant! He secretly plotted to adopt Dixie's baby when it was born—without his wife Brooke ever knowing the child was his. The plan went awry when Dixie refused to give up her newborn baby.

"Brooke or me," she demanded.

"Why, I choose you," Adam lied in reply.

Having overheard the whole disgusting exchange, Brooke packed her bags, divorced Adam, and made a quick retreat to Pine Valley's number-one attorney, Jackson Montgomery, who helped her win half of Adam's fortune. Scrambling to

secure his legacy, Adam persuaded Dixie to marry him.

One person, Tad Martin, refused to accept Adam's actions at face value. After being dumped by Barbara Montgomery, the resilient Tad picked himself up, dusted himself off, and found himself falling in love with Dixie. And he knew she cared for him. But there was a problem. His name was Adam, who just happened to be Dixie's new husband. In part two of his sinister master plan, Adam attempted to drive Dixie insane and get her to commit herself to Laurel Hill, a mental institution. If all went well, Adam, Jr., would be Adam's. All Adam's. Fortunately, Tad saved the day when he realized what Adam was up to and helped Dixie escape from the hospital. From that day forward, Tad and Dixie were inseparable.

Armed with a Caribbean divorce, Dixie married Tad, as Donna Tyler and her daughter, Emily Ann, sang a love song to commemorate the happy occasion. Before the bride and groom departed in a hail of rice and good wishes, Dixie tossed her bouquet, which was grabbed by Tad's recently returned mother, wacky Opal Gardner Purdy.

In 1990 Tad and Dixie's marriage got off to a stormy start when Tad expressed his desire to move out of Pine Valley to start a new life away from his least favorite person, Dixie's demanding

Everything was in place— the guests were in the pews, the bride was ready to take her walk down the aisle, but the groom was nowhere to be found. Tad hitched a ride to the church with his mother, Opal, who had just bought her car from Trask Bodine.

When her car, a lemon, died on the road to the church, Tad had to walk to his own wedding! He arrived, disheveled and dirty, just in time.

Tad and Dixie's path to happiness was a bumpy one—thanks in large part to Dixie's uncle Palmer, who refused to allow his niece to hitch up with Tad the cad! To break them up, Palmer brought Tad's wacky mother, Opal, to town, paying her a healthy sum to try to stop the wedding. Having failed—at least temporarily—Palmer reluctantly walked his veiled niece down the aisle (right). At long last Dixie and Tad became man and wife. During the ceremony, Donna Tyler and her daughter, Emily Ann, serenaded the couple with a special song, "Through the Years" (below).

Uncle Palmer. Dixie refused to go, and the fact that Tad was working close—very close—to Brooke English as they teamed up to investigate kickbacks in the construction industry did not help keep the marriage intact.

Palmer did his worst to break up Tad and Dixie. Paying a woman, Loretta Rutherford, to claim she slept with Tad worked like a charm to convince Dixie that her husband was a hopeless philanderer. Upon receiving divorce papers, Tad soothed his pain by sleeping with Brooke.

Dixie's new "friend," Billy Clyde Tuggle, offered a sympathetic ear to her sorrows. Secretly Billy fantasized about "his southern bride-to-be." When Officer Trevor Dillon warned Billy Clyde to get out of Pine Valley, he dreamed about taking Dixie with him. Billy rented an isolated cabin and, after chloroforming Dixie, dragged her away. Tad frantically probed to find her, and he did—just in the nick of time! Just as Billy was about to rape Dixie, the authorities, led by Trevor Dillon and Officer Derek Frye, arrived on the scene. After a tense standoff, Billy Clyde burst out of the cabin, spraying bullets everywhere. Seriously wounded, Derek was whisked back to Pine Valley Hospital. As Billy Clyde escaped, Tad rushed into the cabin to get Dixie, and she collapsed into his arms.

Billy Clyde's reign of terror came to an end two months later. Tad, having reconciled with his true love, Dixie, promised to keep her safe forever. When Billy Clyde learned of Tad and Dixie's Christmas wedding, he sprang into action, luring Tad to a railroad yard where he'd constructed a bomb.

"I'm gonna blow that Martin boy sky high!" he said to no one in particular.

On a railroad bridge on the outskirts of Pine Valley, Tad and Billy Clyde met for a final showdown. As they struggled, the bomb exploded, sending both men plummeting into the icy, raging waters below. Billy Clyde's lifeless body was recovered. Finding no sign of Tad, Detective Trevor Dillon was faced with the difficult task of telling Dixie that Tad was presumed dead. Unbeknownst to his loved ones, a disoriented Tad, having lost his memory, had accepted a ride from a truck driver and was on his way to California. Dixie grieved, and so did Brooke, especially after discovering she was pregnant with Tad's child!

Tad and Dixie enjoyed a tearful reunion, but their momentary joy was not enough to bring them back together. So much had happened in the months he was gone! The news that Dixie had married both Craig Lawson and Brian Bodine came as a shock to the newly returned Tad. And the news that Brooke had borne him a child threw both Tad and Dixie for a loop too! Though their love was strong, their bruised egos were stronger. Settling back into Pine Valley life and desperately wanting to be a good father, Tad married Brooke English. Dixie divorced Brian and began a flirtation with the newly arrived Ted Orsini, who looked amazingly like Tad.

But Dixie also entered into a secret affair with Tad. Despite their separation, Tad and Dixie could never deny their unmistakable attraction to each other. Tad began lying to Brooke about his whereabouts so that he could spend time with Dixie. And Brooke knew something was wrong with her marriage because in the bedroom, the normally Lothario-like Tad rolled over and went to sleep, resisting her amorous efforts to seduce him.

By now Ted Orsini's feelings for Dixie had developed into an odious obsession. Desperately wanting to eliminate his look-alike, Ted lured Tad away to a remote part of Canada for what he claimed was a hunting trip. What Tad didn't realize was that he was the prey!

Realizing what Ted was up to, Dixie rushed north of the border and managed to talk a murderously jealous Ted out of killing her and Tad. The path was finally clear for Tad and Dixie to remarry. After months of playing emotional hide-and seek, Tad and Dixie finally put their bruised egos aside and admitted that old feelings die hard. Finally reunited, the happiness these star-crossed lovers felt transcended time and space.

Wrongly believing that Tad was having an affair, Dixie served him with divorce papers. On the rebound, Tad slept with Brooke English but reunited with Dixie after rescuing her from the clutches of the diabolical Billy Clyde Tuggle. They planned to marry, but on the day of the wedding, Tad was in hot pursuit of fugitive Billy Clyde. Dixie waited . . . and waited—but Tad never showed up for their wedding. The groom-to-be had been blown off a bridge by a bomb set by Billy Clyde! Dixie was devastated when Tad, whose body was never recovered, was presumed dead.

Could marriage be better the second time around? Wiser and more mature, Tad and Dixie were up to the challenge. The popular couple had endured hardship, trauma, and years of separation before, at long last, tying the knot again on May 16, 1994.

Once again happiness proved fleeting. Tad's teenage flame, Liza Colby, came back to Pine Valley, still harboring deep resentment over his affair with her mother over a decade earlier. Liza was determined to get revenge on Tad but against her will found all her old feelings for Tad reigniting. Working side by side at their TV talk show, *The Cutting Edge*, Liza and Tad fell back into each other's arms. A night of passion was all it took to end Tad's second marriage to Dixie. Hurt and betrayed, Dixie left Tad and returned to her childhood home, Pigeon Hollow, West Virginia. Tad's foolishness had cost him the only woman who could hold his heart in the palm of her hand.

Two years had passed, but thoughts of Dixie never faded from Tad's memory. Then, out of the blue, he was given a second chance. Dixie had come back to town! Could Tad, after all the pain and heartache, regain her love and affection? Only time would tell . . .

TAD AND DIXIE'S WEDDING VOWS
December 29, 1989

TAD

I'm no prize, but I love you. I don't know how I ever got so lucky, but I know that I will guard you and care for you and keep you safe always. Because without you, I have nothing.

DIXIE

*I love you, Tad. And I thank the Dear Lord for bringing you to me.
And I will never take advantage of that gift, because you are my life.*

THE BEST MAN'S TOAST: NICO KELLY

NICO

*To Mr. and Mrs. Thaddeus Martin. Two better people I never knew. You want friends?
They're friends. The best. And that's what I'm wishing them. The best of everything.
A life full of happiness—lots of laughs, lots of fun—and a marriage that's as perfect
as Cecily's and mine. To the Martins! Long may they live and love in bliss!!*

WORDS OF LOVE
Tad Regains His Memory and Shares a 1993 Reunion
with Dixie in New York City.

TAD

*You were always there, always. Inside me. Even when I couldn't remember who
you were. Coming back like this, considering everything that's gone on, I don't want
you the same way I used to. I want you more. And right now, I feel like if can't
walk across the room and kiss you, I'm gonna die.*

Tad and Dixie's Second Wedding

May 13, 1994

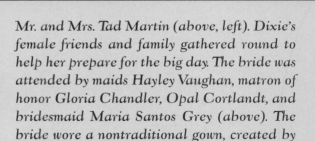

Mr. and Mrs. Tad Martin (above, left). Dixie's female friends and family gathered round to help her prepare for the big day. The bride was attended by maids Hayley Vaughan, matron of honor Gloria Chandler, Opal Cortlandt, and bridesmaid Maria Santos Grey (above). The bride wore a nontraditional gown, created by Richard Schurkamp. The underdress was a column of gold, metallic pleated mesh, with an overdress of olive-green crocheted lace. The style was Gothic empire with a long train. To complete the look, Dixie wore a hair wreath of ivy, lily of the valley, and freesia with a matching bouquet (left).

Cortlandt Manor, Dixie's family homestead, provided the setting for the long-awaited, lush garden nuptials. The Stephen Sondheim song "Not a Day Goes By" added a lilting musical flair to the ceremony. The star-crossed lovers had been torn apart and reunited several times over the years. During the time Tad was presumed dead, Dixie married Craig Lawson, a con artist pretending to be a friend of Tad's, and then Brian Bodine, a friend who helped her through the bad times. When Tad turned up alive, he chose to marry Brooke English, the mother of his son. In the fall of 1993 Tad and Dixie finally rediscovered their love.

Tips from the Pros

At Tad and Dixie's second wedding, the fragrant aroma of fresh flowers filled the set of All My Children. *That's because hundreds of fresh gardenias were brought by (former) set designer Kevin Rupnik to beautify the lush Cortlandt Manor garden, the setting for the nuptials. The gazebo was repainted a creamy yellow to complement the red brick exterior of the mansion.*

Words of Love
Tad and Dixie on Their Honeymoon in Acapulco, Mexico, 1989

TAD

*If we live to be a hundred, it's not gonna
be enough time to spend with you.*

DIXIE

*You promised me something once.
You promised me you'd make my dreams come true,
and you have. I love you.*

TAD

*The only thing I am sure of is you. Without a doubt, you are the most beautiful,
astounding, passionate, funny, wonderful woman I have ever known in my entire life.
And how I was ever lucky enough to get you back, I have no idea. But I do know
that I love you, Dixie. I always have. I always will . . . for the rest of my life.*

Words of Love
Tad's Proposal (in Chicken Suit), October 30, 1989

TAD

*You're a delicate flower with a spine of spun steel. When you look
at me with those eyes, I believe I can do anything. Without even trying,
you make me want to be better than I am. And with you, I know
I can be. Besides, you laugh at my jokes. Don't cry. All I want to do
is make you and Junior happy, now and for the rest of our lives.
Will you marry me, Dixie?*

DIXIE

*I love you. With all my heart and soul.
I thank you for never giving up on me.*

TAD

Will you be my wife?

DIXIE

I'd be honored to.

(Tad puts the ring on her finger and they kiss.)

If I had this day to live over, I wouldn't change one blessed thing. Not one step that got me here with you, right now. I want to be here. I belong here. I love you more than anything. And what's more . . . I don't want to live without you. You are an answer to a very big question: Where's the rest of my heart? Dixie, you're in my blood. You're in a place in me so deep no one else is ever gonna be able to get there again.   —Tad Martin

One Life to Live

Antonio Vega

and

Andy Harrison

August 4, 1997

Growing up on the tough streets of East Llanview, Antonio Vega learned to use his wits and his fists to survive. This smoldering Latino didn't trust the system. He did things his way! Proud and passionate, Antonio wanted to make a difference—so he joined a local gang, the Prides, and eventually became the group's leader. Eventually, Antonio's fervent actions led him to be charged with and convicted of murder—a crime he did not commit.

Like Antonio, Andy Harrison had a strong desire to make a difference in society. However, she chose to work within the system by becoming a police officer. In 1994 an unusual set of circumstances would bring these two strong-willed individuals together.

Mr. and Mrs. Antonio Vega (above). In the weeks before their wedding, Andy and Antonio finally had a chance to bask in the glory of their love. The lovers journeyed to New York City where they enjoyed the sights and a delectable treat from a SoHo bakery (left).

The Llanview boys partied a bit too heartily at Antonio's bachelor party held on a tenement roof in East Llanview. With no women there, the men created a raucous scene as they bid farewell to Antonio's bachelorhood. In the course of their wild night, the men roasted a pig, consumed mass quantities of booze, and dressed in fake animal skins to prove they were indeed "lords of the jungle" (left). While the men partied the night away, Andy held center stage at a soothing "spa-shower" at Serenity Springs (below).

Languishing in jail, Antonio received an incredible opportunity to turn his life around. When Llanview's police commissioner, Bo Buchanan, needed someone to go undercover to determine who was selling guns to kids, he called upon Antonio to ferret out the scoundrel. Bo arranged for Antonio's release and prepared to team him up with Officer Andy Harrison.

Though at first reluctant to cooperate with the police, Antonio agreed to the secret plan in order to protect his kid brother, Cristian, who was in danger of following in Antonio's footsteps. While waiting to meet Officer Harrison, Antonio was approached by a beautiful young blond woman in a flowered skirt and denim vest.

"Hey, you," she called out in a matter-of-fact tone. "Get in the car."

Antonio mistook the tough-talking woman for an East Llanview streetwalker.

"Sounds nice," he replied with a wary grin, "but I've got other plans. So why don't you go peddle it someplace else?"

"You peddle this!" the girl answered sharply, pulling out her badge. "Get in. I'm Andy Harrison, and we've got to talk." Never in his wildest dreams did Antonio believe that his new partner would be a beautiful young woman—and his future wife!

Barely restraining his hostility, Antonio consented to join with Andy on their secret mission. An incredible team had been born—though no one would believe it would last, based on their initial encounter.

Antonio's mother, Carlotta, was given the sweet task of baking the wedding cake—and she prepared a masterpiece! The night before the wedding, Carlotta baked and decorated the five-tiered creation with sugary icing to look like delicate lace.

"The guy's a hotheaded chauvinist pig with an attitude the size of Statesville prison and a macho thing about women, especially women cops . . . I don't trust him at all," Andy informed her brother, Max Holden. Every time Andy and Antonio were together, the air was thick with sexual tension. Still, they remained wary of each other. Andy's romance with Kevin Buchanan had recently gone bust and she was reluctant to share her innermost feelings with another man. Eventually their distrust grew into love. Their private moments, though few, were both intense and romantic.

In the midst of Andy and Antonio's investigation, a full-scale gang war exploded in Llanview's Angel Square. When Andy shot and killed gang member Ice Dixon in self-defense, she was charged with murder. With no one to back up her claim that Ice was carrying a gun, Andy was found guilty—while the real culprit, Detective Nick Manzo, remained free. To make matters worse, Antonio was fingered as her accomplice, and his parole was revoked. Eventually Bo coerced Manzo into confessing that he was the cop selling guns to kids. Andy and Antonio were set free, though she told him she didn't trust him enough to make a commitment.

Andy and Antonio managed to overcome their differences, consummating their love on Valentine's Day, 1996. In their moment of rapture, all seemed right with the world. Trouble, however, was soon to follow the couple in the person of Antonio's new boss, mobster Carlo Hesser.

Antonio hated working for Carlo Hesser. More than that, he hated keeping secrets from Andy. But Antonio felt he had no choice but to accept a secret job working for Llanview's crime kingpin. Though striving to stay on the right side of the law, Antonio desperately needed money to buy back the family diner for his mother and send his brother to college. To accomplish these goals, he made a deal with the devil.

Andy, now a detective, swore to her superiors that her boyfriend was following a straight and narrow path. Eventually a stunned Andy would discover Antonio's criminal ties. Suddenly Andy found herself immersed in a perplexing dilemma—trapped between her love for Antonio and her vow to protect and defend.

What to do? Andy struggled with her dilemma, finally making the painful decision to break up with Antonio. During their separation, Andy grew anguished every time she saw Antonio working his way up the criminal ladder. Antonio's actions were against everything she believed in and everything she believed about the fiery young man she loved. To her astonishment, Andy would soon discover that Antonio had been keeping another secret—and she thanked God for this one! It seemed that Antonio had secretly switched allegiance. Unbeknownst to anyone but Llanview's police commissioner, Antonio was now working with the authorities to bring Carlo down.

A tender reunion followed, and Andy and Antonio's love grew deeper and stronger as they pledged to love each other forever—soul mates for eternity. Their renewed relationship withstood another blow when Antonio was charged with murdering his "boss," Carlo Hesser. Though she was given the incredibly difficult chore of arresting Antonio, Andy stood by her man, believing in him without reservation. Throughout the ordeal, she found strength in her faith in the system, knowing in her heart that the truth would win out. And it did! It was revealed that Carlo's ex-wife, Alex, had committed the dirty deed. She was apprehended, but not before holding Andy hostage in an abandoned beauty parlor.

His name cleared at long last, Antonio hurried to Andy's rescue, heroically saving her from harm. Finally Andy and Antonio could be together. The stage was set for a fabulous wedding and, afterward, a joyous wedding reception—giving the folks in Angel Square a much-deserved cause for celebration!

The streets of Angel Square hosted a rollicking postwedding reception. During the celebration, Antonio played the conga drum and was joined by several musicians who heated up the party with a strong Latin beat. After the wedding reception, the newlyweds bid farewell to Llanview and left for Berkeley, California, where Antonio would be attending law school.

Asa Buchanan
and
Alex Olanov

November 14, 1994

A sa Buchanan wasn't looking for wife number eight when sexy Alexandra Olanov strutted into his life and promptly fell in love—with his bank account! Once Alex set her sights on this crotchety oil baron, any resistance was hopeless. After all, her strongest quality was always her determination. Alex was also one of those people who never knew how to take no for an answer.

Always unpredictable, Asa Buchanan stunned the people of Llanview when he agreed to tie the knot with flighty Alex Olanov in an outrageously decadent ceremony in New York's Central Park. Alex was determined to become the eighth Mrs. Asa Buchanan in grand style!

The sultry blond bombshell yearned to capture a prominent man of wealth, position, and power—someone to fuel her passion for obtaining the best that life had to offer. Someone like Asa Buchanan. Better yet, she would woo Asa Buchanan himself!

With a head for business and a body built for sin, Alex zeroed in on her prestigious prey. Early in 1994 she pulled out all the sexy stops to try to convince Asa to back her master plan to open a fancy new casino-nightclub in Llanview. Despite her flirtatious sales pitch, ol' Asa kept his checkbook tightly closed. After all, this much-married millionaire had learned a valuable lesson from his last wife, Blair Daimler: Don't mess with scheming temptresses! Still, in keeping with her usual style, Alex refused to take no for an answer. Once she convinced Asa to become her business partner, she stepped up her scheme to make the tall Texan her next husband.

Slipping into a slinky dress, Alex idled up to the macho millionaire and tried to melt his icy reserve. But time after time Asa laughed off her seductive overtures. Only when Alex proposed a tempting wager did Asa's ears perk up. Alex, willing to risk it all on this one man, bet Asa that he would offer to marry her within a month. If not, she

Beginning with her grand entrance as Cleopatra (in full Egyptian garb)! Alex arrived at the Central Park wedding on a bejeweled barge paddled by a team of loin-clothed, palm-toting attendants (left). Emulating her heroine, Cleopatra, Alex arrived at her husband-to-be's side in grand style. No matter the outcome of the wedding, Alex was sure to make a lasting impression in her original Cecil B. DeMille–inspired matte gold lamé gown. With its open, pleated bodice, bugle-beaded collar in the shape of a bird, and elaborate embroidered draped train, Alex looked every inch the Egyptian queen! (below)

would hand over ownership of nightclub, Olanov's—lock, stock, and bauble!

Just when it appeared that Alex had lost her bet, Asa realized that he loved this feisty lass after all. To her amazement, he agreed to make her his wife.

The Buchanan clan reacted with horror to the news that the tacky town tramp had finessed her way into the family fold. Convinced that marriage to

Alexandra Olanov was just about to pull off the "wedding of the century" to millionaire Asa Buchanan when two of her former henchmen, Buck Miller and Bulge Hackmann, kidnapped her for ransom. Would the outrageous and determined Alex make it to the altar? Would Asa lose his eighth bride to two bumbling grown men dressed as nuns?

Llanview's leading citizen would put her on top of the social ladder, Alex seized the moment. Now was the time to get back at the blue-haired, high-society dowagers whose approval she had sought for years. Thumbing her nose at convention, she planned to make herself the centerpiece of "the wedding of the century."

Never fear! When he discovered that his fiancée had been abducted, Asa assembled a posse of "Buchanan boys" —sons Clint and Bo and grandson Cord—who grabbed horses from passersby and rescued the damsel in distress, Texas style! After this calamitous event, the bride and groom galloped straight to the ceremony, which proceeded without a hitch (above). To the music of lyres and flutes, the wedding got under way. Then with the march from Aida blaring in the background, Alex descended the stairs of the Grand Ballroom to take her place

next to Asa. As expected, Bo agreed to serve as best man for his pa at the lavish ceremony, held in New York's fictional Royal Plaza Hotel. To Bo's shock, his best gal, Nora, reluctantly agreed to act as maid of honor for her longtime nemesis, Alex. Asa proudly joined his wife-to-be at the altar, handsomely dressed in Western garb— complete with a six-shooter strapped to his side (right).

A self-proclaimed "Egypt-ologist," Alex pulled out all the stops, casting herself in the lead role in a gaudy pageant to be staged in New York City's Central Park. And how would this secret agent–turned–lawyer–turned–gangster–turned–torch singer–turned–socialite make her grand entrance? Dressed as Cleopatra, of course, and delivered herself to her "Caesar" on a gilded barge paddled by a team of loin-clothed, muscle-bound servants!

ALEX AND ASA'S
WEDDING VOWS

REVEREND ANDREW CARPENTER

In the time before time, Osiris, the Ruler King, was betrayed by his evil brother and his body was hacked into fourteen pieces, then scattered far and wide. His loyal wife, Isis, the Great Goddess, searched everywhere for the precious fragments, even diving down into the depths of the Nile, until she had reassembled her husband's body. All but one certain body part, which had been eaten by a crab.

(Thinking fast)

In the spirit of Osiris and Isis, do the bride and groom have anything to say?

ASA

I don't claim to be a god, just a Texan, but that's close enough for me.

(The guests laugh.)

You all have been patiently guzzling my champagne, so I'll make this quick. I love this little lady. Some of you still can't believe that. You're too busy pointing out her faults. Well, guess what? I've heard rumors I may have one or two myself.

(They laugh.)

Fact is, Alex honey, when I met you, I met my match. I promise to love you, and be true to you, and share with you, and get one heckuva kick out of you for the rest of my life. Amen.

(Everyone applauds.)

ALEX

Asa, sweetheart, I knew a long time ago you were the man for me. I met my match too. But today I fell in love with you all over again. With all the Buchanans. When you, your sons, and your grandson came to my rescue, I knew I'd found my true family. At last, I've come home. I'm a Buchanan. I love you, Asa. You're larger than life, you're almost as big as Texas, and as rich, and as much fun. You make me feel safe. I promise to make your days exciting, and your nights—unforgettable.

KEVIN
You've got to hand it to Grandpa. After seven tries, he still hasn't given up on marriage.

CLINT
I guess that kind of optimism runs in the family.

Todd Manning and Blair Daimler

November 14, 1995

Her love soothed his savage soul. His passion saved her from a self-loathing abyss. Todd and Blair's parallel journeys proved to be one of Llanview's most poignant and unconventional love stories.

When, in the fall of 1994, Blair Daimler met up by chance with Todd Manning at Rodi's Bar, she hadn't an inkling that their lives would be entwined forever. Over drinks and conversation, they bonded, commiserating with one another over their mutually sorry and sorrowful lives.

Indeed, Todd Manning had taken a mighty fall. The once-invincible football hero had become the scourge of Llanview, having led a brutal fraternity house rape of Marty Saybrooke. Now, released from jail, this tortured soul continued to flounder, skirting the thin line between good and evil as he searched for meaning in his life.

Like Todd, Blair Daimler remained an enigma—complex, ambiguous, and beautiful. The illegitimate daughter of a mentally ill mother, Addie Cramer, Blair had been shuttled between foster homes throughout her childhood. Blair yearned for affection, for family, and for acceptance.

Todd's niece and nephew, Sarah and C. J. Roberts, never considered Todd a monster, as did most people in Llanview. At the lowest point in Todd's life, the two kids were the only ones to see the good in him. Now, with his life finally on track Todd was proud to include his littlest loved ones in his wedding party.

The sexy vixen had already proven, through her loveless marriage to millionaire Asa Buchanan, that she would sell her soul to get what she wanted out of life. And what Blair wanted was respect, stature, and most of all money!

On that fateful night at Rodi's Bar, Todd and Blair talked into the wee hours. Listening to Todd's story, Blair felt compassion for her fellow outcast. The convicted rapist did not scare Blair with his menacing ways. She found Todd Manning intriguing—and he was equally attracted to her. When the barkeep shouted, "Last call!" they parted, allies against the cruel world. They were platonic, misery-loves-company companions. Soon the two town pariahs, both so much alike, found themselves in bed together. Wrapped in each other's arms, Todd and Blair sought mutual pleasure in order to forget, if just for a fleeing moment, the emptiness in their lives.

It was weeks later that Blair upon an incredible secret: Todd Manning was the son of the late publishing magnate Victor Lord, and as a result, he stood to inherit $27.8 million!

To add to the romance of this special day, Blair's Aunt Dorian presented her with Grandmother Cramer's antique wedding dress. After the wedding, Dorian joined with the families of the bride and groom for this first-ever group portrait. From left: Blair's cousins Kelly and Cassie; Dorian, mother Addie, and Blair. In the foreground, Todd's niece Sarah and nephew C. J. (left). Todd surprised Blair with a private reception at the Palace Hotel, where they vowed their everlasting love. "I've got to share you with everyone else for the rest of my life. Tonight I'm keeping you for myself," whispered Todd to his new bride as they danced the night away in a very private affair for two (bottom, right). "Honored guests, a toast. To my wife—past, present, and future. To life!" (bottom, left)

Golden balloons fell from the heavens to herald Todd and Blair's renewed commitment. Sadly, their bliss was short-lived. Only days later Todd journeyed to Ireland on a mission to bring Marty Saybrooke back home and was shot in the back when he got mixed up in a plot to murder Marty's new boyfriend, Patrick Thornhart. Although his body was never found, Blair, heartbroken, had no choice but to believe that her beloved husband was dead. Early the next year she gave birth to Todd's daughter, Starr.

With calculated swiftness, she set out to snag herself a husband. A wealthy husband is exactly what she needed to pay her mounting bills and cover the high cost of keeping her mother, Addie, institutionalized. Suddenly Blair had an agenda. Playing it coy and seductive, she set out to make Todd Manning marry her.

To fulfill her mission, Blair told Todd she was pregnant. It was a lie! In a simple ceremony on the beach in Key West, Florida, Blair became Mrs. Todd Manning. Soon after Todd discovered the secret that Blair already knew—that he was the long-lost Lord heir! Blair feigned surprise, suppressing her greedy sense of delight as Todd took control of the vast Lord family fortune. Later, when Todd learned that Blair had lied to him, he bought a pregnancy test and immediately forced her to take it. Blair was as surprised as he was when the test revealed she was expecting. In a fortuitous stroke of luck, Blair had really become pregnant—just in the nick of time!

Todd and his wife grew closer as they worked together to turn their publication, *The Sun*, into Llanview's leading newspaper. United in their climb to respectability, Todd and Blair fell in love.

Tragedy struck when Blair was mugged on the docks and lost her unborn baby. Thanks to Max Holden's loose lips, Todd learned the truth that the fetus Blair miscarried was younger than it should have been. He deduced that Blair must have faked her pregnancy when they took the plunge in Florida! Disgusted with his deceitful wife, Todd had their marriage annulled. Then something weird happened. Blair discovered she was pregnant—again! She kept the news a closely guarded secret from Todd.

Even though he always tried to keep his emotions inside himself, Todd could not contain his excitement every time he found himself in Blair's presence. He wanted her completely. To his own amazement, Todd had fallen deeply in love with Blair!

Flying to Key West, the scene of their first, ill-fated wedding, Todd proposed marriage—again! The emotion-laced words did not come easily to Todd, but he spoke them nonetheless, on bended knee.

"We're not going to do what we did last time. No games. No lies, there's no conditions—everything is out in the open. All right. I love you. And I want to marry you, that's all. Nothing else, just that."

To his amazement, Blair broke the news of her pregnancy to Todd. "Do you want to take back the proposal?" she asked anxiously.

"Do you want me to?"

"No," answered Blair, holding back the tears. "I want you to know something. I want to make a promise to you right here, right now, that I am not going to be afraid. Fear is what messed things up for us in the first place. All the lies and manipulations. Todd, I am going to be honest with you. And I'm going to trust you. And I'm going to trust myself. And I am going to trust in our love."

"Are you trying to tell me something, Blair?"

"Yes!" she responded. "Yes!!! I will marry you."

With a tender kiss, Todd and Blair sealed their pact. They were together at last!

WORDS OF LOVE

Blair to Todd on Their Wedding Day

BLAIR
This is the happiest day of my life. I know everybody always says that, Todd, but it's true.

TODD
Right now all I care about is making you happy.

WORDS OF LOVE

Blair and Todd on Their Wedding Night

BLAIR
So this is the new you, huh? A total romantic.

TODD
Well, why not? I'm with my one true babe, floating on a cloud all night.

BLAIR
And our absolutely perfect wedding at the church of St. James.

TODD
I love you, Blair.

BLAIR
I love you, Todd.

I don't want to get dragged down by my past. Or haunted by it. Not my past, or my families. All I want is to be a husband and to have the love and respect of my child.

—Todd Manning

Max Holden and Luna Moody

December 1, 1993

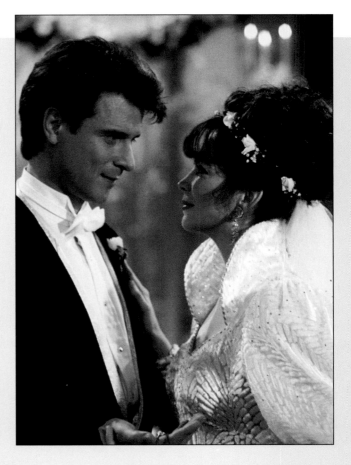

 One unforgettable day, late in the summer of 1991, a lovingly eccentric woman landed in Llanview—with a parachute trailing behind her! Her name was Luna Moody, and this country girl jumped right into the Llanview scene waving crystals and chanting to the almighty goddess.

The moment she laid eyes on the town's blow-dried hunk, Max Holden, Luna was smitten. And Max was . . . well, intrigued. Max and Luna discovered they were kindred spirits, even sharing the same favorite color.

"The pink-purple color the sky gets when the sun's setting," he told her in their colorful first meeting. Luna nodded in an absolute agreement. She had met her man!

Almost immediately, Max and Luna shared an extrasensory bond. But Max considered Luna a friend. While Luna was falling for Max, his wandering eye had set on the dangerous femme fatale Blair Daimler, whom he had first encountered during a sexy midnight dance on New Years' Eve.

While Blair continued to hold Max spellbound, Luna made the most of the friendship he offered, as she not-so-secretly yearned to be with him in body, mind, and spirit. Together with his good-luck charm Luna, Max built his pride and joy—the Serenity Springs Spa.

Throughout their colorful adventures, Luna hid her feelings of love from Max, who insisted that he just wanted to be friends. Meanwhile, she watched with silent sorrow as he chased Blair Daimler. However, Blair

At long last, Max and Luna were man and wife!

had no time for a hopeless dreamer like Max Holden. As it turned out, the best thing that could have happened to Luna's love life was the enigmatic Suede Pruitt, an escaped convict who became obsessed with Luna while listening to her radio show, "Luna's Loveline." Max raced to Luna's rescue and, in the process, came to his senses and realized that he loved her as much as she loved him!

Max gallantly faced danger head-on in his quest to save Luna, who watched in horror as he stepped in front of a bullet meant for her. Max, critically injured, fell into a coma.

Rushed to the hospital, Max fought off death—literally! Inside Max's mind, he was being seduced by the ultimate femme fatale, "Death," who appeared in his visions in the form of an alluring woman. While "Death" tried to coax Max into joining her for eternity, Luna begged Max to hang on to life. Bound and determined to stand by her man, she used her psychic energies to take a cosmic journey to bring Max back to life. With the ordeal behind them, Max finally whispered the words Luna longed to hear: "I love you."

Luna and Max—now joyously in love—moved in together. They were *in* love, but Max quickly became exasperated when Luna refused to *make* love until the stars were in proper alignment. After consulting her astrological charts, Luna decided that February 14, 1993, was the perfect day for a romantic tryst with Max. To Max's relief, her psychic abilities eventually told her that they could make love at a lodge on Lake Serene. However, the plan went awry when Luna encountered a blinding snowstorm and was forced to take refuge in a shack. With the help of a

Max and Luna's unique wedding blended the traditional church service with ritual taken from ancient honors of the goddess Mother Nature and all her aspects. The one-of-a-kind service invoking various rituals including honoring the four directions of nature, taking locks of the bride and groom's hair and mingling them together in a vessel for all eternity, as well as wrapping the couple in

Luna's grandmother's wedding quilt while blessings were shared. The Reverend Andrew Carpenter joined with Sabrina, a New Age priestess, to perform a ceremony in accordance with their belief systems. Andrew and Sabrina found themselves in complete harmony and balance as they united Llanview's star-crossed lovers.

trusty St. Bernard (whom they later named Valentine), Luna found her to way to the Mountain Sunset Inn where she shared a glorious night of love with Max. Appropriately, their Valentine's Day lovemaking coincided with an avalanche that kept them cozily snowed in!

It took a lot of love and patience for Luna to get her man, but when Max finally proposed, Luna seemed vaguely disappointed.

"I somehow expected there to be fireworks going off and bass drums thumping. I figured that when you finally popped the question, the whole world would hear the kaboom."

Max nodded slowly, then charged out the door. Before long, Luna had the proposal she'd dreamed of—in spades! First, Max interrupted WVLE's radio broadcast to tell all of Llantano County that he wanted Luna Moody to be his wife. Then Luna looked out her window to see a low-flying prop plane towing a sign spelling out "Marry me, Luna!" in bright lights. Finally, Max returned in person wearing a plumed *Music Man* hat and beating a bass drum. Reaching into his hat, he pulled out a stunning ring: a moonstone surrounded by diamonds.

"I'm giving you the moon and the stars," he whispered, slipping the ring on Luna's finger. When it came time to set the date, Luna heeded the warning signs from the goddess and decided to wait until the stars were perfectly aligned. Max became exasperated as his spiritually guided fiancée kept postponing the date of their nuptials.

Max was already wondering if Luna really wanted to marry him when all of a sudden she started seeing the ghost of her dead husband, Bobby Ever.

A specially designed set, called the Meditation Center, was built for the wedding. Conceived by One Life to Live set designer Roger Mooney, the center was "a place of serenity" designed to capture the spiritual essence of the couple. With a backdrop of windows that captures sunset—Luna's and Max's favorite time of day—and a ceiling that displayed the night sky and stars, the wedding ceremony literally breathed romance (right). Luna and Max's sunset ceremony was followed by a gala evening reception in Serenity Springs' new Meditation Center (left).

Appearing before Luna, Bobby's "ghost" urged Luna not to marry Max or he would end up like Bobby—dead. Luna nervously agreed to a December wedding, but as the big day approached, she listened to Bobby and ran away.

Max was determined to bring her back—even if it

meant battling a ghost for Luna's love. He followed her, vanquished the ghost, and attempted a daring rescue of Luna from a burning tower.

"You've got to believe that I love you as much as you love me," Max implored Luna. "You're always saving me through the power of your love; now trust that I can do the same for you."

In that moment, Luna knew beyond any doubt that Max was the man for her. Overcoming every obstacle thrown their way, Max and Luna couldn't wait to get back to Llanview to tie the knot. But first they had to climb down a burning tower, parachute out of a plane, and steal Asa Buchanan's prized horse, Copper Beech, in order to make it back in time for their beautiful sunset ceremony with a magically metaphysical twist.

Friends and family were already waiting at the spanking new Meditation Center at Serenity Springs for a remarkably spiritual ceremony—a blend of a traditional Episcopalian service performed by the Reverend Andrew Carpenter and a New Age ceremony based on ancient goddess rituals conducted by Sabrina, the High Priestess of the Daughters of the Earth.

WORDS OF LOVE
Max proposes to Luna

(Max reaches into his hat and pulls out a ring.)

LUNA
Oh, Max. It's beautiful. A moonstone and diamonds.

MAX
That's right, darling. I'm giving you the moon and the stars. That's just for starters. Luna, the whole world heard me ask for this hand, but only you can hear this. I have a vision.

LUNA
What do you see, Max?

MAX
Us. Together. Always. Luna, I want to wake up with you every morning and fall asleep next to you every night. I want to laugh and dream and fight and make up. I want to make babies, mistakes, music, and magic to really live. All with you. And in fifty years or so, when Death comes to take me, I want you right there fighting for me with all that ferocious love in your heart, telling Death "No! It's too soon! It's too soon." Luna, will you make my vision come true? Will you be my wife?

LUNA
Yes, Max. Yes. Yes. I will be your wife!

MAX AND LUNA'S WEDDING VOWS
A Nontraditional Ceremony

REV. ANDREW CARPENTER
Welcome friends, old and new. On this joyous occasion we honor the Great Goddess of Nature,
Our Mother the Earth. We join her rites to the holy sacrament of marriage.
Established by God at the creation, and adorned by Christ at a wedding at Galilee.

SABRINA
Mother of all, bless us and be with us and bless this circle. Bless this couple that come here
today into this circle. And may the spirit elements bless them, fire, air, earth, and water!

(At this time Renee Buchanan emerges from the gathering into the center of the circle,
with a candle, whispering: "Which way is north?" She is gently directed by Sabrina.)

RENEE
I call upon the golden spirit of Earth, of creation, of renewal! Help us that we may
be mindful of Earth, our mother, and live together in peace as her children.

(Tina Lord then emerges with a lit candle and moves to the west.)

TINA
I call upon the spirit of Water, of love, of birth. Help us to take our place
in the ebb and flow of all else that lives.

(Renee moves to the south.)

RENEE
I call upon the spirit of Fire, of passion and warmth and joy. Warm our hearts and our hearths.

(Tina moves facing east.)

TINA
I call upon the spirit of Air, of wisdom, and of mystery. Help us to drink the wind,
and yet find the still center.

(Sabrina chooses a cluster of holly. She moves it from one
shoulder of Luna's to the other in a blessing.)

SABRINA
Luna, nature chooses you, out of the dust and a shower of stars, to be one with Her.
Max, nature chooses you, out of the dust and a shower of stars, to be one with Her.

SABRINA
Luna, do you choose this man to be your husband? Do you dedicate your mind and heart
and will to him, as he to you, joining in an equal partnership that will last your whole life long?

LUNA
Yes I do. I choose you, Max Holden.

ANDREW
Max, will you have this woman to be your wife, to live together in the covenant of marriage,
to love and comfort her, honor and keep her, in sickness and in health,
and forsaking all others be faithful to her as long as you both shall live?

MAX
I will.

ANDREW
Luna, repeat after me . . .

LUNA

I, Luna, take you Max, to be my husband. To have and to hold from this day forward.
For better for worse, for richer and for poorer, to love and to cherish,
until we are parted by death, this is my solemn vow.

SABRINA

Max, repeat after me . . .

MAX

Before my family and friends, I, Max, choose you, Luna, to love and bless in all seasons
in all ways, for all time. I honor you with my soul, I cherish you with my body.
I choose you till my life's end.

(Luna pulls Max to her.)

LUNA

Wherever you go, wherever life takes you, you will always be with me. . . .

MAX

In life, and in death, nothing can ever come between us.

SABRINA

This ring belonged to Luna's mother. It is her daughter's wish to wear it now, completing the circle.

MAX

(Repeating after Andrew)

I give you this ring as a symbol of my vows, and with all that I am and all that I have,
I honor you in the name of God.

ANDREW

This ring belonged to Max's father. He reaffirms a bond. Not only with the men of the
Holden family, but with the traditions and the faith he passes on to his own son.

LUNA

(Repeating after Sabrina)

I give you this ring as a symbol of my vow. And with all that I am and with all that I have,
I honor you in the name of the Goddess!

(Luna and Max address each other.)

MAX

I had this idea that there was someone I had to be. Someone wilder, richer, bigger,
better than myself. And that no one could make that happen but me. Until I met you.
Of all the things you have given me, the real magic is that you have taught me to believe
in things beyond myself. The best part is that I believe in us!

LUNA

When I met you I believed in everything. You name it, I believed in it! One thing that I wasn't too
sure about was me. So when you told me that you loved me, I thought it was an impossible dream.
So I ran from it, I hid from it, you might say I didn't give myself a ghost of a chance!

(Giggling)

But you wouldn't give up on me! You believed in me, and I believe in us!

ANDREW

Now that Max and Luna have given themselves to each other by solemn vows,
the joining of hands, and the giving and receiving of rings, I pronounce that they are husband
and wife. In the name of the Father, Son, and Holy Spirit. Those whom God . . .

SABRINA

. . . and Goddess . . .

ANDREW

. . . And Goddess have joined together, let no man or woman put asunder. Amen.

SABRINA

May God and Goddess bless you and keep you, and may you faithfully live together in this life, and in the age to come, have life everlasting. Amen!

CROWD

Amen!

ANDREW

You may kiss your bride!

MAX

I thought you'd never say it!

(They kiss.)

WORDS OF LOVE

Luna Throws Max to the Ground and for the First Time, Declares Her Love for Him

LUNA

I can't wait anymore . . . can't take this one minute longer! I love you, Max!

MAX

What?

(He struggles underneath her energized frame.)

LUNA

I do! Madly. I fall asleep nights thinking of you, and I wake up thinking of you and in between thinking of you. . . . I'm thinkin' of you!

(She kisses him wildly.)

MAX

Wait . . . Luna . . . Luna!

LUNA

On that very first night we met, when you told me your favorite color was that pink purple the sky turns in the mountains about ten minutes after the sun sets—From that moment I knew I was lost to you! Utterly, hopelessly, blissfully lost! I know I'm gushing. . . . I'm probably making a heckuva fool outa myself but truth is, the truth is, I can't take it anymore! I love you, Max. . . . I love you. O Goddess, I LOVE YOU!

(She kisses him fully and passionately.)

WORDS OF LOVE

Max Saves Luna from the Ghost of Her Late Husband Bobby

MAX

Luna, I don't know any magic words . . . I only know I love you! I love you more than my own life. . . . Luna you are my life. Somewhere along the line everything got mixed up, your heart, my soul, your vision, my hopes. . . . I don't know where you leave off and I begin! When we are together, there is no hope of anything ever breaking us apart, you know that, don't you? I'm not alone, Luna, and neither are you. Every breath we take, every beat of our hearts. . . . one breath . . . one beat. No ghost and no memory will ever change that!

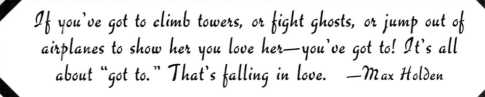

If you've got to climb towers, or fight ghosts, or jump out of airplanes to show her you love her—you've got to! It's all about "got to." That's falling in love. —Max Holden

Jake Harrison
and
Megan Gordon
May 14, 1991

The magnetic attraction of polar opposites isn't just a convention of romance, it's a force of nature. Nowhere was its power more apparent than in the classic soap opera pairing of Megan Gordon and Jake Harrison. She was a spitfire in silk stockings. He was trouble in a tight tank top. How could they help but fall hopelessly in love?

When shady Jake Harrison turned up in Llanview in March of 1990, suffering from a gunshot wound to the stomach, it was obvious that he was in with a bad crowd. And why was this shady but handsome mystery man skulking around celebrated soap celebrity Megan Gordon?

It quickly became apparent that Jake was under the thumb of the villainous Michael Grande, who had ordered his subject to woo the high-and-mighty soap star in order to dig up some dirt on her family and ultimately destroy her mother Viki's campaign for mayor. Reluctantly Jake carried out his mission—which proved quite a challenge. Jake quickly found what the men of Llanview already knew—sassy Megan was a tough nut to crack!

A feisty, career-oriented woman, Megan was leery of close relationships with the opposite sex. Driven by her quest for stardom, she shut out a personal life in order to cover up her insecurities. One man, Max Holden, had managed to break through her facade, but when their love affair went sour, Megan withdrew again behind her emotional wall.

"You have no idea how real people live!" Jake shouted at Megan during one of their many oil-and-water confrontations. He challenged her to come out with him for a night on the town and see for herself how the "other half" lives. Megan, never one to back down from a challenge, accepted Jake's offer. And where did the handsome stranger take the haughty actress for their first date? The local pool hall!

> ### JAKE
> *I love you. No matter what I have to do, no matter what happens from here on in, I always want you to know that my love for you is . . . imperishable. Megan Gordon, will you marry me?*

Deeply in love, Megan and Jake were forced to stage a public breakup so that Jake could undertake a mission to woo mob princess Charlotte Hesser. While everyone believed that Jake and Megan were through, the couple managed to sneak away to Viki's mountain cabin, where they shared a symbolic wedding ceremony, presided over by "the Reverend Simpson," a mannequin on loan from Logan's Department Store.

Despite her protestations, Megan had a great time laughing, shooting pool, and knocking back beers with this raw, earthy, dangerous man. Neither could deny the attraction they felt. Megan and Jake were in love. Only later did Megan learn the terrible truth that Jake had been working for her family's worst enemies. Hurt and betrayed by his duplicity, Megan turned her back on Jake.

"How can I ever trust you again?" Megan asked, her voice laced with anguish.

Jake pulled out all the stops to show the woman he loved that his feelings were real. By now he had broken free from Michael Grande, who was soon gunned down in the lounge of Llanview Hospital. Megan quickly became the prime suspect, and when she was charged with Michael's murder, Jake stood by her side throughout the ordeal, his faith in her innocence unshaken even in the darkest hour.

"Are you ready to begin the first day of your new life?" asked Megan's father, Roger Gordon. Keeping with tradition Roger gave the radiant bride away (left). The bridesmaids and matron of honor wore bright-blue iridescent short, sleeveless silk dresses, along with detachable trains. From left: Andy Harrison, Blaine Adams, matron of honor Tina Lord Roberts, and (right) Jessica Buchanan.

After overcoming a host of obstacles, including Jake's marriage to a mobster's daughter and Megan's first true love coming to town, Jake and Megan were finally able to admit their true, passionate feelings for each other. They were man and wife—at last! (left) In an impulsive move, Jake kissed Megan with love and passion.

Jake couldn't bear the thought of his beloved Megan languishing behind bars in Statesville Prison. Somehow he was going to find the real killer—but not before he broke Megan out of jail! When Megan was nominated for a coveted Daisy Award for her dual role as sisters "Roxanne" and "Ruby" on the hit TV soap opera, *Fraternity Row*, Jake saw the perfect opportunity to set her free. Posing as part of the TV crew hired to tape Megan's acceptance speech from behind bars, Jake sneaked into the prison and kidnapped her! Fleeing the jail, Jake took Megan to an abandoned drive-in movie theater where they shared a tender reunion. Before long Jake heroically unearthed the evidence to reveal the actual killer. Thanks to Jake's perseverence and unwavering support, Megan was set free. Now the two were more hopelessly in love than ever!

Jake and Megan couldn't tell anyone about their renewed relationship because Jake was very busy courting mob princess Charlotte Hesser in a quest to get the goods on her father, Carlo. To help Jake with his undercover mission, Megan staged a very public breakup with him, but they managed to sneak away for a night of romance at Viki's cabin in the mountains. Alone together, they pledged their everlasting love and held a symbolic wedding ceremony.

"Tomorrow doesn't exist," Jake whispered to his bride. "There's just tonight, and tonight there's only you and me, together, in love, forever."

Back home, Megan was forced to conceal her anguish when Jake married the mob princess in order to protect his family.

Megan's first love, Hunter Guthrie, showed up in Llanview at a most opportune time. Still in love with Megan, handsome Hunter was ready to catch her on the rebound when Jake let her down. But he didn't! True to his word, Jake eventually jettisoned Charlotte. His mission complete, the path was clear for a wedding to remember.

On a sunny spring day, Jake and Megan's loved ones gathered inside St. James Church for a blissful day—one that began on an ominous note. On the morning of the wedding, Jake's former wife, Charlotte, made one, last-ditch effort to stop the ceremony

from taking place. Sneaking into the Lord Library, Charlotte stole Megan's Chantilly lace wedding gown! Fortunately, Megan quickly tracked her down and retrieved the gown before Charlotte could destroy the dress. The wedding was on!

A Llanview wedding that was not interrupted by crazed ex-spouses, an explosion, a natural disaster, or someone's return from the dead? Unbelievable but true! On May 20, 1991, the long-awaited wedding of the feisty duo, Megan and Jake, took place with nary a hitch. Though, admittedly, the groom threw a scare into his nervous bride when he and his best man ran out of gas on the way to the church!

Behind the Scenes

Would Megan really marry Jake on *One Life to Live*? Anyone driving by Christ King Church in New Vernon, New Jersey, knew the answer was yes. Seventeen key cast members and twenty-two extras journeyed to the location to tape exterior shots for the long-awaited wedding. Producers from *One Life to Live* scouted about thirty churches in the area before choosing the pastoral setting that fit the bill perfectly with its requisite duck pond in front.

"We wanted to find a small, quaint church, so people would believe it really was Llanview, Pennsylvania," said associate producer Chuck Lioi.

As Megan and Jake left the church, they were pelted with birdseed—Megan's idea—instead of rice. "It's better for the birds," she told the grousing Asa Buchanan, who couldn't comprehend the break from tradition (above). At the conclusion of the emotional wedding ceremony, Megan and Jake ushered everyone in attendance out the door and onto the sprawling lawn of the Church of St. James for a very special tree planting (right).

MEGAN

This tree is a symbol of our love and a way of giving back to God a little of the joy He's given us. We hope that in the years to come, all our friends and our family will think of us as they pass this tree. And, God willing, our own children and grand-children will play beneath this tree. And here are some lines I remember reciting when I was a little girl: "from these roots grow branch, leaf, and flower: Children of the sheltering earth, ripening in the tumult of the seasons, generation after generation.

WORDS OF LOVE
Megan Speaks to Her Family on the Morning of Her Wedding

I never thought that I would love anybody the way that I love all of you. I guess love has a way of sneaking up on you sometimes. But when it's right, you know it and I guess you're hooked. And that's the way I am with Jake. I want to thank all of you for making him a part of this family, and I am so happy that I get to share this day with all of you.

VIKI TO HER HUSBAND, CLINT, AS THE BRIDE AND GROOM LEAVE THE RECEPTION

Oh, Clint, this is another *happiest day of my life!*

CORD ROBERTS TO HIS WIFE, TINA, AFTER THE WEDDING CEREMONY

You know, this is the first wedding in a long time where some kind of disaster hasn't happened. I kept looking over my shoulder waiting for the roof to cave in or something.

You taught me to trust again. You gave me the courage to throw away all the masks and to love again.   —Jake Harrison

Love isn't a mystery but a miracle. Your courage gives me courage, your strength gives me strength, and no matter what the future holds, I'm not afraid as long as I have you with me.   —Megan Gordon

Patrick Thornhart and Margaret "Marty" Saybrooke

September 12, 1997

Call it the luck of the Irish. As Marty Saybrooke sipped a hot cup of tea in a quaint Irish pub on the remote island of Inishcrag, she never suspected that a total stranger was about to steal her heart.

Outside, a full moon brightened the October night, prompting the innkeeper, a sage old man named Kenneally, to share an ancient legend with his pretty young patron.

"The isle of Inishcrag is enchanted, you know," he recounted with a twinkle in his Irish eye. "Who-so kisses a newcomer beneath the full moon on this island—that man becomes yours forever."

Marty chuckled, not noticing the handsome stranger finishing his glass of whiskey and starting out the door. Just then the stranger froze in his tracks, a look of panic in his eyes. Two burly men had walked into the pub, and the stranger knew instantly that they were looking for him.

He quickly turned his back, his eyes rapidly scanning the room. They came to rest on the girl with the long, flowing locks, peacefully seated on a nearby bench. He rushed to her side.

An old Celtic fairy tale brought these eternal lovers together under a full Irish moon. Two years would pass before the lovers were free to marry atop Llantano Mountain (above). "Margaret, I promise you—with all my heart—that our love is going to be a light. And it'll guide us through the dark and the sadness. All the way home." During the days Marty was shipwrecked on a remote island, she finally realized that Patrick was the only man she truly loved.

"Darling, there you are," he said to a startled Marty. Before she could utter a word in response, the stranger planted a kiss on her lips! Breathless, Marty broke from the kiss with an incredulous smile that quickly turned to fear as the impact of the moment set in.

"Let me go!" she cried.

"Please, miss. It's a matter of life and death. We've got to pretend we are lovers."

Without a second to ponder what was happening, Marty played along, engaging in intimate conversation with a man she'd just met. Meanwhile, the two thugs searched the pub but, not seeing their prey, took off into the night. The stranger breathed a hefty sigh of relief and thanked his "wife" for taking part in this hastily arranged charade. By acting casually and posing as his "wife," she had helped him elude his hunters. She had saved his life!

"That was close," he uttered in a thick Irish brogue. "I always thought angels had halos."

In a flash, he was gone, hurrying out the door. Marty sat transfixed, overcome with an uncanny sense of wonderment and fear, attraction and apprehension.

The attractive interloper was Patrick Thornhart, a passionate and articulate man, a writer by profession and a poet by nature. Now this peaceful man found himself in the midst of a nightmare because he was being pursued by the notorious terrorist group, the "Men of Twenty-one," who suspected that he had a piece of coded sheet music that could reveal their militant plans.

Over the next few days Marty continued to assist her rough-hewn stranger, and they grew close.

"Tomorrow I leave and we'll never see each other again," Marty told Patrick. "Time will pass until it's like it never happened at all, like we never met."

"I doubt that'll happen. But if it does then time is my enemy," answered Patrick. A tense, almost unbearable silence followed, as Patrick and Marty sat just apart, aware

Over the course of his tempestuous two years in Llanview, Patrick Thornhart proved himself to be Marty's romantic hero. The duo cherished their midnight picnics under the stars and restful evenings curled up before a fire of smoldering peat.

of every breath the other was taking. Marty broke the silence and moved to Patrick, putting her hand on his face. He took her hand and slowly kissed her palm.

"Maybe we can make time stop," Patrick said in hushed tones.

"Just for tonight, " Marty whispered.

He pulled her close and they made love, with all the abandon and tenderness of two people trying to capture a moment out of time, certain they'd never see each other again.

Afterward, the lovers held each other close and gazed out the window. Naked, Patrick stood behind Marty, relishing the moment. He wrapped a lock of her hair around his hand.

"I am looped in the loops of her hair," he whispered, quoting from "Brown Penny," a poem written by his favorite Irish poet, William Butler Yeats.

They made love again on that magical night, before settling gently into sleep, entwined in each other's arms. When Marty awoke the next morning, reality began to sink in.

Terrified of her feelings for Patrick, Marty fled Inishcrag and returned home. Patrick quickly followed, unwilling to let go of what they had found together. Though they had known each other only a few short days, Patrick knew in his heart that he was meant to spend his life with his beloved "Margaret." The love he felt for her was complete, passionate, and all-encompassing. He had to see her again! Once in Llanview, he was amazed to find the woman he loved engaged to another man, Dylan Moody. On the day of their wedding, Patrick pleaded with Marty to change her mind.

As a violin soloist played softly in the background, Dr. Larry Wolek escorted Marty down the aisle (above). Patrick and Marty chose to marry in a very special place—a clearing high atop Llantano Mountain. "This mountaintop, with these old oaks rising like pillars to hold up God's own roof, seems more cathedral than man could ever devise," Patrick told his bride. Surrounded by their loved ones, the lovers tied the knot in a poetic and passionate open-air wedding ceremony (above, right).

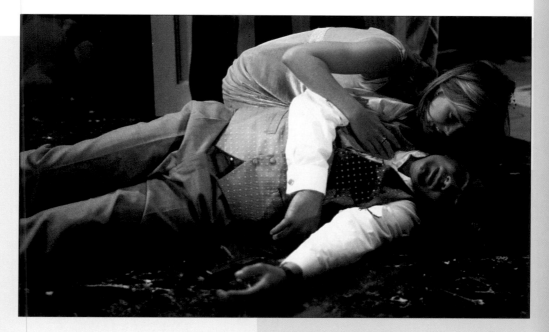

"When the priest says, 'Margaret, do you take this man to be your husband,' and the time has come to answer, the Margaret I know, the woman I love with all my heart, won't be able to utter those words, not to any living man, but me." Marty was torn. She both loved and feared Patrick.

"You say you're a simple man—but that's not true," she countered. "You're complicated, you're secretive, mysterious. And even now when you say the danger's over you're about as calm as a storm in the Irish Sea. It's like any second a tide could turn and a wild current would sweep you away again."

Marty's worst nightmare came to life when terrorists struck at their wedding reception. Mel Hayes (pictured here on the ground) became an innocent victim when he was felled by an assassin's bullet. As shots fired, Patrick pulled Marty to the ground, instinctively covering her with his own body. Later Patrick was shot in the chest. Miraculously, he survived! To keep their dream alive forever, Patrick faked his own death and, with Marty, moved to Ireland just after their wedding.

With tears streaming down his face, Patrick watched as Marty lowered her wedding veil and made the painful decision to honor her commitment to Dylan. Only much later, after months of misery, did Marty realize that she had made a mistake. The only man she wanted to be with was her princely poet, Patrick Thornhart.

Months of pitfalls and obstacles would pass before Marty and Patrick were free to become man and wife. And for a couple as danger-prone as Marty and Patrick, their late-summer wedding atop Llantano Mountain came off beautifully, without a hitch.

Though the reception following the ceremony was marred by violence that forced the newlyweds to flee Llanview, this was the wedding that Patrick and Marty had longed to have. It was truly the happiest moment in the turbulent lives of this unforgettable couple.

WORDS OF LOVE

Nora Calms Marty on the Morning of her Wedding

NORA

You have a real gift to share with the world. All your friends are very proud of you. And what you're doing today is the final step in the journey. The rest of a beautiful fairy-tale—and you're gonna miss it all, if you don't move it, Cinderella! Makeup—twenty minutes! Go!

PATRICK AND MARTY'S WEDDING VOWS

September 12, 1997

JUDGE

*Margaret and Patrick, by coming here today in the presence of your friends,
you are performing an act of faith with each other. Whatever obstacles you may
encounter, nothing will turn you away from the joyful duty of loving each other.*

(In the background Patrick recites "Brown Penny")

*I whispered, "I am too young,"
And then, "I am old enough,"
Wherefore I threw a penny
To find out if I might Love,
"Go and Love, go and love, young man,
If the lady be young and fair."
Ah, penny, brown penny, brown penny,
I am looped in the loops of her hair.*

JUDGE

*By the love you are pledging here today, you will find the entire world in the light of each other's
faces. Patrick, do you take Margaret to be your wife this day and for all your days to come?*

PATRICK

*I do. Margaret, when I met you for the first time under a full moon on Inishcrag
I thought it was by chance, but I was wrong. It wasn't chance at all, it was my destiny
to find you and love you with all my heart for the rest of my days.*

JUDGE

*Margaret, do you take Patrick this day for your
husband and for all your days to come?*

MARGARET

*I do. From the moment I met you, the first
night you kissed me with the full moon shining
on Inishcrag, we were meant to be together.
Now and for the rest of our lives. I love you.*

JUDGE

May I have the rings, please?

(As Patrick places the ring on Margaret's
finger, in the background he recites . . .)

*Love is the crooked thing
There is nobody wise enough
To find out all that is in it,
For he would be thinking of love
Till the stars had run away
And the shadows eaten the moon.
Ah, penny, brown penny, brown penny,
One cannot begin it too soon.*

JUDGE

*And so by the power vested in me by the
Commonwealth of Pennsylvania,
I now pronounce you husband and wife.*

(Patrick and Marty kiss.)

Their friends breathed sighs of relief when Patrick and Marty married without a hitch. But joy suddenly turned to terror when chaos erupted at the reception. Terrorists attacked before the couple could cut the wedding cake.

"Tell it to my face. Lift up that veil, look me in the eye, and tell me that God didn't mean us for each other." On the day she was to marry Dylan, Patrick showed up at the church and tried, to no avail, to convince Marty to change her mind.

PATRICK'S WORDS OF LOVE TO MARTY ON THE DAY SHE MARRIED DYLAN

PATRICK

There's a piece of land in the green hills of County Kildare with a stream as blue as the sky. And the nights are so clear and so crisp you can almost touch them—touch the stars with your fingertips. I want to build our home there, with roses tangled thick over the red front door and a great big fireplace made with the stones cleared from our land—a home made from the very earth it stands on. And we'll be warm there in winter. And by the glow of the peat fire I see you standing there and you're holding our first child—she looks like you, God, she looks just like you. But she'll grow up loved like no other child. She'll not know the fear and the loneliness you felt. She'll be free and fearless and loved—as you are loved, Margaret, forever.

You're a beautiful lady. That's obvious. You're talented and smart, it's just as clear. But even something else—you've got bravery. A man would be lucky to have you standing by his side, Margaret Saybrooke.

I want the same things you do—a home, children, love that lasts a lifetime. But I also want more than that. I also want the passion that I know is in you. I want to free that wild heat inside you, deep inside you.
—Patrick Thornhart

Bo Buchanan and Nora Gannon

June 2, 1995

Call it fate or just plain clumsy luck, but when attorney Nora Gannon strolled into the Palace restaurant and collided with Bo Buchanan, a very unique relationship was born. Nora was instantly taken by the man she ran smack into, but Bo had other things on his mind. His cherished wife, Sarah, had died in a terrible car accident with Bo at the wheel, and the usually affable Buchanan was near suicidal with grief.

Bo was shattered by Sarah's untimely passing. Over and over he replayed in his mind the details of the crash, hoping to understand the unexplained accident. He had tried to swerve to avoid an oncoming vehicle and lost control of his car, which plunged into the Llantano River. But who was driving the car that ran him off the road? Months passed before Bo could deal with the horrible tragedy. Like a godsend, Llanview's newest attorney, Nora Gannon, helped Bo come to grips with the overwhelming loss.

Nora never intended to stay in town. She was a partner in a high-powered legal practice in Chicago. The quick-witted lawyer with the razor-sharp brain had

Mr. and Mrs. Bo Buchanan. For months Bo Buchanan and Nora Gannon avoided making wedding plans. Whenever they took the time to get serious about their big day, something would come along to distract them. Fortunately their closest friends appointed themselves "wedding police," taking matters into their own hands to throw a rock-and-roll wedding, complete with a sock-hop reception! (above, right). Nora's clan—mother Selma, sister Susannah, and father Len—welcomed their new son-in-law into the family (above).

come to Llanview intent on convincing her dropout daughter Rachel to return to college. Before long, Nora decided to settle in town, thanks in part to her budding relationship with Bo.

Week after week Nora fought off her unexplainable migraine headaches to work with Bo, trying to help him find the answers to who was responsible for Sarah's death. Nora helped get his mind off the tragedy by convincing him to join her in a jitterbug during a local

At the rehearsal dinner, Nora joined with the fabulous Norettes (a group of her pals) for a fabulous lip-synched serenade of "Will You Still Love Me Tomorrow?"(above) After they had all but decided to call off their wedding, Bo and Nora got the surprise of their lives when singer Little Richard suddenly appeared on the scene. Propelled by the spirit of rock and roll, they boogied up the aisle to let Little Richard, a real-life ordained minister, officiate at their nuptials. In between bursts of "Good Golly Miss Molly," "Send Me Some Lovin'," and "Tutti Frutti," the flamboyant singer pronounced Bo and Nora man and wife (left).

dance contest. Nora and Bo shared a love of old movies, and Nora brought a sense of joy and fun back to his life. A grieving Bo tried to resist Nora, but his heart won out. She helped him come to grips with the overwhelming loss of his beloved Sarah—and in the process, they fell in love. But as honest as she was in the courtroom, Nora could not bring herself to share a terrible truth with Bo— she may have been the hit-and-run driver who killed Sarah.

A year after they met, Nora and Bo moved in together. Just as Bo was about to propose marriage, Nora admitted that she might have killed Sarah. As it turned out, she was not the guilty party after all! A drunken driver was the culprit. Now, more than ever, Bo knew that this feisty attorney was the woman with whom he wanted to spend the rest of his life. Nora answered Bo's tender proposal of marriage with a resounding yes!

Their troubles were far from over. Nora was diagnosed as having a malignant brain tumor and needed surgery. She reluctantly opted to go under the knife but chose not to inform Bo. Instead, Nora lied, telling her beloved fiancé that she was paying an extended visit to her parents in Chicago. Just after the operation, Bo found out the

At the end of this memorable day, Nora gathered Llanview's eligible women together, then tossed her wedding bouquet. The flowery bunch landed in the waiting hands of her daughter, Rachel.

truth and raced to Nora's hospital bedside, where he stayed throughout her ordeal.

Back home, Nora came to rely on Bo during her recovery just as he had depended on her kindness and strength after Sarah's death. After long days on the job, they longed to spend their nights cuddled under the covers, munching popcorn and watching nostalgic old movies. They were more in love than ever—but when it came to actually making their love official, both Bo and Nora insisted on dragging their feet. Eventually they concurred that a wedding was not what they wanted after all—or did they?

"We're not getting married," Nora reminded Bo. "We have a plan and we're going to stick with it: a permanent engagement with *no* wedding bells."

"Then again, plans can change," answered Bo. And they did. Bo and Nora got engaged!

One after another, things came up to force Bo and Nora to postpone the big event. Finally their exasperated friends stepped in and took charge. To help the procrastinators get their act together, Nora's ex-husband, Hank, his wife, Sheila, and their pals, Max and Luna, dubbed themselves the "wedding police" and planned a tasteful, traditional interfaith wedding for the couple.

Finally the day arrived! Wearing a lavender gown picked out by the wedding police, Nora joined Bo in the Church of St. James, but when it came time to say I do, they didn't! Once the bride and groom stood before the Reverend Andrew Carpenter, Rabbi Heller, and a church full of guests, they had a change of heart. The astonished guests listened as Bo and Nora stopped the proceedings to sheepishly explain that, while they were honored to be given such a flowery and fluffy wedding, something was missing. They had dreamed of having a rock-and-roll wedding—full of fun, music, and dancing!

Thanking their guests, Bo and Nora turned on their heels and started to walk out of the Church. Suddenly Max Holden pulled a curtain behind the reverend and the rabbi to reveal Bo and Nora's favorite rock-and-roller, Little Richard!

As the legendary Little Richard played a mean riff on the piano, Bo and Nora delightfully danced back up the aisle to take part in the most electrifying wedding ever to hit Llanview!

BO AND NORA'S WEDDING VOWS
An Interfaith, rock-and-roll Ceremony

LITTLE RICHARD
Is there anything you want to say to each other?
Nora . . .you're first. Make me cry. Go on, break my heart.

NORA
I don't know why I am really so surprised, you know. . . .I mean, suddenly everything just turned
out right . . . out of nowhere. Just like you, Bo, out of nowhere when I wasn't looking, there you were,
and there we were. And here we are. . . .A few minutes ago, we were gonna call the whole thing off
because something felt wrong, and we're not used to that feeling when the two of us are together.
It's the one thing we've always had. One thing that was never wrong, not for a minute, was this
love we have. . . .You just make everything so easy, easier than I ever thought love could be.
I promise you, Bo Buchanan, with all my heart and all my soul!, that I will love you and cherish
you for as long as I live.

BO
Every time I try to say something, it's not exactly the way I feel anyway,
so I don't want to try. Next wedding, I'll write everything down first.

NORA
Next wedding?!

BO
See what I mean! Look, since the first time I ever saw you when you spilled that club soda
all over the front of my suit, you wound up in my heart and in my life like nobody else.
You know, we've had a problem or two . . .

NORA
Or three . . .

BO
Yeah, it's been some dance though, hasn't it? My life's never felt so full. I've never felt so alive.
I hope the music keeps playing for us as long as it possibly can, because as long as I got you,
that dance can just go on forever.

NORA
For someone who doesn't have the words, you did just fine.

RABBI
Nora, are you ready?

ANDREW
Bo, are you ready?

BO
Ready!

NORA
Ready!

LITTLE RICHARD
All right then, let's get this show on the road!

BO
With this ring, I thee wed.

ANDREW
God made man, male and female. He made them two halves of one whole. And for this reason, a man
leaves his mother and father, the family he has known, and thereafter will join with a wife, and the two
become one. One life. One flesh. Therefore, what God joins together today let no one put asunder.

NORA
With this ring, I thee wed.

RABBI
May your lives be joined mellow and sweet, from this day forward. In every life, there is sweetness and sadness both. And now the groom will step on this glass, and he will break it. And in doing so we pray that all the sorrow and suffering in the world will be broken and passed away. Nora and Bo, we hope you share a very happy life together filled with warmth and contentment.

(Rabbi puts glass in lace bag and places it on the floor.)

BO
If I miss it the first time do I get another shot?

LITTLE RICHARD
Step on it, will you? Let's get to the party!

(Bo steps on the glass.)

EVERYONE
Mazel tov!

ANDREW
By the power vested in me . . .

RABBI
And according to the traditions of Moses and Israel . . .

LITTLE RICHARD
And in the name of good ol' rock and roll, that sweet music that heals the soul, makes your liver quiver, the bladder splatter, and makes your knees freeze, let Little Richard be the first to congratulate you as Nora and Bo Buchanan, husband and wife! Kiss your bride!

Marriage is a wonderful institution—and I'm more than ready to be institutionalized.
—Nora Gannon, 1995

And the Bride Wore . . .

Weddings are always notable occasions on the soaps. Whether the ceremony is filled with intrigue or brimming with romance and emotion, you can be certain that all eyes will be on the blushing bride. Though all brides have that special glow, their individuality is reflected in the gowns they choose to wear on this most momentous day. In the spirit of love, we offer a look at the most glamorous gowns worn by ABC Daytime brides through the years . . .

One Life to Live

"Go for a dress that reflects who you are," advised *One Life to Live* costume designer Susan Gammie. Luna's unique wedding dress reflects both her New Age beliefs and the fairy-tale princess quality of her romance with Max. "The stand-up collar was kind of regal and the material (silk cut velvet) had a thirties quality to it," says designer Gammie. "We kept adding thousands of aurora borealis crystals to the dress," she recalled, "so it really sparkled all through the wedding and reception. I think the dress succeeded in having a real magical quality to it." Design by Susan Gammie; sketch by David Brooks.

*O*ne *Life to Live*'s mightily self-possessed Alex Olanov costumed herself in a queenly Cleopatra-esque wedding dress when she wed a local "ruler" of equal self-possession, Llanview's own Asa Buchanan. In a matte gold lamé gown with a bugle-beaded collar in the shape of an Egyptian bird and a sculpted, burnished headdress made of resin, Alex was certainly dressed to conquer. Says *One Life to Live* costume designer Susan Gammie, who devised the dress, "Since Alex's idea of Cleopatra would have been based on one of those old Cecil B. DeMille movie epics, we decided to do something very Hollywood, sexy, and glamorous." As Alex thought of herself as kind of a queen of all worldly temptresses, the bodice of this not-for-the-demure dress was especially creased to showcase much of Ms. Olanov's legendary cleavage. Design by Susan Gammie; sketch by David Brooks.

Designer Susan Gammie chose a breathtaking wedding gown for Sheila Price when she wed longtime love Hank Gannon. The African-inspired dress, designed by Thereza Fleetwood for Phe-Zula, was fashioned from satin, with touches of gold brocade and beaded with pearls. The bolero jacket was detachable, as was the full overskirt, which enabled the formal gown to be transformed into a sexy evening fashion. In keeping with the theme, the groom wore a genuine African mud-cloth vest and matching bow tie, hand-painted with metallic paint to create a more formal look.

When Blair Daimler married Todd Manning, the storyline presented special considerations to the *One Life to Live* costume department: the bride was pregnant (with baby Starr), and she wanted to wear a dress that was supposedly a Cramer family heirloom. Costume designer Susan Gammie purchased this wide-skirted silk and lace antique dress in a vintage wedding dress shop in Manhattan's trendy Soho district, but had to completely restore the gown and rebuild it "because (actress) Kassie Wesley DePaiva is much taller than women were in Victorian times." The gray crosses on the dress, which specially matched Blair's necklace, were beaded embroidery—very fashionable in the nineteenth century.

"We needed two dresses in one," Susan Gammie says of the dress Nora Gannon wore when she wed Bo Buchanan in a church wedding presided over by rock-and-roll star Little Richard. The ceremony was followed by a sock hop–style rock-and-roll reception, so Gammie designed a pink dupois silk dress that had a dark-pink sequined strapless top to be worn at the reception. To cover Nora's shoulders and keep her arms hidden during

the more conservative ceremony, Gammie devised a matching pink bolero jacket for the dress. Under-lying layers of crinoline and tulle kept Nora's bouffant skirt puffy through the evening as Nora, Bo, and their guests danced to their favorite oldies. Design by Susan Gammie; sketch by David Brooks.

"*C*assie is very romantic, very traditional," says *One Life To Live*'s costume Designer Susan Gammie. So this ongoing personal characteristic was the overriding factor in her choice of wedding gowns. At Cassie's first wedding (to Bo, which was invalidated when Bo's "dead" wife Sarah appeared moments after the ceremony), she wore an ivory silk and lace dress with off-the-shoulder Juliette sleeves heavily edged with pearls. "It had a sumptuous

quality," says Gammie. Cassie's wedding dress (at her next nuptials to Andrew) was designed to be vaguely Elizabethan. The dress was made of blush silk shantung, with dropped shoulders and delicate lace sleeves. "With both dresses, Cassie had a classic natural beauty we wanted to showcase," Gammie says.

At Megan's outdoor wedding to Jake, the bride wore a relatively simple yet elegant Chantilly lace sheath with a scoop neck, long sleeves, and a detachable silk train. Explains designer Taylor Cheek, "Megan was a very sophisticated, elegant woman who liked things simple. She was a real romantic, and I think that came across in the dress she chose."

"Marty was a romantic," says Susan Gammie of the gown Marty wore to her 1996 wedding to Dylan. "We were looking for something that looked like it came exactly from a fairy tale." "(Actress) Susan Haskell has a lovely long neck and a long waist, so we wanted something that would show them both." Note how the tulle veil edged with satin exactly matches the tulle skirt also edged with satin.

It was a double fashion delight when Asa wed Renee and Asa's grandson Cord and his bride Tina renewed their vows at a lavish double wedding held at Llanview Cathedral. Renee wore a gold silk chiffon blouse and pillbox hat and peau de soie skirt designed by Taylor Cheek. Tina wore a tiered white silk dress with a small bodice and a flared skirt designed by high-fashion couturier Scassi.

The White Dress

Two different theories explain why white became a favorite color of brides. One assumption is that the nineteenth-century bride, who had worn grays, blues, and pastels, was influenced by Queen Victoria's pure-white wedding ensemble. The queen wore a delicate white veil and flowing white satin gown that gave her an ethereal, fairy-tale quality. What bride wouldn't want to emulate her romantic royal look? So they did. The other theory is that a Victorian bride wore white to prove she was wealthy. After all, only a woman of means could wear a dress that would presumably get soiled and which she would then have to discard. (There were no dry cleaners in the 1800s.) White also became the symbol of purity in the early twentieth century, and brides were assumed to be virgins. Just like today.

General Hospital

When Ned Quartermaine married Lois Cerullo, the bride wore one of daytime television's most unique and memorable gowns. In the story, the dress was lent to Lois by Ned's grandmother Lila, who had married Edward wearing it in about 1939 or '40. "That's also the time when the movie *Gone With the Wind* premiered," relates designer Bob Miller. "So we decided to do a dress with a Civil War influence." The dress is made of heavy satin ("which was very popular in the forties," says Miller) and has magnolia appliqués cascading down the left side. The dress also had a special long train that *General Hospital* fans got a full view of as they watched Lois run through the streets of her native Brooklyn to the church. Design by Bob Miller.

The actress who played Karen (Carrie Shayne) had lovely shoulders. So when Karen Wexler married Jagger Cates, we did an off-the-shoulder dress. In the story, her mother Rhonda had supposedly made the gown, so we wanted to do something relatively simple," says *General Hospital* costume designer Bob Miller. The shoulder ruffle on the dress was made of corded lace. The bodice was made of lace over organza over taffeta. The skirt was organza over taffeta. Years later on Port Charles, Karen dyed the dress red, cut it short, and wore it to a party she threw celebrating her divorce from Jagger. Since Karen's original dress had in the interim been sold at an ABC event, a copy had to be made. Design by Bob Miller.

Felicia Cummings looked every bit the princess when she married Frisco Jones in 1986. In the story, Felicia was an Aztec princess and Gloria Monty, then *General Hospital* executive producer, wanted something that looked like it had been handed down through generations. "In the design we decided to mix a Spanish style with kind of a Gothic princess look," remembers costume designer Bob Miller. The dress was made of three tiers of Chantilly scalloped lace, dyed in shades of cream, ecru, and peach. The ecru lace mantilla was held in place with a Spanish-style comb. Design by Bob Miller. At Felicia's second wedding to Frisco in 1989, the beautiful bride chose to wear a cocktail-length white velvet dress covered by a bolero jacket and a cocktail hat in the shape of a teardrop. Design by Bob Miller.

When Anna finally married Duke Lavery, *General Hospital* costume designer Bob Miller says, "We decided we wanted it to look like a royal wedding." Duke wore a Scottish kilt. Anna wore a very traditional, classic dress with a corsetlike top. The skirt was light lace over organza, with an underpanel of shimmer lace. Along the edges the dress had a dust ruffle of gathered lace. "The brooch which Anna wore was supposedly Duke's grandmother's," recalls Miller, "but it actually belonged to Ian Buchanan's (Duke) grandmother." Design by Bob Miller.

At her 1990 garden wedding to Robert Scorpio, Anna wore a rose-colored lace dress designed by John Patton. The large picture hat, decorated with roses, was worn for a soap magazine cover shoot but not used at the on-screen wedding. Design by John Patton.

Katherine Bell wore this fitted, long-sleeve light-beige dress in her aborted wedding to Scotty Baldwin. The dress is made of reembroidered Chantilly lace. Designed by Bob Miller.

When Brenda Barrett was scheduled to marry "Jax" in a formal second wedding in the spring of 1997 (she had actually married him once before on a yacht wearing a plain white satin dress), she wore a short-sleeved pearl-gray satin dress with stark cap sleeves. *General Hospital* costume designer Miller says the dress design "was very clean, very Jackie O." Design by Bob Miller.

At Brenda's aborted 1997 wedding to Sonny Corinthos, she wore a form-fitting silk charmeuse-lined dress with an overlay of ornate lace. "The lining was purposely nude-colored, so it looked like all that Brenda was wearing was lace," says Miller. Design by Bob Miller.

All My Children

When Liza Colby married Adam Chandler, the circumstances of the occasion dictated the design of the dress. Remembers costume designer Margaret Delgado: "It was Liza's first wedding, so the dress was white. It was an informal at-home wedding, so Liza wore a long rayon sheath covered by a blazer-type jacket. And the wedding took place at Christmastime, so the jacket's lapel and sleeves were festively beaded with crystals and seed pearls." Design by Margaret Delgado.

Julia Santos married Noah Keefer in a fairy-tale ceremony straight out of the Disney animated movie *Cinderella*. Costume designer Margaret Delgado carefully copied the design of Cinderella's gown. "Our dress is a total knock-off." She laughs. "In the movie, the color of the dress changed from pink to yellow to blue, but ours was white." The dress is made of tulle and has a beaded headdress. Design by Margaret Delgado.

When Erica Kane married Dimitri Marick for the first time, she wore a dress of heavy reembroidered lace. "The characters had just come back from Budapest, so we wanted to do kind of a European princess design," says Carol Luiken, the former Emmy-winning costume designer on *All my Children*. "The veil was incredibly long—about eighteen feet. It trailed down the aisle magnificently. The veil was trimmed with gold. Actually, Erica looked more like a queen than a princess," remembers Luiken. "And this dress played up Susan Lucci's figure perfectly." Design by Carol Luiken.

Erica Kane wore a candlelight-colored gown designed by the trendy designers Badgley Mischka when she married Dimitri Marick for the second time. According to designer Margaret Delgado, the gown is made of a special fabric called "cracked ice," which is jersey covered by pale gold glitter that is actually part of the fabric. "We call this gown 'the Guenevere dress,'" says Delgado. "It had a simple long train in the back." Design by Badgley Mischka.

When Dixie Cooney wed older business mogul Adam Chandler, costume designer Carol Luiken carefully considered her age and background. "Dixie was young and fresh, and we wanted to play on that," recalls Luiken. She simply went to Brooklyn and bought this silk taffeta dress off the rack at Kleinfeld's, the famous bridal emporium. "We wanted to play that back-home charm (Dixie was from Pigeon Hollow, West Virginia) which was something so different for Adam. The dress harks back to another place, another time."

All My Children's most stunning wedding dress ever may have been the silver lace over nude silk sheath gown worn by Natalie when she married Jeremy Hunter. The dress was actually loaned to costume designer Carol Luiken by Calvin Klein from his own personal collection. "The dress had been in his couturier line the year before," Luiken remembers, "and Calvin was kind enough to lend it to me if we agreed not to alter it. Fortunately it fit Kate (Collins, who played Natalie) like a glove." Design by Calvin Klein.

For Nina Cortlandt's marriage to Cliff Warner at Cortlandt Manor, "we planned the quintessential 'Princess marries Prince Charming' wedding," remembers then–*All My Children* costume designer Carol Luiken. Nina's silk dress had an overlay with appliqués of lace on it, which the bride wore with a veiled picture hat. Says Luiken, "Everyone flipped for that hat! That dress was the classic wedding gown. This gown haunted me throughout all my time at AMC. People kept calling me for years asking me where they could get it." Design by Carol Luiken.

All My Children helped to make black a real-life fashion trend, thanks to the dress worn by Nina when she married Cliff for a third time in 1986 at New York's Tavern on the Green restaurant. The black velvet dress, lined in white silk, "shows you how much more sophisticated Nina had become by then," remembers Carol Luiken. "A very dear friend of mine had just gotten married and I stole Nina's headdress (a cocktail hat) design directly from her wedding." Design by Carol Luiken.

When Cindy Parker married Stuart Chandler, recalls Carol Luiken, "It was a heartbreaking time. She had AIDS. We wanted to make her look like the perfect bride—fragile, beautiful, ethereal. The finished effect made Cindy look as if she was on a cameo," says Luiken. The dress is made of silk tissue taffeta appliquéd with lace. The upper bodice is illusion lace. Design by Carol Luiken.

The dress Brooke English wore when she married Tad Martin was based on a blue, off-the-shoulder evening gown that actress Julia Barr had worn previously on the show. "Julia has extraordinary shoulders," remembers designer Carol Luiken. "So I designed the wedding dress similarly." The dress is peau de soie with appliqué lace and pearls. The headdress was a pillbox hat with a veil attached to it by silk roses. Design by Carol Luiken.

When Livia Frye married Tom Cudahy, the story dictated that the gown be an antique. Carol Luiken bought this vintage 1930s silk chiffon gown from an antique dress dealer in New York. "Even though it photographs white, it's actually a pale blue." says Luiken. The unusual headdress, which was designed by Gary Brower, was done to echo the dress's 1930s style, according to Luiken.

Tips from the Pros

"Think about the image that *you* want to project and don't be pressured into accepting what someone else thinks you should be. Getting married is a very stressful experience—you don't want to wake up on the morning of your wedding saying 'What is this costume I'm wearing?' Your wedding dress should be a reflection of you—don't be afraid of expressing who you are."
—Susan Gammie, Costume Designer, *One Life to Live*

"Your wedding should be like naming your child. Make sure it is what you really want. Make it your fantasy—not your mother's or your sister's or your friend's. That's what I did, and I had a great time!"
—Maggie Delgado, Costume Designer, *All My Children*

Wedding Styles

ABC Daytime's design teams agree that one of the first things to decide when planning your wedding is the style of the affair. The style determines what you and the groom will wear and if you are going to follow traditional wedding protocol. A very formal daytime or evening wedding is defined by a large guest list (usually 200 or more people), a majestic setting, such as a cathedral or grand ballroom, and live music, usually provided by an orchestra. If it's a daytime wedding, the ceremony starts before 6:00 P.M., and the bride wears a long dress with a short or long train. The groom rents a cutaway coat with gray-striped trousers, gray vest, wing-collared shirt, and striped tie or ascot. A bride having a very formal evening wedding walks down the aisle in a long train and veil. For the groom, it's time for full-dress tails with matching trousers, white vest, wing-collared shirt, and white bow tie. His other option is a dinner jacket in white or ivory with formal black trousers.

Where They Shop . . .

You too can look like a soap opera bride by shopping at the locations frequented by ABC-TV's costume designers:

B&J Fabrics
263 West 40th Street
New York, NY 10018
(212) 354-8150

Bergdorf Goodman
754 Fifth Avenue
New York, NY 10019
(212) 753-7300

**Beverly Hills Silks
and Woolens**
417 North Canon Drive
Beverly Hills, CA
(310) 271-8389

Hyman Hindler
729 East Temple Street
Los Angeles, CA 90012
(213) 626-5123

**International Silks
and Woolens**
8347 Beverly Boulevard
Los Angeles, CA 90048
(213) 653-6453

Yumi Katsura
907 Madison Avenue
New York, NY 10021
(212) 772-3760

Kleinfeld
8206 Fifth Avenue
Brooklyn, NY 11209
(718) 833-1100

One of a Kind Bride
98-100 Thompson Street
New York, NY 10012
(212) 966-8678

Paul's Veil and Net
42 West 38th Street
New York, NY 10018
(212) 391-3822

Saks Fifth Avenue
611 Fifth Avenue
New York, NY 10022
(212) 753-4000

Vera Wang Bridal House
991 Madison Avenue
New York, NY 10021
(212) 628-3400

Weddings That Weren't . . .

For better or worse, ABC Daytime throws a heck of a wedding. Dead spouses suddenly reappear, bombs threaten to burst lovers' bubbles, and dogs have been known to race up the aisle to take a bite out of the bride! Witness these calamitous weddings featuring doomed couples who never made it to death before parting . . .

General Hospital

Sonny Corinthos
and
Brenda Barrett

September 19, 1997

Brenda Veronica Barrett
And
Michael Corinthos, Jr.
request the honor of your
presence
at their wedding
Friday, the nineteenth of
September
Eight O'Clock in the Evening
Saint Timothy's Episcopal Church

With a flash of his sexy dimples and a touch of charm, mobster Sonny Corinthos won the heart of model Brenda Barrett. Their romance began with a ritualistic mating dance that kept viewers on the edge of their seats for months. Sonny and Brenda's tempestuous relationship was grounded in lust and passion, but their egos kept the lovers from finding eternal happiness. Even when they broke up, it wasn't because they didn't love each other. Mob machinations, stubborn pride, and foolish choices constantly forced the angst-filled couple apart.

When Sonny and Brenda first started dating, life was magic. Because Sonny had

September 19, 1997, was to be the happiest day of Brenda's life. Wearing a form-fitting, custom-made silk and lace gown, the beautiful bride waited in the flower-festooned church for her dashing groom to arrive at the church (opposite page). Despite their estrangement, Brenda sat vigil at Sonny's bedside when he nearly died after being injected with an overdose of heroin. In his delirium, Sonny pledged his love to Brenda (below).

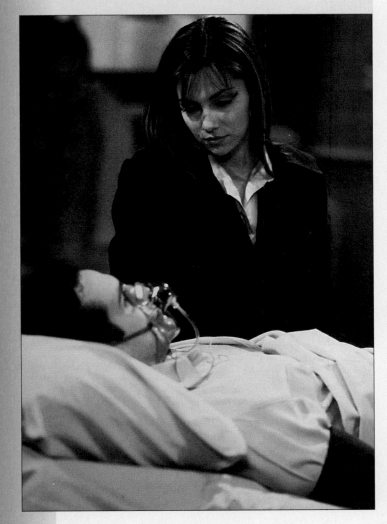

a bad rap, Brenda dated him on the sly. He dazzled her with fancy meals at mob restaurants, where Mr. Corinthos and his lady love were treated like royalty. On the night of Karen and Jagger's wedding, Sonny was shot, and Brenda saved his life with a blood transfusion. Upon his recovery, Sonny knew that this gorgeous young woman was someone special. He gave Brenda a diamond bracelet inscribed with the words of William Wordsworth: "Sensations sweet, felt in the blood, felt in the blood, felt along the heart. This will always remind you of what I can't forget."

Eventually, Brenda could not help but see Sonny for what he was—an underworld crime boss. As she realized the danger he brought to her life, Sonny's shady dealings did not sit well with Brenda. Eventually she reluctantly agreed to wear a wire to help the authorities get the goods on the man she loved. Unfortunately, trust and loyalty meant everything to Sonny—and when he discovered her deception, he threw her out. Brenda's tears and apologies couldn't melt Sonny's icy heart. Stubborn pride forced the two to go their separate ways. Brenda became involved with singer Miguel Morez, while Sonny romanced mob princess Lily Rivera, but they never got over each other.

Eventually Brenda moved on to dashing billionaire Jasper "Jax" Jacks, convinced that his safer lifestyle would finally bring her the happiness she coveted. After a whirlwind courtship, Brenda married Jax on a yacht in the Pacific Ocean—just as Sonny's new wife, Lily, died in an explosion meant to kill him.

Though she implored Sonny to stay away from her, Brenda found herself once again drawn to his side when he was mysteriously injected with heroin and almost died. As he was whisked into the emergency room at General Hospital, Sonny expressed his love to Brenda. Weeks later Sonny and Brenda were together again—trapped in a cave by a vengeful mobster who blamed Brenda for Lily's death. The ex-lovers, certain that they would die, made love for the first time in almost two years.

"I love you. It's the only thing in my life I've ever really known. And I don't know whether it's right or wrong. But it's real. I love you," Brenda tenderly admitted to Sonny. As they pledged their love for each other, Sonny was convinced that Brenda was finally his again, but still she was torn.

Upon their rescue, Brenda made a difficult decision to leave Jax but not to be with Sonny. Instead, she chose to move out on her own. Brenda needed time to sort out her turbulent life while she recovered from a lingering dependence on prescription painkillers. Once free of her addiction, Brenda enjoyed a newfound clarity. She realized that Sonny was the only man for her. Jax, understanding her decision, let Brenda go—and she went straight to the Port Charles docks to find the man she belonged with all along—Sonny. Together they faced danger in the form of Lily's father, Rivera, who tried to exact revenge on Sonny and Brenda for the death of his beloved daughter. This time the peril united Brenda and Sonny instead of driving them apart.

Rivera gave Sonny and Brenda twenty minutes to say their final good-byes. Brenda couldn't believe her ears when Sonny proposed with words she never expected to hear.

"You're asking me to marry you?" she asked.

"I mean it," responded Sonny. "I love you. And I want you to be my wife."

"You know, since the day I met you, this is the only thing I ever wanted you to say to me," a tearful Brenda responded.

After this heartfelt moment, Rivera held a gun to Brenda's head, and Sonny heroically shot him dead before he could kill her. The wait was over—at last Sonny and Brenda could be together. Back in Port Charles, Sonny decided to make it official.

"I've waited for a lot of things in my life," he admitted to Brenda as he got down on one knee. "To grow up. To get respect. To get over . . . things. But the hardest waiting I ever had to do was the waiting I had to do for you. Will you marry me?"

With the guests gathered at the church, a tortured Sonny chose to spare Brenda a life filled with death and danger. He instructed his best man, Jason, to go to the church to break the news to Brenda that there would be no wedding. He didn't want to hurt Brenda, but Sonny knew that there was no other way. As Jason left to deliver the awful news, Sonny resolutely stared straight ahead. A lone tear rolled down his cheek as he instructed the limo driver to take him to the airport so he could leave Brenda forever.

"I was born to be Mrs. Corinthos," Brenda answered as Sonny slipped his mother's engagement ring on her finger.

With the threat of mafia retribution to their marriage, Sonny and Brenda agreed that he would leave the mob and, together with his new wife, leave Port Charles forever just after their wedding ceremony. They were giving up everything to be together. Sonny trained his best man, Jason, to take over his mob duties. But as Brenda dizzily planned their wedding, danger once again lurked around the corner—and Sonny knew it. Just days before the wedding, he received yet another threat from his mob enemies. There was another hit out on him! Now even if they departed Port Charles, how could Sonny possibly keep Brenda safe?

As the wedding day drew near, Brenda ignored all the warning signs, trusting in Sonny's love. At the same time, Sonny's persistent nightmares made him grow more conflicted about the future. He agonized over what this marriage would do to the woman he loved. He had already buried one wife, and he couldn't bear to see Brenda pay the ultimate price for loving him. The only thing more important to Sonny than his love for Brenda was her safety. Finally the big day was here . . . would Sonny break Brenda's heart?

Brenda looked forward to a bright future with Sonny, but when she turned back from the altar to greet her groom, she was stunned to see his messenger, Jason, standing in the back of the church prepared to deliver the news that everyone in the church already knew: Sonny was not showing up. Not today, not ever (above). When she realized that Sonny had deserted her at the altar, Brenda exploded with anger at Jason, the bearer of the bad news. Her feelings of devastation were more than matched by feelings of betrayal. With her heart broken, Brenda took immediate steps to banish thoughts of Sonny Corinthos from her life forever (left).

WORDS OF LOVE

Sonny Formally Proposes to Brenda

SONNY

(On bended knee)

Will you be my wife?

BRENDA

I can't believe that you're on your knees.
That you're asking me to marry you.
And that we're not even facing certain death.

SONNY

The way I see it, you have three options. Yes. No. Or maybe.

BRENDA

There really is no other option for me. Yes.
You know I'll be your wife.

SHARE A ROMANTIC RENDEZVOUS IN SAN JUAN, PUERTO RICO

Puerto Rico looks, feels, and smells like the Caribbean, even though it sits in the Atlantic Ocean. Like Sonny and Brenda, you can luxuriate at the gorgeous beach resorts in San Juan, then spend time discovering the historical treasures of the Old Town.

When to go: The weather is beautiful year round. Prices are highest from mid-December to mid-April. Hurricane season runs from August to October.

What to do: Start your own exploration along the narrow blue-stone streets of Old San Juan. A top attraction is the six-level, four-centuries-old El Morro Fortress, at the entrance to San Juan Harbor. This intriguing twenty-seven-acre maze of tunnels, dungeons, moats, and barracks was used by Spanish soldiers to defend their city against European pirates. The Catedral de San Juan is a medieval showcase with vaulted Gothic ceilings and the tomb of explorer Ponce de León. Excellent resorts include Condado and Isla Verde. You also can go fishing, windsurfing, Jet Skiing, and scuba diving in the area.

"Tomorrow we'll still be who we are—except without the loneliness," Sonny whispered to Brenda before they made love on a deserted beach in Puerto Rico in the autumn of 1994.

Romantic rendezvous: Take a break at Parque de las Palomas at the top of the city wall to drink in a spectacular vista of the harbor, city, and mountains. Cruise San Juan Harbor to see the sights of the Old City at twilight by ferry or tour boat.

Stepping out at night: There's no shortage of evening entertainment in the San Juan area. You can dance to the sounds of salsa and merengue and other Latin music. Many of the major hotels offer Las Vegas–style revues and have casinos and nightclubs. Theater, opera, and concert performances also are a part of the legendary night life.

For more information: The Puerto Rico Tourism Company has branches in Los Angeles, New York, and Miami.

Luke Spencer and Jennifer Smith

July 11, 1980

Luke Spencer should have known better than to allow naive mob princess Jennifer Smith to fall in love with him. To work his way into good favor with her father, mob boss Frank Smith, Luke courted Jennifer while secretly carrying a torch for Laura Baldwin. To protect Laura from the wrath of the mob, Luke agreed to Frank Smith's demand that he marry his daughter! The wedding date was set for July 11, 1980, but the nuptials would never take place.

On the morning of the wedding, Laura Baldwin's husband, Scotty, discovered that, months earlier, Luke had raped his wife. In a rage, Scotty showed up at mobster Frank Smith's yacht just moments before Luke and Jennifer's wedding. Leaping aboard the yacht, Scotty punched Luke, sending him flying overboard. When Luke failed to surface, he was presumed dead. In reality, he surfaced, then went on the run with Laura.

Mac Scorpio and Felicia Jones

February 9, 1994

They were business partners and best pals, so it seemed only right that Felicia and Mac would fall in love eventually. After fighting her true feelings for Mac Scorpio, Felicia finally saw the light and agreed to marry her handsome Prince Charming. On their wedding day, Felicia was the picture-perfect bride in a buttercup-yellow gown that matched her golden tresses. But her dream shattered when a double dose of trouble spoiled this Valentine wedding.

Hell-bent on stopping the wedding, Felicia's psychotic stalker, Ryan Chamberlain, escaped from prison and hurried to Port Charles. After knocking out his twin brother, Kevin, Ryan traded places with him! Then, just before the bride and groom exchanged vows, Ryan showed up at the wedding with a bomb strapped to his body. He grabbed Felicia, but Mac raced to her rescue and wrestled the explosive device away from Ryan and tossed it to Paul Hornsby, who safely detonated it outside the church.

The groom, Mac, and the mad trespasser, Ryan, struggled and crashed through the church's second-floor choir balcony and plummeted to the floor below. The fall injured Mac, who was rushed to the hospital, forcing the postponement of the nuptials. The wedding day wasn't a total disaster. Paul Hornsby and Jenny Eckert, who had longed to be together, took advantage of the ready-made wedding and took the plunge themselves. Sadly for Mac and Felicia, this explosive day was the first in a series of difficulties that may have permanently derailed their wedding plans.

Jasper "Jax" Jacks and Brenda Barrett

November 5, 1996

On the rebound from Sonny Corinthos, Brenda married the rich and charming Australian Jasper "Jax" Jacks in California. Returning to Port Charles, Brenda and her billionaire husband planned to publicly renew their commitment to each other at the Quartermaine mansion. But Sonny refused to let Brenda go. He worked feverishly to uncover a secret that Jax desperately tried to keep hidden—his other wife!

Moments before Brenda and Jax were due to repeat their solemn wedding vows before friends and family at the Quartermaine mansion, Sonny interrupted the ceremony with a surprise guest—Mrs. Jasper Jacks! Jax, utterly shocked, believed that his wife, Miranda, had been killed in an explosion. Now, after extensive cosmetic surgery to repair her scarred face, she was back—in time to stop the wedding.

Brenda showed Sonny exactly how she felt about the surprise scheme that destroyed her glorious wedding to Jax.

WORDS OF LOVE
Jax Woos Brenda

JAX
I love you, Brenda—more each day. I promise you I'll never hurt you. You don't have to prove yourself to me, or turn your life upside down to show you're loyal. I'll never scream at you, I'll never frighten you or hurt you knowingly in any way. You're safe with me.

WORDS OF LOVE
Brenda Shares Her Feelings with Jax on the morning of "the Wedding That Wasn't"

BRENDA
I didn't want to tell you this in front of a room full of people . . . I love you. I love you so much I feel dizzy. I can't even see straight. I can't think straight. I don't even know when this happened. All I know is I want to marry you again right away.

JAX
Thank goodness for small mercies.

BRENDA
I want to live with you forever, and have a family with you. Do everything and nothing together. I even want to get old and lumpy with you. I don't even feel this way because it's the smart thing to do anymore, or because I like you. I am crazy, head over heels, in old-fashioned love with you! I don't know what I ever did to deserve you.

JAX
I ask myself that question about you all the time. I swear to you, Brenda . . . I never thought I could love so much in my lifetime. I didn't think I was capable of it, that I wasn't that lucky.

BRENDA
Hey, I'm the original do-everything-wrong girl. Falling in love with you is the first perfect, right thing I've done in my whole, entire life!

THE PERSONAL VOWS THAT JAX NEVER
HAD THE CHANCE TO DELIVER TO BRENDA

JAX

Brenda, you know me. I don't make promises as a rule, I've learned not to.
Most promises seem so imaginary, with a life span as short as a firefly's.
In fact, most things people hold dear or say they do don't seem to last.
What is valuable one day may be worthless the next.
No one knows that better than I do.

How can I say, so soon and so surely, that my happiness in you will never fade?
I can't say. It's like waking up with the answer to a puzzle and not knowing
where it came from. I never make promises as a rule. But now every word between
us from morning until night is a promise to me. I collect them in my head and,
at the end of each day, I turn them over and set them in place, like bricks.
They are that solid, they are that real. They have built us a home,
and fire and wind and flood cannot touch it. They give me a place
where I can love you from this day forward, for better, for worse,
for richer, for poorer, in sickness and in health until death do us part.

Marriage means work, attention, care, unconditional love, acceptance of each other's imperfections, and adjustments. But if you've chosen the right partner, then nothing in your life can be more rewarding.
—Mrs. Jane Jacks
(mother of the groom)

All My Children

Trevor Dillon and "Jane Cox"

December 2, 1994

Trevor Dillon had good reason to despise Janet Green, the deranged sister of his late wife, Natalie. Years earlier Janet threw her sister down a well, then proceeded to trick Trevor into sleeping with her. As a result, Janet gave birth to Trevor's daughter, Amanda. Eventually Janet murdered Will

Cortlandt and was shipped off to jail. However, she managed to get out of prison early by undergoing experimental cosmetic surgery that gave her a new face. Desperate to get close to her daughter, Janet infiltrated the Dillon household under the guise of a woman named Jane Cox. Before long she had the man she wanted—Trevor. Janet was just a heartbeat away from marrying Trevor when disaster struck!

After being drugged by Jane Cox (a.k.a. psychotic Janet Green) and hidden away on a moving van bound for California, Harold the dog went on a cross-country quest to return to his devoted owner, Tim Dillon. Just as the minister asked if anyone could show just cause why these two people should not be wed, there was a loud commotion at the back of the room. A waiter opened the door to Harold, who clutched in his mouth an empty prescription bottle—proof that Janet had drugged him. The purloined pooch then made a beeline up the aisle and lunged for Janet's throat!

Harold's quick "thinking" exposed "Jane." Armed with the evidence that his bride-to-be was an imposter, Trevor confronted Janet, who was forced to admit her charade. The wedding was off!

In an unlikely twist of fate, Trevor and Janet eveually fill in lone, and on May 27, 1998, they tied the knot. Janet's longtime enemy, harold the dog, made a surprise entrance at the wedding and barked his approval of the new marriage.

Sean Cudahy and Cecily Davidson

February 17, 1989

Poor Cecily Davidson. All she wanted was a man to love. Money-hungry Sean Cudahy set his sights on Cecily Davidson's hefty trust fund from the day he came back to Pine Valley after serving time for the murder of nurse Sybil Thorne. Cecily fell victim to Sean's snaky charms, and before long they were engaged to marry. But Cecily's society matron mother, Bitsy, saw her daughter's fiancé for the fortune hunter he really was—and made it clear that she did not consider the ex-con a suitable husband for her blue-blooded daughter.

To keep Sean from Cecily, Bitsy set out to seduce him for herself. At Christmas Bitsy maneuvered Sean under the mistletoe and kissed him passionately. Behind

Cecily's back, they began a sizzling affair! On the night before the wedding, Cecily eavesdropped on a seductive conversation between Sean and Bitsy and heard Sean confess his initial motives for pursuing her to the altar. She waited until the wedding to spring her surprise. When the minister asked, "Will you . . . ?", Cecily answered, "No! Never!" She blasted Sean as a fortune hunter and damned her mother as a liar—then took off without saying "I do!"

Stuart Chandler and Gloria Marsh

February 22, 1993

In the winter of 1993, sweet Stuart Chandler's tender love made Gloria Marsh blossom. After being raped by the evil Will Cortlandt and caught in a scandalous affair with Craig, the husband of her best friend, Dixie, Gloria had hit rock bottom. She attempted suicide and might have succeeded had it not been for Stuart's kindness and sensitivity. Stuart saw a kernel of goodness in the troubled young nurse and asked her to be his wife.

Stuart's fiercely protective twin brother, Adam, was highly suspicious of Gloria and tried to trick her into revealing what he thought were her true colors—that she was after Stuart only for his money. Adam resolved to drive Gloria out of Pine Valley, but before long he realized he was falling in love with her himself. One night he passionately kissed Gloria, who shocked herself by responding in kind. In the days after, Gloria told herself that her future was with Stuart, not his passionate and exciting brother, Adam! Still, she could not get Adam's kiss out of her mind. On the morning of her wedding, Gloria woke up in Adam's arms—after having made love with him the night before. Gloria knew in her heart that she loved Adam, not Stuart. However, she couldn't bring herself to jilt her fiancé at the eleventh hour. Consumed by guilt, Gloria insisted to Adam that she had to go through with the wedding—unaware that Stuart was listening in to their revealing conversation!

Furious and deeply hurt, Stuart listened to Gloria's explanation before blasting her for living a lie. Then he stormed into the chapel and told the gathered guests that the wedding was off!

Jeremy Hunter and Erica Kane

November 26, 1986

When her beau, Jeremy Hunter, was sent to jail for a murder he did not commit, Erica schemed to break him out—by marrying him! Without breathing a word of her plan to her groom, Erica convinced Matt Connelly to fly a helicopter over the prison at the time of their behind-bars wedding. Their wedding ceremony screeched to a halt when Erica suddenly pretended to pass out! In the ensuing melée, she waved Jeremy to follow her to the prison roof where Matt waited in his chopper to whisk them away to freedom.

"Erica, I love you with all my heart, but I can't let you do this!" Jeremy shouted over the din of the hovering helicopter that waited to whisk him to freedom. "We'll be on the run for the rest of our lives!"

"We'll still be together. We'll make a wonderful life. It's our only chance. Come on, Jeremy!" she countered. Despite Erica's pleas, the ever-noble Jeremy chose to remain behind and was eventually freed from jail—the legal way!

One Life to Live

Marco Dane and Edwina Lewis

September 8, 1980

Dr. Mario Corelli felt nothing but disdain for snooty journalist Edwina Lewis—until the day he saw her appear as guest on Pat Ashley's TV talk show. As Edwina spoke at length on having been shunted from foster home to foster home as a child, Mario suddenly saw a different side of Edwina, a side with which he keenly identified. Mario asked Edwina out on a date and, in a matter of days, they were hopelessly in love.

In Mario, Edwina had found a man whom she felt could be completely open and honest with her. However, there was one thing that he could not possibly reveal to her. Mario was actually Marco Dane, his own miscreant brother. As their romance progressed and they made plans to marry, a built-in threat remained—would Marco's secret ever be revealed?

What should have been the happiest day in Edwina's life turned into a nightmare when her groom was arrested for impersonating his own late brother, Dr. Mario Corelli. Though he had curbed his evil ways, Marco's dastardly past had just caught up with him!

Traditions

Blooming Bouquets

The classic bridal bouquet is a cluster of flowers anchored in a plastic holder. A more informal choice that's equally beautiful is a loosely assembled collection of flowers hand-tied with ribbon. One of the most popular styles, a cascade forms a teardrop shape that's usually anchored in an oasis for support. The flowers and greenery are positioned to taper downward gracefully. A nosegay, or posy, is a tight round arrangement of flowers that may be hand-tied with ribbon or set in a holder and often backed by a paper doily. They were once carried primarily by bridesmaids but are now popular with brides too. A crescent-shape posy is centered and two trails are pointed slightly downward. A tussie-mussie features stems tied together with ribbon. The bouquet often is inserted into a special silver cone-shape holder. A Biedermeier is a small tight nosegay featuring concentric rings of varied colors and blooms. Each ring is usually one type of flower. A composite is individual petals of a flower or a cluster of individual blooms wired or glued together to create the impression of a single flower. A pomander is a blossom-covered globe suspended and held from a satin ribbon.

Flowery Language

Every flower tells a story, thanks to the Victorians, who assigned meanings to many popular blooms.

Amaryllis: beauty, pride
Apple blossom: preference
Azalea: temperance
Bluebell: constancy
Buttercup: childhood memories
Camellia (white): perfect loveliness
Carnation: bonds of affection, love
Chrysanthemum (red): I love you
Chrysanthemum (white): truth
Cornflower: hope
Daffodil: regard
Daisy (white): innocence
Fern: fascination
Forget-me-not: true love
Geranium: bridal favor
Holly: foresight
Honeysuckle: generosity
Hyacinth: constancy
Ivy: fidelity
Jasmine: joy, amiability
Larkspur: levity
Lilac: first love
Lily (white): purity
Lily of the Valley: return of happiness
Mimosa: sensitivity
Myrtle: love, remembrance
Orange blossoms: fertility, purity
Pansy: love, courtship
Rose (white): innocence
Rose (red): desire
Stock: beauty
Sweet pea: pleasure
Sweet William: gallantry
Tulip (red): declaration of love
Violet: faithfulness
Water lily: purity of heart

Circles of Love

Nothing says engagement like a sparkling diamond ring. But just like people, no two diamonds are alike. How will you and your fiancé know which one to buy? By understanding the four C's, defined by the Diamond Information Center as cut, clarity, color, and carat.

- Cut: A diamond's cut directly influences how much it sparkles. The cut also allows the stone to make the best use of light, which is reflected from one facet to another and then dispersed through the top.
- Color: The less color a diamond has (most have yellow or brown traces), the better its ability to reflect and refract light and the more valuable it is. The stone is rated from D (totally colorless and very rare) to Z (yellow).
- Clarity: This refers to the diamond's degree of flawlessness. Most have natural carbon traces and slight imperfections like bubbles, specks, and inner cracks. Like color, less is more. Diamonds with the fewest flaws are the most precious.
- Carat: A diamond is measured in carats. One hundred points equals one carat.
- Diamonds come in a wide variety of shapes to suit different tastes. The favorite is round, or brilliant, but others are popular too: oval (egg-shaped), pear (round on one end, pointed on the other), marquise (oblong with pointed oval stones), emerald (rectangular with steps on sides and corners), and heart. Because hands come in various shapes and sizes, some stone configurations look better than others on different women. The lucky bride-to-be with long fingers can wear just about any style. A woman with thin hands will look beautiful wearing an oval or round diamond. Shorter fingers will look elongated showing off a pear, oval, or marquise shape.

The Wedding Ring

All My Children's *Lanie* and David exchange rings.

True love never ends, and a circular symbol—a ring—is the perfect way to express that sentiment. Gold bands became the rage in ancient times. Egyptians wore them to show off their wealth. By giving his new wife a gold ring, a husband was telling the world that he trusted her with his money. It became fashionable in ancient Rome to wear the ring on the fourth finger of the left hand because it was believed that the nerve of that hand led directly to the heart.

The Cake

Besides being a sweet finale to a wedding feast, a layered cake is a symbol of good luck and fertility. But the cake wasn't always the pile of frosted tiers decorated with flowers and topped with a miniature bride and groom that we know today. In Roman times, the groom broke a small wheat bun over his beloved's head as a symbol of fruitfulness when the ceremony was over. Guests were encouraged to scramble for crumbs and share in the couple's good luck. Later, sweet buns baked by the bridesmaids replaced the wheat cakes. In the seventeenth century, a French baker decided to put sugar frosting on several buns so he could stack them, thus creating the first tiered wedding cake.

Lois's mother, Gloria, spent hours baking "every excruciating inch" of the divine wedding cake. As the pastry was rolled in, Lois eyed it suspiciously. "Just checking it for false bottoms," she said with a laugh, alluding to the fact that she once jumped out of Katherine Bell's birthday cake to surprise Eddie/Ned with her knowledge that he was a fraud (above). All My Children's Erica Kane and new husband Dimitri Marick sweetly celebrate their nuptials (right).

Old, New, Borrowed, and Blue

The much-followed Victorian wedding tradition goes: "Something old, something new, something borrowed, something blue, and a silver sixpence in her shoe." To satisfy the "old" part, which represents the bride's connection to her family and past, some women wear a piece of heirloom family jewelry, carry a family Bible down the aisle, or cut the wedding cake with an antique cake knife. Representing "new"—for good luck in her new life as a married woman—the bride can count on her recently purchased dress, headpiece, or lingerie. The "borrowed" item—from a happily married friend or relative whose own good fortune will rub off on the bride, it is hoped—could be a veil or pearls. As for "something blue," which signifies loyalty and fidelity, a bride might wear an undergarment or garter that incorporates blue ribbon or lace, or paint her toenails with blue polish. The sixpence is a wish for future wealth. (A dime, by the way, works just as well.)

SOMETHING OLD, SOMETHING NEW . . .

General Hospital's Bobbie and Stefan's Wedding

JUDGE
Now that the bride is here, shall we begin?

STEFAN
Just a moment. Forgive me. I am a traditionalist.
Something old . . .
(He opens a jewelry box, revealing a stunning necklace.)

BOBBIE
It's gorgeous.

STEFAN
This has been in my family for generations.
(He places the necklace around Bobbie's neck.)

LUCAS
You look like a princess, Mommy.

STEFAN
That's exactly what I was thinking. The dress will serve as something new.
Now we just need something borrowed.
(Nikolas steps forward, handing Bobbie his handkerchief.)

BOBBIE
It's perfect.

The Wedding Party

Before flowers, candy, and the threat of jail time, a man was expected to secure a bride in an unusually aggressive manner—by kidnapping her. He'd round up his closest buddies to help him and defend him against any threats from her family. Later it became fashionable for the bride and her female pals to travel to the man's village. The friends would protect the bride and her dowry from potential suitors and robbers. Male attendants started dressing alike to ward off evil demons preying on the bride. The idea was to dress everyone similarly so that the demons wouldn't know which woman was getting married. That's what friends are for.

Marty Saybrooke and Dylan Moody (left). Tom Cudahy and Livia Frye (below).

Being Gifted

Every year of marital bliss means new and exciting gifts from friends and family! Though the first year's bounty traditionally consists of modest offerings involving paper, the gifts get more extravagant as time goes by. Work your way up to seventy-five years of togetherness, and you're due some diamonds! Traditional anniversary gifts:

First	paper
Second	cotton
Third	leather
Fourth	linen
Fifth	wood
Sixth	iron
Seventh	wool
Eighth	bronze
Ninth	pottery
Tenth	tin
Fifteenth	crystal
Twentieth	china
Twenty-fifth	silver
Thirtieth	pearl
Thirty-fifth	coral
Fortieth	ruby
Forty-fifth	sapphire
Fiftieth	gold
Fifty-fifth	emerald
Sixtieth	diamond
Seventy-fifth	diamond

Edward and Lila Quartermaine have been married for over fifty years.

The Melody Lingers On

*A*ll eyes are pealed on the bride and groom when they take the floor for their first dance as husband and wife. ABC's music directors carefully select songs that best characterize the way in which the soap opera bride and groom feel about each other. To locate a particular song of your own, head to a music store that has a self-help computer. You type in the title to get a listing of artists who've recorded the song and albums the title is on. "Cherish the Day, Romantic Music from ABC Daytime Dramas" for your wedding, Cherry Lane Music © 1997.

Frisco and Felicia proved that love really can conquer all. During their first dance, Frisco serenaded his new bride with an a capella rendition of their special song, "Lady of My Heart."

"Lady of my heart
Tell me who you are
you've waited in the dark
and I need you with me."

ABC Daytime's Music Directors Recommend the Following Musical Selections for a Bride and Groom's "First Dance". . .

"All of My Life"	(Michael Randal) by Diana Ross
"Always and Forever"	(Rod Temperton) by Heatwave
"As Time Goes By"	(Herman Hupfeld) by Carly Simon
"Because You Loved Me"	(Diane Warren) by Celine Dion
"Come Rain or Come Shine"	(Harold Arlen and Johnny Mercer) by Frank Sinatra
"Here and Now"	(T. Steele and D. Elliot) by Luther Vandross
"How Sweet It Is (To Be Loved by You)"	(B. Holland, L. Dozier, E. Holland) by James Taylor
"In Your Eyes"	(Michael Masser and Dan Hill) by George Benson
"It Had to Be You"	(G. Kahn, I. Jones) by Frank Sinatra
"Love Is Here to Stay"	(George and Ira Gershwin) by Tony Bennett
"Love of My Life"	(Jimmy George and James Auspitz) by George Benson
"On My Way to You"	(Michel LeGrand, Alan and Marilyn Bergman) by Barbra Streisand
"Our Love"	(David Pack) by Michael McDonald
"Ribbon in the Sky"	by Stevie Wonder
"Starting Here, Starting Now"	(R. Maltby, Jr., and David Shire) by Barbra Streisand
"Theme from Ice Castles" (Through the Eyes of Love)	(Carole Bayer Sager and Marvin Hamlisch) by Melissa Manchester
"The Sweetest Days"	(Wendy Waldman, Jon Lind, Phil Galston) by Vanessa Williams
"Valentine"	(Jim Brickman) by Martina McBride
"A Whole New World"	(Alan Menken and Tim Rice) by Regina Bell and Peabo Bryson

Musical Selections From ABC Soap Weddings

Song: "Through the Years"
Couple: Tad and Dixie

Song: "Just You and I"
Couple: Greg and Jenny

Song: "All in Love Is Fair"
Couple: Robert and Anna's love theme

Song: "Someone to Watch Over Me"
Couple: Scotty and Dominique

Song: "You and I"
Couple: Trevor and Natalie

Song: "Woman to Man"
Couple: Jagger and Karen

Song: "Not a Day Goes By"
Couple: Tad and Dixie
  (second wedding)

Song: "A Dream Is a Wish
  Your Heart Makes"
Couple: Julia and Noah

Song: "Lady of My Heart"
Couple: Frisco and Felicia

Song: "All I Ask of You"
Couple: Andrew and Cassie

Wild Weddings-- Marital Mayhem

When two people make that ultimate commitment to each other, wedding plans are put in motion. Invitations are dispatched, guests gather and, sometimes, all hell breaks loose! The outcome of soap weddings is amazingly unpredictable. Anything can happen—and often does—in these wildest of weddings . . .

One Life to Live

Bo Buchanan and Cassie Callison

November 27, 1991

After the disappearance and apparent death of his wife, Sarah, Bo Buchanan found new love with sweet Cassie Callison. Together they walked down the aisle and spoke their vows in a traditional wedding ceremony, surrounded by friends and family at the newly decorated Llanfair, home of the groom's family.

This romantic duo overcame many obstacles in their roller-coaster relationship, including the constant threat of the dangerous Alex Olanov, who was obsessively in love with Bo. During the wedding ceremony, the devious Alex lurked just outside, prepared to destroy anyone who kept her from her beloved Bo. Bo may have been marrying Cassie, but he wasn't quite free of his "late" wife, Sarah. During their wedding reception, Llan-view's police commissioner, Troy Nichols, unwrapped a mysterious gift box and found both a poem and a music box that played "As Time Goes By." That was Bo and Sarah's song!

BO AND CASSIE'S WEDDING VOWS

An Episcopalian Ceremony

REVEREND ANDREW CARPENTER

*Bless, O Lord, these rings to be a sign of the vows by which this man
and this woman have bound themselves to each other.*
(Andrew gives Cassie's ring to Bo, then nods to Bo.)
You may place the ring on her finger.

BO

*I give you this ring as a symbol of my vow, and with all that I am,
and all that I have, I honor you.*

ANDREW

(Gives Bo's ring to Cassie, then nods to Cassie)
You may place the ring on his finger.

CASSIE

*I give you this ring as a symbol of my vow, and with all that I am,
and all that I have, I honor you.*

ANDREW

*Let us pray. Eternal God, creator and preserver of all life, look with favor upon
this man and this woman whom you make one flesh in holy matrimony. Amen.*

GUESTS

Amen.

ANDREW

*Give them wisdom and devotion in the ordering of their common life;
that each may be to the other a strength in need, a comfort in sorrow,
and a companion in joy. Amen.*

GUESTS

Amen.

ANDREW

*Give them grace when they hurt each other, to recognize and acknowledge
their fault, and to seek each other's forgiveness. Amen.*

GUESTS

Amen.

ANDREW

*Bestow on them, if it is your will, the gift and heritage of children
and the grace to bring them up to love and honor their parents
as they themselves honor their own. Amen.*

GUESTS

Amen.

ANDREW

Grant that all married persons who have witnessed these vows may find
their lives strengthened and their loyalties confirmed. Amen.

GUESTS

Amen.

ANDREW

Now that Bo and Cassie have given themselves to each other by solemn vows
and the giving and receiving of a ring, I pronounce that they are husband and wife.
Those whom God has joined together let no one put asunder.

GUESTS

Amen.

ANDREW

You may kiss the bride.
(Bo kisses Cassie.)
Congratulations.

Could Sarah be . . . alive? Bo raced onto the Llanfair terrace where he discovered,
to his astonishment, Sarah standing before him!

Cordero Roberts and Kate Sanders

May 12, 1987

It was the wedding of the year! Noted archeologist Kate Sanders was marrying widower Cord Roberts, whose pregnant wife had recently disappeared in a raft over the Iguazu Falls in Argentina. Cord buried his grief and prepared to embark upon a new life with his new bride. But deep in the jungles of Argentina, a feverish woman washed up on a remote shore and was revived by a local tribe of Indians. Now fully recovered, she returned to her home, Llanview, with a baby in her arms—only to make the startling discovery that her beloved Cord was about to tie the knot with another woman!

The unsuspecting bride and groom assumed that Tina had perished in a tumble over the Iguazu Falls. As they prepared for their beautiful interfaith ceremony, Cord and Kate were blissfully unaware that Tina, tot in tow, was rushing back to Llanview. Would she make it in time to stop Cord from marrying Kate? (top) Moments after the wedding ceremony, Tina burst through the chapel door, handed a stunned Cord a baby, and asked, "Am I too late?" before collapsing on the floor. (right)

KATE AND CORD'S WEDDING VOWS

An Interfaith Wedding Ceremony

FATHER WALKER AND RABBI HERSHORN PERFORM THE CEREMONY.

PRIEST

Today, standing together at this holy altar, are a bride and groom of different faiths. Some may see only how different they are. Yet, if we look at their shining faces, we see the love and harmony they feel for each other; the common faith they share in a God of love. Katherine, Cordero, your love and your faith are a lesson for all of us. As you have come together, so may we, your friends and family, come closer to one another. May your differences be a source of vitality. May your faith and love be your strength. The sacrament of marriage will be yours to share, now and for all time. As it is written, so let it be said: This is the day the Lord has made, let us rejoice and be glad in it. Amen.

RABBI

Katherine, Cordero, my friend Father Walker has spoken eloquently of your differences and of your common faith in a God of love. Let the words of the Hundredth Psalm be our prayer for you and for all of us on this glorious day. (In Hebrew) Rejoice in the Lord all the earth. Serve the Lord with gladness, come before His Presence with cheerfulness. Enter His gates with thanksgiving. Elohenu veilohey avo taynu. (Then in English) Our God, and God of our Fathers, grant your choicest blessing to Cordero, and to Katherine, as they enter the Holy Covenant of Marriage. May their devotion gain favor in your eyes. May their home gain your protection. May their lives be filled with love, loyalty, and dedication to each other's happiness and well-being. . . . Bless their love, bind their lives together, and help them face the future with faith in one another and unshakeable confidence in your Divine Providence. . . . Guide them through trial and temptation. With Your grace, embrace them with a love that shall not falter nor fade. . . .

. . . And now, O Lord, come Cordero and Katherine before you—to enter the time-tested, age-old institution of marriage. Their hearts are filled with love, and courage, and confidence, and faith. So let it be now, and for all their days to come. Amen.

PRIEST

He cannot know the future. Its hopes, its disappointments, its triumphs, its failures, its pleasures, its pains, its joys, its sorrows—all are hidden from our eyes. Yet, unafraid, come Katherine and Cordero to pledge their love and their union. Their love will guide them; their union will sustain them. Now and through the great unknowable future—even unto death.

PRIEST

Cordero wishes to marry Katherine. In this does he have the blessing of his father and mother?

CLINT

He does.

PRIEST

Cordero, do you wish to have Katherine as your wife?

CORD

I do.

PRIEST

Katherine, do you wish to have Cordero as your husband?

KATE

I do.

PRIEST

Cordero, repeat after me: Katherine, I take you to be my wife.

PRIEST

I promise to be true to you in good times and in bad, in sickness and in health.
(He repeats.)

PRIEST

I will love you and honor you all the days of my life. (He repeats.)

PRIEST

Katherine, repeat after me. Cordero, I take you to be my husband. (She repeats.)

PRIEST

I promise to be true to you in good times and in bad, in sickness and in health. (She repeats.)

PRIEST

I will love you and honor you all the days of my life. (She repeats.)

RABBI

Katherine and Cordero, to symbolize your union, have you tokens of your love?

CORD and KATE

We do.

RABBI

Avinu She-ba-Shamayin barech at ha-Tabo-oth ha-zoth/ha-Eleh . . . *Heavenly Father, may it be good in Thy sight to bless these rings. May they bring cheer, joy, gladness, success, and harmony to Katherine and Cordero in the holy wedlock of matrimony. Cordero, will you take Katherine's hand? Dear Katherine, with this ring I thee wed . . .* (He repeats.)

RABBI

*. . . And by it be Thou consecrated unto me, as my wedded wife,
according to the Law of God and Man.* (He repeats.)

RABBI

Katherine, will you take Cordero's hand? Dear Cordero, with this ring I thee wed. . .
(She repeats.)

RABBI

*. . . And by it be Thou consecrated unto me, as my wedded husband,
according to the Laws of God and Man.* (She repeats.)

RABBI

(Sings Hebrew blessing over the wine, then)
. . . As together you now drink from this cup, so may you, under God's guidance in perfect union and devotion to each other, draw contentment, comfort, and felicity from the cup of life that is in store for you, now that you are united in the holy wedlock of matrimony. Amen. Thou, Source of all life and all joy, sanctify the covenant which Katherine and Cordero consummate in Thy Name. Grant them Thy gifts of friendship, of love, and of peace. Make them rejoice in the sweetness of that family union which is founded on purity and fidelity, on duty and religious consecration. Be with them at this hour of their gladness, bless their convenant and seal their bond of wedlock with love everlasting. Amen.

KATE and CORD

Amen.

SHARE A ROMANTIC RENDEZVOUS IN BUENOS AIRES, ARGENTINA

Like Cord and Kate's dynamic tango, Buenos Aires will sweep you off your feet! With its distinctly European flavor and cosmopolitan personality, it's no wonder that the city is considered the most suave capital of South America. Trendy boutiques, outdoor cafés, and nightclubs give the city a modern edge, but it is the historical reverence that gives Buenos Aires its heart.

When to go: Summer runs from November to March. Crowds tend to thin out from March to May, but the weather is still gorgeous and warm.

What to do: Start exploring Buenos Aires at the Plaza de Mayo, a downtown square decorated with palm trees and flower gardens that's set off by impressive colonial buildings, including the Casa Rosada, a pretty-in-pink government building, the Cabildo (Town Council), and the majestic Metropolitan Cathedral. Take a stroll down the wide sidewalks of Avenida de Mayo, past gilded lampposts, chocolate shops, and clothing stores. If you're interested in buying leather, silver, or the latest fashions, plan to spend your pesos on Calle Florida, a pedestrian-only street that serves as the main shopping area.

Romantic rendezvous: Head to the tree-lined Palermo district to walk hand in hand through the park, which boasts botanic gardens and a zoo. Have an exciting day at the races (horses) at either the Palermo or San Isidro racecourses.

Stepping out at night: The night was made for dancing, especially the tango, and you'll find plenty of clubs that keep to the beat. Avenida Corrientes, Latin America's version of "the street that never sleeps," is the center of night life for dining and entertainment and even shopping past dark. For a big night out, head to the Teatro Colón, the world-famous opera house.

For more information: The Argentina Government Tourist Office has branches in Los Angeles, New York, and Miami.

Cord and Kate in Buenos Aires.

"Prince Raymond" and Sarah Gordon

March 5, 1990

Sarah knew that if she didn't agree to marry Prince Raymond of Mendorra, she could be killed by his maniacal brother, Prince Roland. But unbeknownst to the reluctant bride, Sarah's true love, Bo Buchanan, had daringly infiltrated the Royal Palace, and took Raymond's place at the altar.

In the kingdom of Mendorra, Sarah Gordon was happily stunned when she realized that the bearded man in full military regalia standing next to her at the altar was Bo—in disguise! She joyously spoke her vows and married her phony "prince"!

SHARE A ROMANTIC RENDEZVOUS IN SALZBURG, AUSTRIA

One Life to Live viewers took a fairy-tale journey to the incredibly picturesque city of Salzburg, which served as the setting for the fictional Mendorra. This beautiful baroque city is best known as the birthplace of Mozart and *The Sound of Music*. (The 1965 movie was filmed there.) Perched between mountains along the Salzach River, Salzburg is the embodiment of Old World elegance.

When to go: The weather is gorgeous from April through October; the least crowded times to visit are May and early June, September, and October.

What to do: Most of the top sights are in the Old City, which is connected by squares and narrow streets and looks as if it hasn't changed much since Mozart lived there in the late eighteenth century.

Romantic rendezvous: You'll feel like you're on top of the world when you ride the elevator up Mönchsberg to Winkler Terrace for an all-encompassing view of the city.

Stepping out at night: Life is a symphony in Salzburg, especially at night, when there are numerous musical performances.

For more information: The Austrian National Tourist Office has branches in Los Angeles and New York.

Bo and Megan in Salzburg.

Michael Grande
and Brenda McGillis

April 27, 1990

Michael Grande was obsessed with power, money, *and* Brenda's baby son. The evil manipulator would stop at nothing make to Brenda his bride, even if it meant dragging her to the altar in a semiconscious state.

Could anything save her from this trumped-up marriage? The one man who was determined to prevent this dangerous charade was Dr. Dan Wolek. He correctly deduced that Brenda was being drugged—but he couldn't prove it! Dan truly loved Brenda, and was determined somehow to head off this wicked wedding. Rushing to the church on the morning of the nuptials, Dan stopped Brenda in the foyer just as she was about to walk down the aisle. He pleaded with her not to get married, but a befuddled Brenda repeated the rote phrases Michael had taught her and numbly marched into the church where the wedding proceeded as planned.

General Hospital

Sean Donely and Tiffany Hill

December 23, 1988

The hilarious courtship of volatile former "B" movie star
Tiffany Hill and globe-trotting spy Sean Donely
culminated in the nuttiest nuptials in soap history.

An unlikely pair, Sean Donely and Tiffany Hill began dating in 1987, but Sean, a longtime bachelor, did not even entertain the notion of marriage until he received some rather pointed prodding from his business partner, Anna Devane. Anna practically pushed Sean into popping the question, but when he finally did, he asked Tiffany in such a lackluster fashion that she ordered him to be more romantic and kicked him out of her house! Sean countered with more elaborate efforts, but once again Tiffany gave him the cold shoulder.

"I'm holding out to make Sean sweat after all the misery he's given me!" she admitted to her sister, Cheryl. But Cheryl cautioned Tiffany not to wait too long in case Sean

changed his mind. Refusing to take no for an answer, Sean pressed on. He escorted Tiffany to a gourmet dinner at the Versailles Room and produced a gigantic emerald ring—but still she put him off. He bought her a yacht—and again Tiffany held Sean at bay. Finally she disguised herself as Madame Olga, a gypsy fortune teller, and counseled Sean to propose yet again. Sean held back a laugh as he recognized Tiffany under the elaborate disguise. Exasperated, she whipped off her veil and announced, with fury, that she loved Sean. This time, when he proposed yet again, Tiffany answered with a resounding yes!

Several troubling predicaments caused the wedding to be postponed. Tiffany grew frantic when, because Sean's

work forced a change in the wedding date, she lost the site she had chosen to hold the affair. Fortunately, Lila offered the Quartermaine mansion after some discreet prompting from Sean. Robert Scorpio's new cottage in the woods served as the ideal place to hold Sean's bachelor party, during which Tiffany jumped out of the cake instead of the preplanned cutie!

On the morning of the wedding, Sean received some devastating news from his employer, the WSB, which he knew would make Tiffany furious. Because of a breaking case, the Bureau forbade Sean to go on his honeymoon. When Sean broke the news to his bride-to-be only moments before the ceremony, she refused to marry him. By then all the guests—including Tiffany's outrageous relatives from Tennessee—had assembled in the Quartermaine mansion!

"I won't repeat the vows!" she warned Sean.

"You'll say every word . . . and act like you mean it! You should be damned thankful I'm willing to go through with this at all! A woman your age can't be too picky about husbands."

"How dare you?!" Tiffany countered as she kicked her groom in the shin and proceeded, stomping and screaming, down the aisle.

Tiffany's garishly garbed parents wouldn't have missed their daughter's wedding for the world. Mr. and Mrs. Crumholz came all the way from their home in Tennessee to witness the nuptials. Tiffany's maid of honor, Cheryl, and friend Anna Devane shared in the homespun fun moments before the wedding.

Tiffany had to be dragged kicking and screaming to the altar to marry Sean after the lovers had a major tiff on the morning of the wedding. Sean began the day by ticking off Tiffany when he announced that he was being "dragged, kicking and screaming, down the aisle of doom!" At that, she threatened to call off the wedding. Later, when Tiffany learned that her honeymoon would have to be postponed because of business, she again announced she was calling off the wedding. Sean became exasperated when she refused to come out of her dressing room. Determined to make Tiffany his wife, Sean broke down the door and literally dragged her down the aisle.

The Quartermaine mansion erupted in laughter when the minister called out Tiffany's real name—*Elsie Mae Crumholz!* Sean couldn't contain himself upon hearing this heretofore unknown revelation. Elsie Mae Crumholz?

The more Sean tried to suppress his laughter, the worse it became. The giggling became infectious. Robert Scorpio faked a coughing fit to hide his laughter. Duke Lavery grinned from ear to ear. The other guests, with the exception of sweet-faced Lila Quartermaine, joined in too, which only added to Tiffany's anger and embarrassment. Even the minister had trouble keeping a straight face as he pronounced Sean and Tiffany man and wife.

> **TIFFANY**
> *Sean Donely, if you don't take your hands off me this instant!*
>
> **SEAN**
> *Shut up and march!*

Grant Putnam and Celia Quartermaine

June 6, 1983

With her husband-to-be, Grant Putnam, working long hours at General Hospital, Celia Quartermaine found any excuse to spend time with rugged Jimmy Lee Holt. Though her love for Grant was real, Celia's passion for Jimmy Lee was too dynamic to deny.

Celia forged ahead with plans to marry Dr. Grant Putnam, though she continued a torrid affair with her secret lover, Jimmy Lee Holt. The jealous groom nearly canceled the wedding because of Celia's continued "interest" in Jimmy Lee. Just days before the nuptials, Grant presented Celia with an ultimatum: Get Jimmy Lee out of your life or the wedding is off! Reluctantly Celia broke off her affair.

On Celia's wedding day, Jimmy Lee made a last-ditch plea for her love. Kidnapping her to a cabin in the country, he tried in vain to get her to admit that she loved him, but Celia couldn't break Grant's heart. Escaping from Jimmy Lee, Celia, wearing only a blanket, flagged down a truck filled with live chickens to take her to the church on time. In front of the church, an angry Grant encountered Jimmy Lee and knocked him out.

Grant Putnam was tempted to cancel his wedding to Celia— but he had no choice but to marry her. Grant, a Russian spy, was forced to adhere to the demands of his DVX superiors and go through with the marriage.

Kevin O'Connor and Terry Brock

February 1986

As her wedding day to fiancé Kevin O'Connor drew near, Terry Brock could not shake the strange feeling that something was terribly wrong. When the bride and groom returned to their hometown of Laurelton for the wedding, Terry began having disturbing flashbacks. She tried to suppress the painful memories, but on the way to the wedding in a limousine, the haunting images nearly overwhelmed her. Still, the troubled young woman forged ahead with her wedding to the handsome Dr. Kevin O'Connor.

Although Terry and Kevin's hometown wedding was a very romantic affair, dark secrets doomed their marriage before it even began. In the end, Terry came to the harsh realization that she should have listened to her inner self. When she finally pieced together the fragmented memories, Terry realized that she had witnessed Kevin killing his uncle, Earl Moody. Soon after, the murderous husband tried to kill his new wife on their honeymoon in Catalina.

SHARE A ROMANTIC RENDEZVOUS
IN CHARLESTON, SOUTH CAROLINA

General Hospital journeyed to historic Charleston, South Carolina, to tape the wedding of Terry and Kevin. A gracious southern town steeped in tradition and charm, Charleston is a showcase of beautifully preserved Colonial and Victorian architecture as well as bountiful formal gardens.

When to go: Year round but especially during the spring and fall. July and August are most humid.

What to do: Several historic homes are open to the public and offer a peek into the town's past, including the Aiken-Rhett House, a palatial antebellum showcase featuring nineteenth-century American and European furnishings; the Edmondston-Alston House, with a sweeping view of the harbor; and the Nathaniel Russell House, with its Federal-style architecture and graceful spiral staircase. The Charleston Museum, the oldest museum in the United States, has impressive collections of clothing, furniture, and photographs.

Romantic rendezvous: Take a moonlit cruise on Charleston Harbor or a cozy horse-drawn carriage ride through the historical district.

Stepping out at night: Charleston has an ear for music. If you're honeymooning in late May or early June, get tickets to the Spoleto Festival, which features jazz, dance, opera, theater, orchestral, chamber, and contemporary music. Year round, the Charleston Symphony Orchestra and Charleston Music Hall offer outstanding entertainment.

For more information: Contact the Charleston Area Convention and Visitors Bureau, P.O. Box 975, Charleston, SC 29402; phone (800) 868-8118.

Alan Quartermaine and Lucy Coe

April 26, 1990

Who would have believed that lusty Lucy Coe could successfully parlay her sordid affair with wealthy Dr. Alan Quartermaine into marriage? Through some shrewd scheming, Lucy landed her man. Lucy—the very embodiment of a Jezebel for the 90s—had managed to snare Alan for one of the most bizarre daytime television weddings ever. It's true that Jezebel wore red and so did Scarlet O'Hara—but Lucy didn't intend to, not for this event. It seemed that the wedding dress she ordered didn't arrive—a bright red one did—and red-faced Lucy had no choice but to wear it for the nuptials.

H is friends and family tried to convince Alan not to go through with the ceremony. Lucy was nothing but a money-hungry vixen, they said, but her seductive charms and unquenchable sexual appetite proved irresistible to the middle-age doctor. Though he had reservations about making his scandalous lover his wife, Alan was forced to go through with the wedding in order to save face at the family company, ELQ. On the big day, everyone showed up—and snickered through the ceremony. Lucy's outrageous gown was a jungle-red, off-the-shoulder cocktail dress with a matching hat that was so big that she could hardly make it through the doorway. Still, she held her head high throughout the ceremony—which was no easy feat!

Scott Baldwin and Katherine Bell

November 23, 1993

Just days after the untimely passing of his true love, Dominique, sorrow-ridden Scotty Baldwin received a letter from her old friend, Katherine Crawford. Longing to maintain a connection with his late wife, Scotty asked Katherine to join him in Port Charles. Before long the conniving Katherine was joining him—at the altar!

Drawn together by their shared loss, Scott and Katherine found instant comfort in each other. Before long they were engaged to be married. At the same time, Lucy Coe hated her! She didn't trust Katherine—and she was right. Lucy Coe raced to the church with a piece of juicy news for the groom. Stopping the wedding before the I dos, she informed Scotty that his bride was a greedy con artist who was scheming to stake her claim to the money he inherited from Dominique. In a bizarre counterrevelation, Katherine swore she was really Dominique's half sister. Fuming at the deception, Scotty left Katherine at the altar.

All My Children

Trevor Dillon and Laurel Banning

May 23, 1995

Determined to keep Trevor from marrying Laurel, Janet Green constructed a bomb that she planned to explode in the church during the wedding ceremony. However, she scrapped the destructive scheme upon discovering that her daughter, Amanda, was a member of the wedding party. Instead, Janet planned to shoot her way into Trevor and Laurel's wedding!

On the morning of her wedding, Laurel accepted some good-natured teasing from Brooke and Hayley—unaware that Janet Green was plotting to ruin the nuptials.

As the ceremony began, the bride and groom were blissfully unaware that Janet Green lurked in the shadows, gun in hand, waiting to strike. She might have followed through with her mission had not her confidant, Kendall Hart, convinced Janet to give up her evil plan. As a storm raged outside, Janet fled the church, then was struck by lightning! Trevor and Laurel married without incident, but when Kendall burst in to the reception with news that Janet was "dead," the party was abruptly canceled.

Tad Martin and Hillary Wilson
February 14, 1986

In 1986 ex-gigolo, Tad Martin, seemed finally to have curbed his flirtatious ways as he prepared to marry unassuming, virtuous Hillary Wilson. Hillary's aunt, Phoebe Tyler Wallingford, still had her doubts about Tad the Cad's worthiness as a husband, but reluctantly she tended to the arrangements for a splendid Valentine's Day wedding.

As Tad and Hillary's wedding was about to begin, the groom was nowhere to be found! Lucky for him, Tad's no-show was not his fault. He had been locked in a bank vault by robbers during a holdup!

"I'm gonna be Tad's wife today if it's the last thing I do!" With that declaration, Hillary took off through the snow-covered streets of Pine Valley in her wedding gown—to find her groom. In her haste, Hillary stepped into the path of a car and was knocked unconscious! When the calamity was cleared up, Tad and Hillary finally married in a simple ceremony at the Wallingford Mansion.

Tom Cudahy and
Barbara Montgomery
November 10, 1989

*Barbara Montgomery was always falling for the wrong guy—until
she met good-guy Tom Cudahy. She really needed a friend in the
fall of 1989 when her ex-husband and current lover Travis
Montgomery suddenly skipped town. Soon after Barbara found
herself pregnant! Labeling Travis irresponsible for leaving
so suddenly, Tom Cudahy made a pledge to Barbara.*

*"Tell everyone that I'm the father of your baby," he offered.
Overwhelmed by Tom's magnanimity, Barbara accepted
Tom's proposal of marriage.*

T hough she was pregnant by Travis, Barbara told Tom that in her heart he was
the father of her baby. Although she began having contractions while she was
dressing for the wedding, she insisted on going through with the ceremony so that she and Tom could be officially married when the child came into the world.

Tom and Barbara's wedding began as scheduled but quickly went awry when Travis rushed in and interrupted the ceremony. As he demanded to know the paternity of the baby, Barbara's contractions worsened and she was rushed to Pine Valley Hospital. Tom and the minister followed, and in the delivery room, the wedding continued between Barbara's contractions. Huffing and puffing, Barbara married Tom seconds before giving birth to a baby girl.

Loveless Weddings

What's love got to do with it? Some of ABC Daytime's most memorable unions were forged in the name of greed, ambition, and lust, not love. Here, for *bitter* and for worse, are a collection of some hateful nuptials. . . .

All My Children

Tad Martin
and
Dottie Thornton
September 28, 1984

Tad dated Dottie Thornton for one reason alone: money! Dottie's mother, nouveau riche Edna Thornton, paid Tad a small fortune to date her daughter in order to boost the overweight teenager's confidence. Though he truly loved Hillary Wilson, Tad "the cad" was forced to marry Dottie when she became pregnant with his baby. They married in a civil ceremony, but soon after Dottie miscarried, this loveless union collapsed.

JUDGE PERRY'S PRONOUNCEMENT TO TAD AND DOTTIE

Dearly beloved, we are gathered together in the presence of these witnesses to join together this man and this woman in holy matrimony. It is with great personal pleasure that I look upon these two young people who have come before me—soberly and advisedly—with due reflection of the true meaning and responsibility that such a union entails. They have found a true and lasting love—and their faith in that love has brought them to this moment of pledging their troth before their family and friends. It is my privilege to seal their promise through marriage.

Wade Matthews and Phoebe Wallingford

August 28, 1986

Slick young con artist Wade Mathews slithered into Pine Valley and set his sights on rich dowager Phoebe Tyler Wallingford. By soap standards, it was a quick courtship for the ill-suited twosome. In swift fashion, wily Wade succeeded in splitting Phoebe from Langley, then lured her to the Caribbean isle of St. Justin, where he plied her with liquor, then proposed.

"You've always represented the perfect woman to me," he said with sheepish charm. "You're beautiful, cultured, intelligent, vulnerable. I love you, truly. Marry me, Phoebe."

Bowled over and besotted, Phoebe married wicked Wade in an outdoor tropical garden ceremony with their hotel manager and a chambermaid as witnesses. Back home in Pine Valley, the new lord of the manor plotted to poison his new bride, but his treachery was discovered in the nick of time!

Adam Chandler and Natalie Hunter

September 3, 1990

his was a marriage forged in hell! Desperate for money, Adam Chandler set his sights on the newly rich Natalie Hunter during the summer of 1990. He proved a formidable contender to Natalie's current beau, Trevor Dillon. Adam was everything that Trevor wasn't. Suave. Slick. Wealthy. But she didn't love him. Still, she agreed to elope with him—just to spite Trevor. When Trevor found out, he sped off to stop the wedding. Arriving at the justice of the peace, he made a last-ditch appeal for Natalie to dump Adam and marry him. "You're making the mistake of your life, doll!" he told her. Natalie turned Trevor down flat and forged ahead with her disastrous marriage to Adam.

One Life to Live

Steve Holden and Gabrielle Medina

January 4, 1988

Gabrielle Medina wanted Max Holden, but when he rejected her in favor of sexy Tina Lord, Gabrielle opted for the next best thing—his handsome brother, Steve! Steve, smitten with Gabrielle, proposed at just the right time, and she accepted to spite Max. Though Gabrielle married Steve on the rebound, she never stopped pining for Max. Max continually declined Gabrielle's romantic overtures until Steve was critically injured and fell into a coma. As Steve Holden hovered between life and death, Gabrielle and Max found comfort in each other's arms—and made love!

After their night of passion, Gabrielle's obsession for Max grew even more powerful. She knew now that her marriage to Steve was a mistake. Still, Max urged her to make it work. But Gabrielle had other ideas. One night, in desperation, she attempted to kill Steve by smothering him with a pillow, backing off just in time to spare his life. Upon his recovery, Steve became aware of his wife's feelings for Max. Though Max insisted that Gabrielle work things out with his brother, Steve filed for divorce. The ill-fated union had come to an end.

Jake Harrison and Charlotte Hesser

October 16, 1990

Jake Harrison engaged in a dangerous game when he agreed to woo mob princess Charlotte Hesser. By romancing the innocent girl, Jake hoped to get close to the inner workings of the organization run by her father, Carlo. Though he truly loved Megan Gordon, Jake had no choice but to marry Charlotte when Carlo threatened the lives of his loved ones. When the time was finally right to dissolve the bogus union, Jake couldn't bring himself to divorce Charlotte because she had developed a case of hysterical blindness. When her sight eventually returned, Charlotte continued to feign blindness to hang on to her husband. But when Jake discovered her charade, he quickly called an end to the unromantic marriage.

David Vickers and Dorian Lord

March 24, 1995

Dorian Lord detested David Vickers! The last thing she ever wanted to do was marry him. But when Viki Carpenter's alter ego, Jean, blackmailed her, Dorian had no choice but to tie the knot with the smarmy devil. Her stomach turned every time

David, with saccharine sweetness, called her "Gumdrop." She grimaced with pain whenever David bought himself expensive gifts—charged to her credit card!

When the path was finally clear to end their unholy alliance, David decided to stick it to Dorian. He wouldn't agree to a divorce without a million-dollar settlement. But devious Dorian devised a sinister scheme to get David to commit adultery so that she wouldn't have to fork over a penny! Dorian donned a blond wig and seduced a drunk, amorous, and blindfolded David. Later, when David saw photos of his scandalous affair with "Madame Helmore," he realized he'd been duped. Because of his adulterous act, David had to forfeit his hefty divorce settlement. After he signed the divorce papers, Dorian divulged that she had been his secret seducer. David's anger turned to passion—and the newly divorced couple shared one last night of wild sex!

Todd Manning and Téa Delgado

July 15, 1997

Todd and Téa tied the knot for all the wrong reasons. Todd Manning proved that he would do anything to keep custody of his precious daughter, Starr. Reasoning that he needed a respectable wife to keep his ex-wife, Blair, from taking back their daughter, Todd made an indecent proposal to his lawyer, Téa. In exchange for two words—"I do"—Téa would receive a cool $5 million! Weighing the tantalizing offer, Téa realized that by marrying Todd, she would have financial security for the rest of her life. Of course she said yes!

The no-nonsense civil ceremony, held in the Llantano County clerk's office, had less to do with love than it did with big business. The bride showed up at the ceremony with flowers in one hand and a briefcase in the other. With little fanfare and without the blessings of their loved ones, Todd and Téa tied the knot. When it came time to kiss his new bride, Todd sheepishly declined. "I have a cold," he dispassionately told the justice of the peace.

General Hospital

Robert Scorpio and Holly Sutton

February 7, 1983

Holly's marriage to Robert began as one of convenience. The quickie civil ceremony, held at the courthouse and presided over by the mayor, was over just moments after it began.

The morning after Holly and Robert made love for the first time, Luke "returned from the dead." Realizing that the woman he loved had married his best friend, a humiliated Luke rushed out the door before Holly could explain that she had agreed to marry Robert only to avoid deportation.

For Robert and Holly, the wedding came *before* the relationship. Although it wasn't love that brought them together initially, it was love that kept their marriage together. In early 1983 Holly was deeply in love with Robert's best friend, Luke Spencer. After Luke's apparent death in an avalanche, Holly discovered she was pregnant and about to be deported back to England, straight into the hands of members of her corrupt family who were certain to murder her.

Spurred by deep loyalty to his best pal, Robert decided to make Holly his wife—if he could find her! After writing thank-you notes to her Port Charles friends, Holly had boarded a plane bound for her homeland. When Robert found out her whereabouts,

he raced to the airport, intercepted the plane, and proposed, assuring her that the marriage would be temporary. Over her protests, Robert insisted that "after you're a U.S. citizen and have Luke's baby, you can have a divorce." Holly reluctantly agreed to Robert's gallant act of kindness. In a quick and somber ceremony held in the mayor's office, Holly Sutton became Mrs. Robert Scorpio.

While she refused to sleep in the same bed with Robert, Holly soon began to enjoy his company. Helping Robert with his police work, Holly became his partner and confidant. When she miscarried the baby, Holly lost the last link to her dearly departed Luke. Robert comforted his bride in her time of grief and their platonic relationship became passionate. Before long Robert and Holly were madly in love. Not even Luke's surprising return from the dead could split up the Scorpios.

ROBERT AND HOLLY'S FIRST WORDS AS MAN AND WIFE

Robert
Well, that wasn't too painful, I hope. The bottom line is they can't make you leave now or ever. Well, shall we go?

Holly
Where?

Robert
I haven't really thought about that!

Ned Ashton and Katherine Bell

July 1, 1994

Ned Ashton has the cold-hearted business resolve of his mother, Tracy Quartermaine, and approaches romance with the same conquering philosophy. That's why he was never more miserable than when he was forced to marry Katherine Bell in 1994. Although Lois Cerullo had stolen his heart, Katherine Bell held Ned in her grasp as she manipulated his family from within their luxurious mansion.

Katherine blackmailed the Quartermaine clan with evidence proving that eldest son Alan accidentally killed abusive bad-guy Ray Conway, then covered up his part in the incident. Ned had no choice but to do what his grandfather told him to do—marry Katherine in order to keep her quiet! The marriage was illegal because Ned was already secretly married to Lois. When Lois found out about "the other Mrs. Ashton," she called Ned's bluff by jumping out of Katherine's birthday cake.

Stefan Cassadine and Bobbie Jones

December 4, 1996

After catching her husband, Tony, in bed with a woman half his age, Bobbie Jones felt hurt and vulnerable. Reeling from the shock, she flew into the waiting arms of sinister Stefan Cassadine. In a dizzying series of events, Bobbie fled to the Dominican Republic to divorce her wayward husband. Hot on her trail, Stefan arrived on the island, seduced Bobbie, and convinced her to marry him—as soon as possible. Stefan lusted after Bobbie but didn't love her. Instead, he loved the idea of earning the ire of his arch-enemy, Luke Spencer, by making his sister his bride.

Before Bobbie could reconsider the marriage, Stefan had made all the arrangements for a quick and small wedding inside his Gothic mansion on Spoon Island.

He even presented Bobbie with four potential wedding gowns to wear during the hurried, somber ceremony. With only her son, Lucas, Stefan's cousin Alexis, and nephew Nikolas in attendance, Bobbie, wearing a sleeveless beaded gown, took her fourth husband.

Paul Hornsby and Tracy Quartermaine

October 25, 1991

Tongues wagged throughout Port Charles when the brilliant and well-chiseled Paul Hornsby pledged his love to Jenny Eckert, then inexplicably proposed marriage to diva Tracy Quartermaine. Tracy, though flattered by Paul's attentiveness, wondered why he was conducting their courtship at breakneck speed. Unbeknownst to her, Paul was being blackmailed into wooing Tracy by an evil cartel that sought to gain control of the Quartermaine family conglomerate, ELQ. To get Paul

to do their bidding, the cartel slipped a potentially lethal drug into his daughter Susan's milk. To keep his daughter alive, Paul had no choice but to convince Tracy to become his bride.

Wowed by Paul's relentless pursuit, Tracy jumped at the chance to exchange I dos. Only later did she learn the truth behind the loveless marriage. Finding out that Paul had been forced to marry her was the greatest humiliation of Tracy Quartermaine's life. Still in love with Paul, Tracy announced her unplanned pregnancy just in time to prevent Paul from dissolving their withering marriage.

Sonny Corinthos and Lily Rivera

February 5, 1996

Lily intended to wear her mother's white Chantilly lace wedding gown when she married Sonny Corinthos. However, her dream became a nightmare when Brenda Barrett accidentally burned the dress. Still, Sonny refused to let the catastrophe interfere with their plans. To appease his devastated bride, Sonny promised to buy her the most beautiful gown they could find in Port Charles.

Both Lily and Sonny were on the rebound from failed romances when they forged their imperfect union. Betrayed by his true love, Brenda Barrett, Sonny took up with Lily, who had broken her engagement to singer Miguel Morez. Only his most intimate friends knew that Sonny didn't love his fiancée, having agreed to marry her as part of a devil's bargain with Lily's father, Puerto Rican gangster Hernando Rivera, who had pulled strings to get Corinthos acquitted of racketeering charges. In exchange for his freedom, Sonny reluctantly turned his back on Brenda, sacrificing true love to make decidedly unromantic wedding arrangements with Lily.

Knowing her groom still had deep feelings for Brenda, Lily suddenly called a halt to the ceremony. Standing in the back of the church, Brenda's heart was filled with hope as she strained to hear what would happen next. Suddenly Brenda's hope turned to heartache as Sonny quelled Lily's fears by telling her—in front of everyone—that he wanted to spend the rest of his life with her. The wedding continued, and Brenda tearfully looked on as Sonny and Lily were pronounced man and wife.

Vintage Weddings— Bride and Joy!

These meant-to-be-together couples can look back on their lives and remember sharing one extraordinary wedding day to remember. . . .

General Hospital

Steve Hardy and Audrey March

February 15, 1965

November 24, 1976

August 26, 1977

*I*t's been said that love is better the second time around. But what can possibly be said about the *third* time? In the case of Dr. Steve Hardy and nurse Audrey March, the third trip to the altar proved to be the charm! Steve was a hard-working doctor at General Hospital when he first met Audrey, an airline stewardess with a nursing degree, in March of 1964.

They fell in love and planned to marry, but when it came time to set the wedding date, lifelong bachelor Steve dragged his feet. Audrey, convinced that Steve loved his job much more than he loved her, broke their engagement and planned to leave town with another man, Randy Washburn. However, just before leaving, Audrey collapsed! Diagnosed with lymphoma, Audrey might have died without Steve's steadfast determination to make her well.

Nearly losing Audrey convinced Steve that he couldn't bear to be apart from the woman he loved. He summoned up the courage once again to ask for Audrey's hand in marriage. Beaming with joy, Audrey readily accepted Steve's heartfelt proposal.

Audrey's near death convinced Steve that he loved her more than life itself. In February 1965 they tied the knot in a solemn church wedding. The discovery that they could not have children proved devastating to Steve and Audrey's marriage. After they divorced in 1968, Audrey endured two ill-fated marriages before realizing that her heart belonged to Steve (top). Flanked by best man Mark Dante, matron of honor Diana Taylor, and Audrey's son, Tommy, Audrey and Steve remarried in November 1976. The newlyweds happily left for a Hawaiian honeymoon, oblivious to the fact that Audrey's believed-dead husband had come back to Port Charles! (middle) It took Audrey nearly a year to extricate herself from a long-dead marriage to Tom Baldwin. Obtaining a divorce, Audrey hurriedly arranged a repeat performance of her wedding vows with Steve. The Hardys blissfully married for the third and lasting time in September 1977 (bottom).

Dr. Peter Taylor and Jessie Brewer

April 1970

After her husband, Phil Brewer, perished in a plane crash, Nurse Jessie Brewer sought the counsel of her friend, Dr. Peter Taylor, a compassionate psychiatrist. Like Phil, Peter was tall and handsome. Unlike diabolical Phil, Peter was kind and honorable. They spent countless hours together, provoking the gossipy staff members to take notice. Worried about the whispers they were hearing in the halls of General Hospital, Peter and Jessie made it abundantly clear to their superiors that their involvement was friendship—nothing more.

But Peter and Jessie could not resist the inevitable. In time, their friendship turned to passion and, early in 1970, they married. Far away, in Venezuela, a critically injured Phil slowly recovered from his accident and made plans to gather enough strength to return home.

Al Weeks and Lucille March

June, 1974

General Hospital's nursing staff lived in fear of strict, no-nonsense Head Nurse Lucille March. Lucille could be abrupt and bellicose, but anyone who really knew her understood that beneath her tough exterior beat a heart of gold. One man who became a victim of Lucille's wrath was widower Al Weeks, who had been admitted to General Hospital suffering from bleeding ulcers. When Lucille barked, Al barked right back. They balanced each other's temperaments perfectly. Al busted through Lucille's tough exterior and found a softer side that utterly delighted him. Proving that the heart has no schedule for love, Al asked Lucille to share her golden years with him as man and wife.

Al and Lucille's wedding was held in the General Hospital chapel. Lucille's sister, Audrey, served as matron of honor in the much-anticipated 1974 wedding. There wasn't a dry eye in the chapel as Lucille's once-and-future brother-in-law, Steve Hardy, crooned "O Promise Me" to mark the occasion.

Cameron Faulkner
and
Dr. Lesley Williams
May 1975

Dr. Lesley Williams married millionaire Cameron Faulkner, though he nearly died on his way to the altar. Lesley, thrilled by Cam's sudden decision to tie the knot, hurried home to pack her bags for the trip to Baltimore for the wedding. Before she could gather her belongings, a deranged former patient who had fallen hopelessly in love with her showed up, gun in his hand.

"The wedding is off!" he shouted, waving the pistol in Lesley's face. Cameron arrived on the scene and valiantly attempted to wrestle the gun away from the lovelorn loser. Lesley watched in horror as a shot rang out. Cameron fell to the floor, with a bullet wound to the chest! The police rushed to the scene and arrested the unbalanced assailant. An ambulance hurried Cameron away to General Hospital where an emergency operation saved his life.

"You nearly gave your life for me," Lesley tearfully exclaimed weeks later, as she tied the knot with her heroic millionaire.

Lee Baldwin

and

Caroline Chandler

February 13, 1976

Attorney Lee Baldwin spent many years alone after the untimely death of his wife, Meg. In 1976 adoption agent Caroline Chandler arrived in Port Charles and, while working on a case together, they fell in love. At long last Lee had found his perfect match—Caroline was as generous and levelheaded as he was. On the eve of Valentine's Day, they made their love official in a civil wedding ceremony.

Dr. Rick Webber and Dr. Lesley Faulkner

October 1977
December 1981

Rick Webber proved to be Lesley Faulkner's savior after her husband, Cameron Faulkner, died in a car accident. Alone and pregnant, Lesley found a compassionate friend in Rick, her fellow doctor. Though she subsequently lost the baby, Lesley stayed close to Rick, much to the displeasure of the manipulating Monica, who yearned to be with him. In the autumn of 1977 they married in a glorious ceremony held in a rustic ski lodge.

In a quiet, intimate ceremony held in their poinsettia-festooned Port Charles home, Rick and Lesley exchanged simple vows and became husband and wife again.

Sadly, Rick and Lesley's marriage came apart at the seams after Lesley was released from jail after serving months for a murder she didn't commit. Rick and Lesley reunited after the ordeal, but their marriage suffered irreparable damage when Lesley became frigid in bed. In his loneliness, Rick had an affair with his former lover, Monica, who became pregnant. With her heart breaking, Lesley filed for divorce so that Rick would be free to marry Monica. Eventually the truth came out that the child belonged to Monica's husband, Alan Quartermaine, not Rick.

Although they tried to live separate lives, Rick and Lesley's love had never died. When Rick caught the garter belt at their daughter Laura's wedding to Luke, he knew that destiny had called him back to Lesley.

"Les, I know I've made mistakes. A lot of mistakes. I hope I've learned from them. And I know I'm not gonna make them again," Rick admitted to his ex-wife. "I've learned just how much I love you. And I always will. Lesley . . . I want you to be my wife."

Without delay, Lesley agreed. "What took you so long?" she quipped as they shared a laugh and a hug in celebration of their renewed commitment.

Bryan Phillips
and
Claudia Johnston
April 1983

The wedding of longtime lovers Bryan Phillips and Claudia Johnston was nearly called off. At the eleventh hour, the groom suffered a case of last-minute jitters. Bryan's friend, Rick Webber, soothed his shattered nerves, and he managed to head for the chapel—before realizing that he had forgotten the ring. Waiting anxiously for her man to appear, Claudia began to suspect that Bryan had backed out on their marriage. Worse, her wealthy father was just about to call off the wedding when Bryan appeared out of the blue—and the wedding was on!

Will they or won't they? It was four years in the making, but not until the last minute did anyone know for sure if Claudia and Bryan would get married. When they finally took the plunge, the entire hospital turned out to wish them the best.

Jimmy Lee Holt and Celia Quartermaine

August 1985

Though she tried for years to make a go of her marriage to Grant Putnam, Celia Quartermaine's fires continued to burn for Jimmy Lee Holt. Early in 1985, their paths crossed again when Jimmy Lee acquired an art gallery in New York and arranged to give Celia, an artist, a one-woman show. Celia was delighted, but Grant felt that her thriving career and continuing friendship with Jimmy Lee threatened their marriage.

Grant's inkling proved accurate when Celia gave in to temptation and made love with Jimmy Lee in New York. Soon after divorcing Grant, Celia accepted Jimmy Lee's proposal and they married in an adventurous Gay Nineties–style wedding held aboard a train in a Pullman car that was specially outfitted for the occasion.

Dr. Tom Hardy and Dr. Simone Ravelle

February 26, 1988

While interning at New York City's Bellevue Hospital, young Dr. Tom Hardy became engaged to marry Simone Ravelle, a beautiful black doctor. However, they called it quits when Simone's parents frowned upon her engagement to a white man. Heartbroken, Tom moved home to Port Charles—and several months later Simone followed to take a new job at General Hospital. Working side by side, Tom and Simone pledged to stay friends, but it was apparent to everyone that they were still very much in love!

Tom and Simone finally were able to admit their feelings for each other—thanks to a fortuitous blizzard that left them stranded in a mountain cabin. Alone together in front of a roaring fire, their hostility thawed—and passion ignited. Overcome with emotion, Tom proposed marriage and Simone accepted. Tom's parents, Audrey and Steve, were thrilled upon hearing the news, but Simone did not receive the same positive response from her own parents. To help them see the light, Audrey invited Mr. and Mrs. Ravelle to a dinner. After a shaky start, the evening proved to be a hit for everyone! Delighted with their new kin, the Ravelles gave Simone and Tom their blessing, and the couple prepared to marry in February.

Psychiatrist Tom Hardy and pediatrician Simone Ravelle overcame the outside pressures of their interracial romance and became man and wife in a ceremony held in the General Hospital chapel in 1988. In a touching moment Tom's father, Steve Hardy, who had been confined to a wheelchair because of a ruptured spinal disk, was able to walk down the aisle.

Tony Jones
and
Bobbie Spencer
October 13, 1989

"Friends can become lovers," Tony Jones told his longtime pal, Bobbie Spencer, as he handed her a jar brimming with cotton balls. Inside, to Bobbie's astonishment, was a sparkling engagement ring.

Anthony Jones and Barbara Jean Spencer had been friends for many years before they fell in love. Bobbie Spencer hadn't had the best luck with men. After a string of failed marriages and broken hearts, she was leery of getting deeply involved with a new man. At the same time, Tony was still smarting from his ill-fated marriage with Lucy Coe. Together, Tony and Bobbie found love among the ruins.

Tony planned an elaborate surprise wedding for Bobbie in, of all places, Puerto Rico. He "tricked" his fiancée into following him to the island paradise, and only then did she make the pleasant discovery that there was a wedding in the works! The groom's brother, Frisco, and Bobbie's stepdaughter, Terry, were among the hand-picked contingent of loved ones who flew down to San Juan to join in the festivities.

"I love you and it is a love different than any love I have ever had," Tony whispered as he got down onto one knee. "It's good and strong and beyond friendship. Will you marry me?" Bobbie couldn't help but say yes to such a sweet proposal of marriage.

"This is the most wonderful surprise I've ever had in my life," proclaimed a radiant Bobbie just before marrying Tony in the bridal suite of a small tropical hotel.

TONY AND BOBBIE'S WEDDING VOWS

TONY

Bobbie, I give you this ring as a symbol of my love, but more importantly, I give it to you as a symbol of our friendship. Love may be the spark that started the flame, but friendship is the timber that keeps it burning. So when you wear this ring, always remember that this flame keeps me warm when I'm cold and lights my way through all my dark hours, and that I will always love you and always cherish you and keep you for the rest of my life.

BOBBIE

Well, you just said everything I was going to say! But I guess that's what happens when you marry your best friend. And you are my best friend. My best and dearest friend. And I love you very much. I feel real lucky to have you and the kids and family and friends and my heart is very full right now and I feel blessed! And I think we're both very fortunate, Tony, because we don't have any illusions about one another. And we're a lot alike in a lot of ways. But in some ways we're very different. But what really matters is that we still respect each other and we trust one another. And I think that's the greatest gift of love that two people can give one another. So please accept this ring and know that I will love you for the rest of my life.

Colton Shore
and
Felicia Jones
June 15, 1989

As she prepared to marry Colton Shore, Felicia Jones knew in her heart that she still cherished her late husband, Frisco. That kind of love doesn't die. It is too deep, too strong. But the love she felt for Colton was separate and apart. And it was just as deep. Colton, compassionate and spiritual, had been Felicia's supreme source of strength in the most difficult period of her life.

Colton and Felicia might have married sooner had not Colton's first wife, Arielle, arrived in Port Charles to try to recapture the love of her one-time mate. Felicia became fiercely jealous of the beautiful Arielle, but Colton wanted only one thing from her—a divorce. As soon as the marriage was dissolved, Colton and Felicia decided to get married before anything else got in their way. Meanwhile, in a Middle East prison, a bearded man was being tortured by guards in the days before his execution. It was Frisco Jones—alive! Miraculously, he escaped his captors and was in the midst of a long and arduous journey home to his wife.

On the morning of the wedding, Colton showed up at Felicia's door.

"You can't see me yet," Felicia said, laughing, as she reached for her groom's hand through a slit in the door. "It's not because it's bad luck but because I don't look very good."

"Oh, that's all right. I can wait a few more hours," Colton answered. "Can you believe this? In a few more hours we're going to be married! We're going to be Mr. and Mrs. Colton Shore! We're going to have the perfect wedding, I promise you."

An ominous clap of thunder shook the walls of the apartment building. Just then Frisco Jones, exhausted from his round-the-world journey, arrived home in Port Charles.

The skies cleared in time for Felicia and Colton's nuptials to take place in Port Charles Park. Just as the minister stated, "If anyone can show just cause why they may not be lawfully married, speak now or forever hold your peace," Frisco arrived on the scene. Stunned by the sight, he opened his mouth but stopped and said nothing. Lurking in the shadows, he closed his eyes so as to not witness the painful sight of Felicia marrying another man.

Drs. Alan and
Monica Quartermaine
August 1991

After countless affairs and endless misunderstandings, Alan and Monica finally realized that they had never stopped loving each other. Just to be sure, they drew up a comprehensive prenuptial agreement. Then, after deciding the document was a ridiculous formality, they tore it up!

In August 1991 the entire Quartermaine clan showed up at Port Charles City Hall to surprise Alan and Monica as they waited in line at the Marriage License Bureau. After a quickie ceremony, Lila invited everyone in line to attend a party back at the Quartermaine mansion.

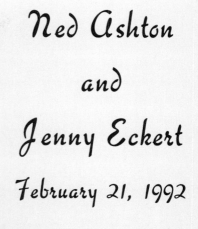

Ned Ashton and Jenny Eckert

February 21, 1992

The courtship of Ned Ashton and Jenny Eckert culminated in a traditional church wedding in Port Charles. Because of the couple's stormy engagement, which weathered murder, blackmail, and family turmoil, the guests were keeping their fingers crossed that nothing further would trip up the couple as they marched toward the altar.

Complicated love affairs are frequent events in Port Charles. However, few raised as much interest as these nuptials, which united the powerful and opinionated Quartermaines with their business rivals—and social opposites—the Eckerts. On their wedding day, the emotional turmoil of the wedding participants proved as complex as the intricate design of the bride's hand-beaded gown.

Scott Baldwin and
Dominique Stanton
February 15, 1993

Although it wasn't love that brought them together, it was love that kept them together. Dominique Stanton and Scott Baldwin weren't in love when they got married in a drunken night on the town in Las Vegas in the fall of 1992. When they awoke the next morning, neither "bride" nor "groom" could believe what each had done. Before their divorce became final, the bickering Baldwins realized that they were inseparable! The charismatic couple mapped out a promising future together, but fate dealt them a cruel blow with the revelation that Dominique was suffering from an inoperable brain tumor. With her days dwindling down to a precious few, Dominique wanted desperately to give Scott a child. But how? Dominique came up with a plan: She asked Scotty's ex-girlfriend, Lucy Coe, to carry a child for her. In a revolutionary procedure, Dominique's fertilized egg was transplanted in Lucy's womb. Before long, lucky Lucy became pregnant with Scotty and Dominique's child.

On a blustery winter day, Scotty and Dominique renewed their vows in a poignant ceremony held in a candlelit, gardenia-festooned chapel in Port Charles. A special song, "Someone to Watch Over Me," musically illuminated the occasion. Their vows were especially bittersweet since the friends and loved ones in attendance all knew that this enchanting wedding would be no happily-ever-after affair.

WORDS OF LOVE
LEE BALDWIN'S WORDS OF LOVE
TO HIS SON, SCOTTY

LEE

*I can't think of a better way to get through this life than with your best friend.
It's a place where those loving feelings that we have can be nurtured. And can flower
and bloom. You see, when friends become lovers and then husbands and wives, well,
two is definitely better than one, to themselves and to everyone they touch.*

SCOTTY AND DOMINIQUE'S
WEDDING VOWS

SCOTT

*I love it when you smile. Prettiest girl I've ever seen. I'm so in love with you.
And I'm going to give you the best because you deserve the best. And I'm so grateful
that you're in my life. So grateful. You know, um, this may sound a little hokey,
but this, this love is the greatest thing in the world. I never thought that I'd ever,
ever feel this. I made you promise me that, you would never leave me,
so, how do you feel now?*

DOMINIQUE

*Listen to me. You must know by now that I will never really leave you.
The love that we are and the spirit of us is always going to be around. Forever.
I promise to love you, to support you, to treasure you, and to never hurt you.
I promise to laugh at all your jokes regularly so you will know how deeply happy
you have made me. And right now, I think we're going to need all the laughter we
can get in our lives. I promise to tell you often how much I really like you.
Because I really do. And I don't think it's every wife who can honestly say that
they like their husband the way I like you. 'Cause you are such a fine, good, caring
man and I respect you. And you are a fighter. I am so proud to be your wife.
And I'm never going to leave you. I'll always be by your side.*

One Life to Live

Carla Gray
and Ed Hall

October 5, 1973

Carla Gray married her longtime love, Police Lieutenant Ed Hall, in an intimate ceremony in the fall of 1973. A guest, celebrated jazz pianist Hazel Scott, serenaded the bride and groom with a special song during the wedding. Ed and Carla's new marriage was immediately put to the test when they adopted a rebellious teenage son, Joshua West.

Mark Toland
and
Julie Siegel
May 1971

Young Julie Siegel yearned to meet a man as kind and sincere as her father, attorney Dave Siegel. She thought that former high school football hero Jack Lawson was *the* one—but Jack turned out to be a philander. When Julie discovered that her live-in lover was cheating on her, she nearly suffered a nervous breakdown. On the rebound, she met Dr. Mark Toland (played by Oscar-winning actor Tommy Lee Jones). Julie and Mark married in 1971, but Dr. Toland soon discovered that his new wife, still emotionally scarred by her breakup with Jack, was passionless in bed. In time, his patience with her frigidity wore thin, and he had an affair with fellow doctor Dorian Cramer.

Vince Wolek
and
Wanda Webb
February 14, 1975

Much to the delight of the residents of Llanview, Police Officer Vince Wolek made waitress Wanda Webb his bride in 1975. The pair were lucky to make it the altar. While on assignment in the weeks before the wedding, Vince was shot. Fortunately, his injuries were minor. Then Wanda consulted an astrologer who told her that she must marry Vince on January 17. However, when the big day arrived, the groom came down with measles! They reset the wedding date for February 14, and, on schedule, Vince made Wanda his very special Valentine.

Tim Siegel and
Jenny Vernon

April 5, 1976

After dropping out of law school and returning home to Llanview, Tim Siegel fell head over heels in love with a young nurse, Jenny Wolek. Jenny was equally captivated by her handsome escort, but she could not act upon her feelings because she was a novice nun, about to take her final vows.

Jenny, torn between her feelings for Tim Siegel and her commitment to God, decided to leave the sisterhood to marry the man she loved. Jenny's decision to forgo her spiritual vows angered her cousin Vince—who took out his wrath on Tim in the halls of Llanview Hospital. During their verbal sparring match, Tim stumbled and took a terrifying tumble down the hospital stairwell. Knowing that Tim was dying from his injuries, Jenny arranged a bedside ceremony in Llanview Hospital. With Jenny's cousin Larry and Tim's mother Eileen in attendance, a minister married Tim and Jenny. The next morning Tim Siegel died in his new wife's arms. (Photo by Al Rosenberg)

Larry Wolek and Karen Wolek

March 31, 1977

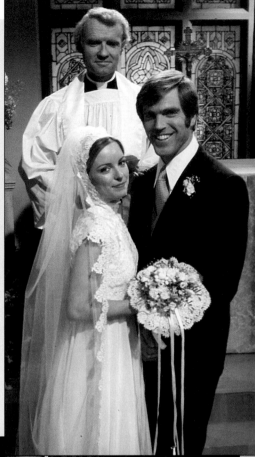

Karen Wolek, a young woman of modest means and cosmopolitan tastes, wanted a husband who could give her the finer things in life—a fancy car, extravagant jewelry, and designer clothes. Her second cousin, widower Larry Wolek, was just such a man. With her gorgeous looks and seemingly sweet smile, Karen had Larry wrapped around the very same finger that he soon decorated with the biggest, most expensive engagement ring in Llanview's local jewelry store.

Larry and Karen's engagement went smoothly until a week before their church wedding. Suddenly a young man named Marco Dane—a shady figure from Karen's shady past—came to town with sinister plans to blow the whistle on Karen by telling Larry all about her sordid, criminal past. The bride-to-be panicked when Marco threatened to make his move during the ceremony. Terrified, Karen went ahead with the wedding, and as planned,

Marco showed up—but rather than stop the wedding, he kept mum, allowing the marriage to take place. The wedding party (including Larry's son, Dan, the ring bearer) was all smiles as they gathered for this group photograph after the wedding. Karen breathed a sigh of relief when her former boyfriend, Marco, left the wedding without interrupting the affair as he had threatened.

Herb Callison and Dorian Lord

January 7, 1981

Dorian Lord satisfied her penchant for power when she accepted Herb Callison's proposal of marriage. Their romance benefited Herb too because, if he played his cards right, the rich Widow Lord would finance his financially strapped campaign for the governorship of Pennsylvania.

Once she got her hooks into Herb, Dorian tried to take charge of his campaign and his life. To ensure his victory, Dorian persuaded Asa Buchanan to make an illegal campaign contribution in exchange for certain "political favors." Indeed, the election was a close one, but when it was over, Herb was elected. Even before she took up residence in the sprawling Governor's mansion, Dorian was already acting the part of the First Lady of Pennsylvania. She was too involved in her wedding plans to do more than deny the rumors that they had bought the election.

On the day of the wedding, the scandal finally broke! Herb, fearing that Dorian might back out of the wedding if she found out, chose not to tell her before the wedding. However, Dorian learned the awful news during the reception, turning what should have been a happy occasion into a wake.

Peter Janssen and Jenny Vernon

September 2, 1981

Jenny and Peter's romance was complicated by former lovers who were determined to keep them apart. The couple endured an endless wait before they could finally overcome the obstacles that stood in the way of their marriage. First, Peter had to obtain a divorce from his mentally ill wife, Melinda Cramer. This became impossible when she attacked Jenny Vernon with a letter opener and was sent to a mental institution. Melinda's crazed act of violence meant further postponement of Jenny and Peter's wedding. Peter realized that he would have to wait months before Melinda was mentally fit enough to sign divorce papers.

Peter nearly died when he was shot by a gunman who aimed a pistol at Asa Buchanan but inadvertently struck down the innocent Dr. Janssen. With Jenny by his side, Peter made a full recovery. However, Brad Vernon, still hopelessly in love with his ex-wife, Jenny, vowed to stop her from marrying Peter. Despite Brad's threat, Peter and Jenny forged ahead with their plans to have a small wedding ceremony with Jenny's sister, Karen, as maid of honor and Peter's colleague, Dr. Larry Wolek, as best man.

Complicating the situation further, Brad threatened to stop the ceremony by revealing a sizzling secret that he had just discovered—Jenny's baby daughter, Mary, was not really hers. (The child had been switched in the hospital nursery with Katrina Karr's dead child.) However, on Jenny and Peter's wedding day, Brad could not bring himself to hurt the woman he still loved with this dreadful secret. As a disheveled but quiet Brad was escorted out of the church, Peter and Jenny *finally* became man and wife.

Tony Lord
and
Pat Ashley

August 27, 1982

Pat Ashley and Tony Lord proved that first love can be lasting love. The couple first met and fell in love sixteen years earlier in Rio de Janeiro. Circumstances kept them apart for years until 1982, when they were finally free to be together.

Days before their wedding, Tony (who always had a thirst for adventure) volunteered to perform a dramatic parachute jump as a stunt for a new movie that was shooting in Llanview. During the jump, his main chute failed to open! A backup chute engaged in time to save his life, but Tony's injuries required hospitalization. Despite his brush with death, the wedding went on as scheduled. As Tony recovered, he and Pat married in the hospital garden.

David Renaldi

and

Jenny Vernon Janssen

June 1, 1984

Llanview eagerly awaited the June wedding of Jenny Vernon Janssen and David Renaldi. And no one loathed the idea more than Jenny's ex-husband, Brad, and David's former flame Dorian Lord. Both had tried scheme after scheme to keep the lovers apart.

When Brad discovered that David's first marriage to an Asian woman had never been officially annulled, he used the woman, Liat, to stop David and Jenny's first wedding in February. Weeks later Dorian went to work. To keep David and Jenny from tying the knot, she falsely claimed to Jenny that David had pushed her down a flight of stairs. Months later Dorian's scam was finally exposed. With no obstacles in their path, Jenny was finally free to marry her man! On June 1, 1984, Jenny and David finally shared the enchanting church wedding that they had waited so long for. The newlyweds looked forward to a long and happy life together.

Rob Coronal
and
Cassie Callison

August 26, 1985

Spooky circumstances brought two teenagers—Cassie Callison and Rob Coronal—together in an abandoned movie theater. Rob, a reluctant member of a mob family, escaped to Llanview after being wounded in a mob shooting in Atlantic City. He hid out in the empty, crumbling Atheneum Theater—but soon found he was not alone. At first, Rob tried to chase Cassie out of the building by trying to make her think the theater was haunted. Despite Rob's terrorizing attempts to scare her off, Cassie remained undaunted. She refused to leave and soon took a job as caretaker of the theater so that she could find the elusive "ghost."

One night a mysterious figure made a move toward her, then fainted. Cassie was shocked to see that her "ghost" was a sick young boy, weak from a bullet wound that had never been treated. She obtained medical aid for him, and before long they were hopelessly in love.

Rob and Cassie became engaged, but soon after Rob backed out of their impending nuptials. Afraid that his mob ties would endanger her life, Rob reluctantly asked Cassie for his engagement ring back. For weeks Cassie was miserable. Still, she refused to believe that their love had ended. Cassie simply would not let Rob walk out of her life. And Rob, heartbroken himself, could not run away from Cassie. They reunited and shared a lavish Llanview wedding.

Bo Buchanan
and
Didi O'Neill

January 10, 1986

When Bo introduced himself to his future wife, Didi O'Neill, he told her his name was Bill Brady, and that he was an unemployed laborer. Little did she know that this blue-collar guy was actually one of Llanview's richest men looking to see how the other half lived. "Bill" romanced Didi, who eventually forgave him when he revealed his true identity. Bo's love for Didi grew deeper when she was blinded in an explosion at the Lord-Manning plant.

Nearly two years later they wed in a ceremony held at St. Barnabas Church; then the newlyweds spent the night at the O'Neill house. The following morning Didi checked into Llanview General Hospital where Bo had arranged for a renowned eye doctor to perform a corneal transplant that enabled her to see again.

Wade Coleman
and
Mari Lynn Dennison

June 9, 1988

Love was in the air when Wade Coleman and Mari Lynn Dennison tied the knot in a glittering 1988 ceremony. Sturdy Wade helped sweet Mari Lynn overcome the trauma of accidentally shooting and killing her own mother. Through this tumultuous period, Wade comforted the blonde beauty, and they came close to making love, but Wade held off. Decidedly old-fashioned, he wanted to do the right thing by Mari Lynn. In a beautiful June wedding, this perfectly paired young couple were united in holy matrimony.

Bo Buchanan and Sarah Gordon

March 21, 1990

Bo and Sarah's fairy-tale romance culminated in a wedding at Llanfair in the spring of 1990. The simple ceremony took place just weeks after their first majestic marriage in a royal castle atop a mountain in the magical kingdom of Mendorra. Now, on this memorable March day, Bo and Sarah found something special that has proven elusive to so many—paradise.

WORDS OF LOVE
BO'S VOW TO SARAH

BO

You have filled my heart with a love and a happiness I never thought that I'd find. And in the presence of our Lord, I pledge to you to honor you, to be faithful to you, to love you in sickness and in health, in prosperity and adversity, and to keep you safe forever. In token and in pledge of our constant faith and abiding love, I take thee for my wife.

The Reverend Andrew Carpenter and Cassie Callison

January 18, 1993

Cassie and Andrew were both mourning lost loves when they found each other. Cassie's marriage to Bo was over even before it began, and Andrew sorrowfully stood on the sidelines and watched as his love, Megan, died in the arms of her husband, Jake. As time passed, a strong bond of friendship developed between Andrew and Cassie. Andrew reaffirmed Cassie's faith in the power of love, and she stood by the reverend when troubled teenager Marty Saybrooke spread vicious rumors that he had tried to seduce Billy Douglas, a young gay parishioner. Cassie's faith in her maligned minister never wavered.

Ultimately, the crisis brought them even closer together. During this trying time, Andrew and Cassie's friendship blossomed into love. Truly a modern woman, Cassie

Joey Buchanan consulted the Yellow Pages under "Entertainment" and hired Miss Bubbles for the Reverend Andrew Carpenter's bachelor party, believing she was a stripper. The joke, however, was on Joey and the rest of the guests—Miss Bubbles made her living as an entertainer at children's birthday parties. When the bubbly Miss Bubbles showed up, clad in a clown costume and balloons in tow, she decided to stay. The men may have been older than she expected, but boys are boys, and Miss Bubbles was determined to show them a good time nonetheless. Luckily for Andrew, his wedding to Cassie was being planned by others, and therefore went off without a hitch.

took the reins of their romance and proposed to Andrew, who seemed stunned by the out-of-the-blue overture.

"So, do you like the idea?" Cassie quizzed.

"I'm in love with it as much as I am with you!" Andrew said gushingly in response. "I've been taking as many walks as I could stand these last few days, and I'd watch my favorite birds. But it seemed like their color and liveliness were so far away. As if that kind of vitality was something I myself would never get close to. But I was wrong. Because here you are. And for the benefit of all my feathered friends who may not have heard—yes, Cassie Callison, I am going to marry you!"

Would Cassie Callison's third wedding be the charm for a life full of happiness? It was an extravagant, storybook wedding for Cassie when she walked down the aisle to marry the Reverend Andrew Carpenter. The happy day also had its share of drama. Andrew's father, Sloan Carpenter, had to calm the frayed nerves of the anxious groom; Cassie and her mother, Dorian, made amends for a lifetime of battles; and the presence of Cassie's manipulative cousin Blair had many guests feeling uncomfortable. Worst of all, unbeknownst to the couple, a drunken Marty Saybrooke, who was in love with Andrew, lurked in the vestibule threatening to interrupt the ceremony. However, Viki Buchanan intervened and managed to hustle Marty away before she caused trouble. "All I Ask of You," the love song featured in the Broadway musical, The Phantom of the Opera, provided musical accompaniment to the grand occasion.

Hank Gannon
and
Sheila Price
February 14, 1995

Cupid fired his mighty arrow on Valentine's Day, 1995, as Sheila Price and Hank Gannon headed down the aisle in a highly anticipated wedding. After a three-year courtship, the romantic duo finally were ready to tie the knot. With wedding plans set and Hank's threatening, evil brother R. J. safely tucked away in prison, it seemed as if nothing could spoil Hank and Sheila's happiness—that is, until R. J. was released on bail and decided to make a special guest appearance at the ceremony. Lurking in the back of the church, R. J.—in an atypical moment of compassion—allowed Hank and Sheila to marry without a hitch.

Dylan Moody
and
Marty Saybrooke
February 23, 1996

Dylan Moody, a brooding ex–Merchant Marine, was the very first man to unlock troubled Marty Saybrooke's oft-bruised heart. He was a source of strength and stability throughout Marty's sojourn toward self-esteem. However, never were Marty's feelings more confounded than when she came home from Ireland after taking part in an unexpected and highly romantic affair with handsome poet Patrick Thornhart. What could have been going through her mind? How could she allow herself to become so involved with this charming Irishman?

Marty returned from Ireland a changed woman—braver, but still fragile when it came to matters of the heart. She knew that she didn't share the electric, once-in-a-lifetime bond with Dylan that she had with Patrick. But Dylan made her feel safe and secure. She accepted Dylan's proposal of marriage, and after ignoring a last-ditch appeal by Patrick to reconsider, she married Dylan in a glittering wedding ceremony at Llanview's St. James Church.

All My Children

Dr. Joe Martin and Ruth Brent

April 1972

Long before they became man and wife, Joe and Ruth worked side by side at Pine Valley Hospital. Joe, a widower, worshiped Ruth from afar. He was there for Ruth every step of the way when her husband, Ted Brent, died in a tragic car accident. Observers might have thought they were "keeping company" before they even realized it themselves. Joe and Ruth had already become the couple most everyone in Pine Valley turned to for comfort, counsel, and friendship. And even before they married, everyone took it for granted that one day they would become man and wife. In 1972 the Martin living room provided the homey setting for their wedding ceremony. Decades later the Martins are still happily married.

Paul Martin
and Anne Tyler

May 1975

Paul Martin remarried Anne Tyler in a small but beautiful ceremony at the
Tyler mansion in 1975. For the couple, this was a chance to remedy a regret-
table mistake made years earlier by Anne, when she let her love for Paul slip away in
favor of an ill-fated romance with Nick Davis.

By the mid-1970s, Paul had been manipulated into a loveless marriage with
scheming model Margo Flax. Too late did he realize that he had never loved Margo
because he had never stopped loving Anne. And, of course, Anne still carried a torch
for Paul. Slowly they rekindled their romance from the embers of the past, and married
again.

Philip Brent

and

Tara Martin

December 30, 1976

When the road to marital bliss proved too winding, Pine Valley's first teenage sweethearts, Phil and Tara, chose to take matters into their own hands. On the night before Phil was to depart for Vietnam, he proposed marriage to Tara. They chose to elope, but a blinding snowstorm prevented the kids from reaching a justice of the peace. Escaping the storm, they took shelter in a roadside chapel.

"I wanted to marry you. But now we won't be able to," Tara cried. "Oh, Phillip, I'm so, so sorry."

"Don't cry, Funny Face. We're here together, and that's all that matters." As they sat in each other's arms, they sensed the quiet and peace and isolation. It felt spiritual, holy. Then Philip got a wonderful idea.

"We can marry ourselves! This place can be our church." Hearing Phillip's suggestion, Tara was more in love with him than ever. They lit candles and exchanged their vows. With only God as their witness, right there in the middle of nowhere, on Phillip's last night before leaving for Vietnam, they became husband and wife. They made love, passionate, tender love, for the very first time. When Phil was declared missing in action, Tara married his pal, Chuck Tyler, and told the world that the child she was carrying was his. When Phil miraculously returned, he was devastated to learn that his "wife" had married someone else. In 1976 Phil and Tara finally overcame their many obstacles, and married again—legally—in a church ceremony.

Throughout her obstacle-laden romance with Phil, Tara received sage advice from her grandmother, Kate Martin. "Gran" was delighted when the lovers finally tied the knot in a radiant pre-Christmas wedding ceremony in 1976.

Chuck Tyler
and Donna Beck

September 1, 1977

August 15, 1990

Dr. Chuck Tyler first met teenage hooker Donna Beck when she was brought to Pine Valley Hospital with a broken leg after being thrown out of a moving car by her pimp. Chuck became the knight in shining armor who rescued her from a life of shame. Donna began to fantasize about a life with him. Still, she was very insecure about herself. She was a nothing, an ex-hooker! Surely Chuck could never feel about her the way he did about his smart and decent ex-wife Tara.

Soon Donna's dreams came true. When Chuck's grandmother, Phoebe, found out about the engagement, she was appalled! How could her beloved grandson marry someone so beneath his stature? Desperate to prevent the marriage, Phoebe tried to bribe Donna into leaving town. Donna defiantly threw the wad of bills back into Phoebe's face.

"Soon you'll be Mrs. Charles Tyler," Chuck said, beaming, as he hurried Donna off to the justice of the peace.

Sadly, the marriage did not last. Afterward Donna married wealthy Palmer Cortlandt, but their union was disastrous from its inception. She followed that ill-fated union with a doomed marriage to her old pal Benny Sago. Chuck left Pine Valley to accept an out-of-town job but returned in 1989 and reunited with Donna. Thirteen years after they first tied the knot, the former sweethearts discovered that love could be even sweeter the second time around. Donna's best friend, Natalie Hunter, hosted a touching wedding ceremony and a gala reception for the reunited couple. "A new name to go along with the new me," Donna gushed to Chuck moments after they were remarried. "Golly, no matter what I was in the past, I think I'm the luckiest girl in the world now." They waited more than a decade to find each other again and rekindle their love, but for Chuck and Donna, it was a wait well worth taking. By 1990 they were older, wiser, and more in love than ever!

SHARE A ROMANTIC RENDEZVOUS IN THE SWISS ALPS

While honeymooning in Switzerland with her new husband, Palmer, Donna shared an unexpectedly romantic encounter with her ex-husband Chuck—while they were trapped together in a cave during a storm! The storybook land of Heidi, yodeling, chocolate, and cheese has a magical appeal. The Alps in particular are stunning—whitecapped mountain peaks, colorful gingerbread chalets, quaint villages, and cows grazing on rolling green meadows.

When to go: The winter season runs from mid-December to mid-April; the weather is more moderate the rest of the year.

What to do: From extreme vertical drops to the gentlest hills, the Alps offer downhill skiers lots of variety and thrills plus breathtaking scenery. On cross-country skis, you can make tracks around rustic villages and hills. Even nonskiing honeymooners can have a great time—there's snowboarding down a mountain, ice skating on a frozen lake, and tobogganing. When most of the snow has melted and the temperatures climb in the spring, the action still remains outdoors.

Chuck and Donna in Switzerland

Romantic rendezvous: Go dashing through the snow in a one-horse open sleigh, or climb onto a sled and pretend you're kids again. Plan to ride a cable car up a mountain and have lunch. (The spectacular panoramic view at the top is free.)

Stepping out at night: After dinner at your chalet, curl up in front of a roaring fireplace to sip brandy or hot cocoa and gaze at the flames and each other.

For more information: The Swiss National Tourist Office has branches in Los Angeles, New York, and Miami.

Lincoln Tyler
and
Kitty Shea
April 1975

Phoebe Tyler nearly fainted when she learned of her son Linc's involvement with tawdry tap-dance teacher Kitty Shea Davis. Snooty Phoebe was determined to stop her blue-blooded son from making "the mistake of his life." However, her vehement objections fell on deaf ears. Linc had fallen deeply in love with Kitty, and nothing Phoebe could say or do, which included falling into a dead faint in the middle of their wedding ceremony, could keep them from saying their I dos.

Sadly, Linc and Kitty's time together was brief. Kitty contracted a terminal illness in the summer of 1977, and knowing that the end was near, she made an impassioned plea that she not be taken to the hospital to have her life prolonged by artificial means. Late in the summer Kitty passed away peacefully in her sleep, with Linc at her side. Several years later Linc found love again when Kitty's much wilder but equally enchanting sister, Kelly Cole, captured his fancy.

Dr. Jeff Martin
and
Mary Kennicott
May 1972

After his tumultuous marriage to the flamboyant Erica Kane, Dr. Jeff Martin found love in the halls of Pine Valley Hospital. Nurse Mary Kennicott, a down-to-earth, hardworking though somewhat plain young woman, was the kind of woman kind-hearted Jeff deserved. Throughout his ill-fated union with Erica, Mary had been Jeff's closest friend and confidante. But Mary was not the type to become "the other woman." She remained silent and supportive, happy to be a friend to Jeff in his loneliness.

Erica had dazzled his eyes and fueled his fantasies. But Mary had entered his soul. Jeff loved her dearly, and when she told him she felt the same way, he melted. Jeff welcomed a divorce from Erica so that he could live happily ever after with his soul mate Mary. Sadly, Mary was killed a few short years later, leaving Jeff lonely and heartbroken once again.

Dr. Charles Tyler and Mona Kane

May 1, 1980

Mona Kane served as Dr. Charles Tyler's loyal secretary for many years before they admitted to each other what others had whispered for years—they were in love.

In the late 1970s, Charles began to grow tired of the incessant meddling of his busybody wife, Phoebe. For decades he'd learned to overlook her faults. When life with Phoebe became overbearing, Dr. Tyler could always seek refuge at Pine Valley Hospital, where he was chief of staff. As the years passed, he began to spend more and more time there with his secretary, Mona, who didn't mind working overtime. She loved the way Dr. Tyler had come to rely on her. She loved calming him down after Phoebe's excesses put him in a black mood. She simply loved him—and the feeling had become mutual.

Langley Wallingford and Phoebe Tyler

June 2, 1980

On the heels of the marriage of her ex-husband, Charles, to Mona, Phoebe Tyler agreed to tie the knot with erudite Professor Langley Wallingford—unaware that he was really a con man out to get his hands on her fortune!

Only one person—Myrtle Fargate—could possibly provide an impediment to Langley's plan. Every time she laid eyes on the professor, she had the oddest sensation that she knew him. But she couldn't remember where they'd met. Langley recognized Myrtle too and prayed that she would never recall that, some twenty years earlier, he'd snatched her purse at a carnival in Topeka, Kansas, where she knew him as roustabout Lenny Wlasuk!

While leafing through an old scrapbook on Phoebe's wedding day, Myrtle's long-forgotten memories came flooding back. She phoned Phoebe to warn her, but the blushing bride-to-be refused to take the call. Kelly Cole convinced Myrtle to drive to the Tyler Mansion, where the ceremony was taking place, but after their car broke down, they arrived too late. Myrtle confronted Langley in the kitchen, where he pleaded for mercy, swearing that he loved Phoebe and that he was not a fortune hunter. After getting Myrtle to agree to keep mum, Langley, fearing exposure, whisked his blissfully unaware bride away to their honeymoon earlier than planned.

> *You're living in the wrong age. In another time, when beauty was more appreciated, your face alone would have inspired painters and poets, not just a humble scholar like myself.*
> —Langley Wallingford

THE REVEREND MULLINS SPEAKS OF "COMMITMENT" DURING PHOEBE AND LANGLEY'S WEDDING

Dear friends, we come together today to share in the celebration of a marriage, an event rooted in the emotions of two people wanting to share with family and friends the fact that they love each other and that this love has changed their lives now and forever. Phoebe and Langley have chosen to share their commitment to one another with us in this ceremony. Let us rejoice and celebrate the love and happiness they have found together. That we may be mindful of the giver of all life and love, let us pray: Eternal God, Creator and sustainer of all people, giver of all grace, father of salvation: look with favor upon this man and this woman that they may grow and love in peace together.

We thank you for the joy which they find in each other and for the love and trust with which they enter into this holy covenant. And since without Your help we cannot do anything as we ought, we pray You to enrich them with Your grace that they may enter into this marriage in Your sight and truly keep their vows through Jesus Christ, our Lord, Amen.

Wedding Styles

A typical semiformal daytime wedding takes place at a relative's or close friend's home and is witnessed by a hundred guests or less. The bride wears a short white or pastel dress with a short veil. The groom wears a suit. The semiformal evening bride chooses between a long or short dress in either white or pastel. A train is optional, and the veil can be floor-length or shorter. Her man puts on a tuxedo or dinner jacket with a vest or cummerbund.

Dr. Frank Grant and Nancy Grant

November 27, 1980

"If at first you don't succeed, try, try again."

Frank and Nancy Grant proved that old platitude true when they married for a second time in 1980. Their first union had faltered several years earlier when Nancy accepted a fabulous new job opportunity in Chicago. Frank stayed behind. For a poor black kid from the inner city, he liked the life he'd made for himself in Pine Valley. But with his wife living hundreds of miles away, Frank grew lonely. When their geographic separation strained the marriage to the breaking point, this once-happy couple decided to divorce in 1977.

Still in love with Frank, Nancy eventually moved back to Pine Valley, and although they shared one last night of passion, Frank went ahead with the divorce. Nancy learned she was pregnant with Frank's child the day he married Nurse Caroline Murray. On the rebound, a devastated Nancy Grant agreed to marry Carl Blair, a white man who loved her dearly. With her ex-husband Frank married to Caroline, Nancy convinced everyone the baby she was carrying was Carl's. Tragically, Nancy married Carl on his deathbed after he'd been in a plane crash.

Frank doted on Nancy and her fatherless baby, and the attention placed an enormous strain on his marriage to Caroline, which began to unravel. Dr. Grant came to realize that he had never stopped loving his ex-wife—and he was overjoyed to discover that her precious son, Carl, was actually his own flesh and blood. Frank finally softened Nancy to the idea of remarriage. On Thanksgiving Day, with son Carl by their side, Frank and Nancy renewed their commitment to each other.

Ross Chandler
and
Ellen Shepherd Dalton
November 23, 1984

"Happy is the bride the sun shines on!" Myrtle Fargate gushed as she toasted Ross and Ellen Chandler on their new marriage. Nexus, New York City's dazzling supper club, provided the stylish backdrop for the autumn wedding of Ellen Dalton and Ross Chandler. The reception was clouded by the unwelcome appearance of Ross's ex-wife, Cynthia Preston. Ellen politely asked the sassy Ms. Preston to leave the restaurant. When she refused to go, the bride lost her cool and stuffed cake in Cynthia's face! Cynthia got her revenge two months later when she used her sexual wiles to lure Ross back into bed. Unbeknownst to either party, their clandestine tryst was photographed by the soon-to-be-murdered Zach Grayson. Ellen, stunned and embarrassed to learn of Ross's betrayal, took a long time to forgive her wayward new husband.

Jasper Sloan

and

Myra Murdoch

December 1984

Palmer Cortlandt's maid and two-time mother-in-law, Myra Murdoch, spent years sternly lurking about the Cortlandt estate in her long black gown, always up to her gray bun in Gothic intrigue. It was only when English butler Jasper Sloan joined the staff that maudlin Myra began to mellow. A new wardrobe and a new man were all she needed! Sloan and Myra discovered love in the golden years, and they married in a festive Christmastime ceremony at Cortlandt Manor in 1984.

Jeremy Hunter and Natalie Cortlandt

November 21, 1988

As teenagers growing up in Canada, Jeremy Hunter and Natalie Marlowe had been sweethearts. Natalie, full of life and passion, broke Jeremy's heart when she married his wealthy father, Alex Hunter. Now, years later, fate had given Jeremy and Natalie a second chance at love.

As their wedding day approached, Jeremy began having disturbing dreams and memories about Marissa, a long-ago lover who had died in an air strike that Jeremy himself had ordered. Natalie comforted her troubled fiancé as he recalled this painful chapter of his life.

On their wedding day, Marissa showed up—alive and well—and sat in the wedding chapel undetected as Jeremy and Natalie became man and wife. Ironically, the beautiful wedding ceremony turned out to be the last bit of happiness for the newlyweds. Immediately after the wedding, Marissa stunned Jeremy, both with her return from the dead and the revelation that she had given birth to their son, David, now a strapping teenager. Marissa's appearance unsettled Natalie, who stood on the sidelines as her new husband doted on his newfound son. Marissa's return succeeded in tearing Natalie and Jeremy apart. The lovers—who had waited for so long to be together—were left with nothing but memories of a wonderful wedding day.

Jeremy and Natalie's Wedding Vows

JEREMY

Natalie, the three bands of this ring represent my past, my present, my future. For when I look at you, I see my first love and my last. I see beauty, strength, understanding, kindness, and even though we've been separated for years, you never left my heart. I don't think it's an accident that we're here today. We were led to this moment by our love and our faith. Our marriage represents more than the joining of hands and hearts. It's the binding together of what's good and true in each of us. You know how much I've always believed in the power of love, but never so much as right now. With you by my side, I feel everything is possible. I give you this ring as a symbol of my abiding love for you.

NATALIE

You're my best friend and my greatest love and we accept and love each other as we are and trust each other. And if I can make you as happy as you have made me, then I will ask no more of myself. As we exchange our vows, I feel blessed to be sharing this moment with Timothy and with our friends. Jeremy, I promise I will share your joys and sorrows, your hopes and fears, and I will do everything to make our life all we dream it to be. I give you this ring as a symbol of my eternal love for you.

Mark Dalton and Ellen Shepherd

March 2, 1988

Seeking a fresh start, Ellen Shepherd left St. Louis and returned to her childhood home in Pine Valley after her husband deserted her for another woman. Still hurting from the betrayal, the last thing she was looking for was another man. Music professor Mark Dalton was feeling equally aggrieved. His budding romance with Erica Kane had just come to a devastating halt upon discovering that she was his half sister. Out of Mark's misery and feelings of rejection sprang a friendship with older woman Ellen—one that turned to love.

Putting aside their ten-year age difference, Mark and Ellen married in 1980. Although Ellen told Mark that she wanted to have his child, she still had lingering doubts about having a baby so late in life. When Ellen became reluctant to make love with her husband, Mark confided his woes to a student, Pamela Kingsley. When Ellen learned of their steamy affair, she separated from Mark. Their once-promising marriage, further ravaged by Mark's rampant cocaine abuse, came to an end.

Ellen tried marriage again with Ross Chandler, but their volatile union, racked by his dissolute behavior, ended in divorce. Ellen wasn't about to sink into a depression—not while a clean and sober Mark was still in town. Having overcome his own multiple battles with drug abuse, Mark was older, wiser, and more smitten than ever with his ex-wife. He was not about to let her get away again! Sharing old memories and future dreams, Mark and Ellen exchanged vows again in 1988.

Nico Kelly and Julie Chandler

December 26, 1988

Julie Rand Chandler was in the throes of a sweet teenage romance with Charlie Brent when she was bowled over by a sultry newcomer, Nico Kelly. The darkly handsome Nico appeared, at least on the surface, to be as cold and ruthless as his Uncle Creed, the madman who had kidnapped and terrorized Julie. But Julie came to see that beneath Nico's frosty exterior beat a heart of gold.

Though she accepted Charlie's proposal of marriage, Julie could not shake the sexual attraction she felt for Nico. He possessed her every waking thought, and his handsome visage fueled her erotic dreams at night. It was only a matter of time before Julie broke her hopeless engagement with Charlie and ran off with Nico to get married.

Arriving at a wedding chapel, Nico and Julie encountered a minister—who turned out to be Nico's vengeful uncle, Creed! Just before Creed could kill Julie, he was gunned down by the arriving police. In the aftermath of the near tragedy, Nico and Julie raced into each other's arms, then accepted the invitation of the local mayor to officiate at their wedding ceremony. In a simple country ceremony, Julie and Nico put their turbulent courtship behind them and became man and wife.

Returning to Pine Valley as man and wife, Nico and Julie remained blissfully unaware that their marriage was invalid because Harry, the small-town mayor who officiated at the simple ceremony, was not authorized to perform marriages. By the time they made this astounding discovery, their romance had cooled considerably.

Nico Kelly and Cecily Davidson

May 15, 1989

August 29, 1989

Cecily and Nico's unconventional love story produced two weddings in one short year. Their first marriage came as a result of a business arrangement. Nico, left penniless after a fire destroyed his nightclub, needed to get his hands on some fast money. Cecily was out for sweet revenge against her mother for having an affair with her former fiancé, Sean Cudahy. So she turned to Nico for help, informing him that if he married her, she would instantly come into her trust fund. *They'd both be rich!*

Cecily conveniently neglected to inform her fiancé that, according to the terms of her trust fund, they would have to stay married for six months before coming into the fortune. Only after the wedding (which was interrupted by Sean) did Nico learn this upsetting news. Six months! To the bride and groom, it seemed like an eternity. After a quarrelsome honeymoon in New York, Nico and Cecily started married life together—in separate beds.

Even though Nico and Cecily quarreled incessantly, the longer

Nico and Cecily cut a deal, then cut the cake. Their May 1989 marriage began as a loveless business arrangement. Only later did these warring lovebirds realize they were made for each other.

they remained in this bogus marriage, the more sexual tension arose between them. One night Phoebe slept on their couch, forcing Nico and Cecily to share the same bed. To their astonishment, both parties found themselves mutually aroused by the unexpected closeness. Though they tried to cover their feel-

Marriage, Hawaiian style. Cecily and Nico reaffirmed their love in a romantic sunset ceremony on the beach in Maui. The couple, who had decided to remain celibate until their honeymoon shared a passionate night of lovemaking and pledged to overcome all future obstacles together.

ings, it was only a matter of time before Nico and Cecily confessed their love to each other!

By then, Cecily's mother, Bitsy, had discovered that the marriage was a sham, and she filed fraud charges to keep Nico's hands off her family fortune. But Nico and Cecily could not have cared less about money. Relinquishing all claims to the trust fund, Nico and Cecily, hopelessly in love, flew to Hawaii for a romantic second wedding.

SHARE A ROMANTIC RENDEZVOUS IN MAUI, HAWAII

Exotic scenery and forty-two magnificent miles of beaches earn Maui its well-deserved reputation as a tropical Eden. With a mountainous landscape made up of lush rain forests, deep valleys, open plains, and flowery fields, the island is a quintessential honeymoon oasis. And it's got the sweetest pineapple you'll ever eat!

When to go: Year round. Maui has a steady climate that's warm and balmy.

What to do: If you're looking for a great beach, you've come to the right place. On the eastern shore is Hana, an unspoiled town of legendary natural beauty that boasts Kaihalulu Beach, which has red sand, and Waianapanapa State Park, with black sand. Kapalua, on the northwest coast, is lined with gorgeous white-sand beaches. Its Honolua Bay offers some of the best snorkeling in Hawaii. With up to fifteen-foot waves, Hookipa Beach has exceptional windsurfing. When you dry off, head to Maui's center where the top draw is Haleakala Crater, the world's largest dormant volcano, which rises almost 11,000 feet from sea level and has wonderful hiking and horseback-riding trails. Since Maui is the winter home of humpback whales, if you're honeymooning from late November to early May take a cruise to see the action up close. Maui has earned the nickname "the Golf Coast" with sixteen of the world's top-rated golf courses.

Romantic rendezvous: Saddle up for a guided overnight horseback ride into Haleakala Crater or set sail at sunset off the Kapalua Coast with your sweetie and some chilled champagne.

Stepping out at night: A popular spot for dining and night life is in Lahaina, the historic whaling town and former Hawaiian capital. It's also a good place to pick up local arts-and-crafts souvenirs for the envious in-laws back home.

For more information: Contact the Maui Visitors Bureau at P.O. Box 580, Wailuku, HI 96893; phone (800) 525-MAUI.

Jeremy Hunter and Ceara Connor

December 31, 1991

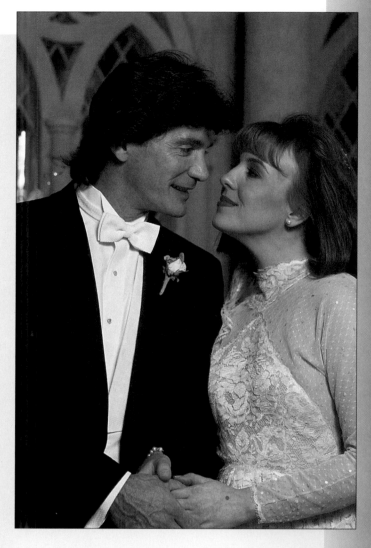

Jeremy Hunter always suspected that Ceara Connor was a gold-digging manipulator, and when she became engaged to his son, David, he set out to prove it. Determined to keep her from marrying David and ransacking his trust fund, Jeremy seductively schemed to break them up. Jeremy believed it was his fatherly duty to woo Ceara from his son. So with great subtlety, he romanced Ceara until she gave in to his charms. She gave in, but so did Jeremy! Caught up in his own game, Jeremy fell hard for the money-hungry beauty. Whisking Ceara off to New York, the pair shared a romantic champagne-and-caviar supper and a first kiss. David was incensed to discover his father's scheme but eventually came to accept Ceara and Jeremy's love. Jeremy and Ceara's love deepened when he helped her through the trauma of dealing with the sexual abuse she had endured as a child. When Ceara suffered a nervous breakdown, Jeremy stood by her during her recovery. In the end, they proved that love can conquer all when they became man and wife in a majestic New Year's Eve wedding.

Trevor Dillon and Natalie Hunter

June 8, 1992

Trevor marveled at the fact that an elegant "doll" like Natalie could fall for a guy like him. Natalie saw through his grumpy and gruff exterior and loved him just the same.

It was a rocky ride, but Trevor and Natalie finally made it to the altar in 1992. Theirs was a most unlikely alliance. By the way they acted in each other's company, it seemed like gruff cop Trevor Dillon and classy Natalie Hunter despised each other. But beneath their warring facades simmered a sexual attraction that finally overflowed while the couple were shipwrecked together on a deserted island. It did not take the sparring twosome long to realize that they belonged together!

The first time that Trevor and Natalie tried to tie the knot, Natalie's demented sister, Janet, threw her down a well and took her place at the altar. Several weeks later Janet's vicious scheme was exposed and Natalie was rescued by Dimitri Marick, who took her back to his Gothic mansion, Wildwind, to recover. Natalie swore that she and Trevor were through! She could never forgive him for failing to recognize Janet's cha-

rade—and sleeping with her. However, she began to soften her stance when Trevor tenderly proposed marriage, giving Natalie a symbolic cigar band in lieu of a ring. They slowly maneuvered into a passionate kiss, but Natalie pulled back, unable to shake the thought of Janet kissing Trevor. Making matters worse, Janet made a stunning announcement that she was pregnant with Trevor's child!

After Janet gave birth to a beautiful baby girl (Amanda) and was shipped off to jail (for the murder of Will Cortlandt), Natalie finally forgave Trevor.

This time *she* proposed marriage, and Trevor eagerly accepted! With a wedding planned for the following week, friends of the bride and groom pitched in to make it an affair to remember. Family friend Edmund Grey charmed socialite Phoebe Wallingford into hosting the reception. Natalie's ex-husband, Adam Chandler, found a church on short notice, and Ruth Martin loaned Natalie Kate Martin's wedding dress for the occasion.

In keeping with their topsy-turvy romance, Trevor and Natalie's wedding plans faced a last-minute glitch. While planning a prewedding rendezvous with Natalie in the Chandler boathouse, Trevor fell through a trapdoor and plummeted into the root cellar below. The next morning Natalie found him, and together they sped to the church, with Trevor quickly getting dressed in the back of the car. Inside the chapel everything went smoothly, as Trevor and Natalie relished every second of their long-awaited wedding.

WORDS OF LOVE

A year after their marriage, Natalie was gravely injured in a car accident. As she slipped away, a grief-stricken Trevor spoke his final words to his wife.

TREVOR
For the rest of my life, every second I live will have been better for having lived it with you. I love you, doll.

Proud of his mom's decision to marry Trevor, Natalie's son, Timmy, picked out a white tuxedo to wear to the wedding—exactly like the one worn by his new dad (above). Beaming with joy, Trevor danced with his bride to the romantic ballad, "Just You and I" (right).

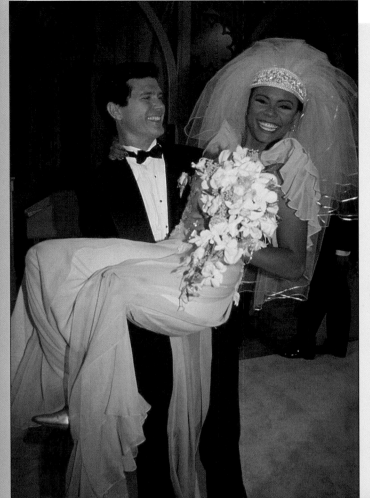

Tom Cudahy and Livia Frye

October 12, 1992

After failing in his marriages to Erica, Brooke, Skye, and Barbara, Tom Cudahy's spirits received a lift when he married attorney Livia Frye. The interracial pair vowed to overcome bigotry as they exchanged vows in an elegant and sophisticated wedding. Tom and Livia's stylish reception featured a touching duet between Livia and special wedding guest Peabo Bryson. The celebrated vocalist joined the bride as she sang a memorable rendition of "Tonight I Celebrate My Love for You" to her new husband.

Tad Martin and Brooke English

May 31, 1993

In 1990 journalist Brooke English joined forces with Tad Martin to expose a Pine Valley housing scam. In the midst of the intrigue, they began an affair that was doomed from the start because Tad was still in love with ex-wife, Dixie. Although Brooke loved Tad, she nobly stepped aside so that Tad and Dixie could reunite. While chasing the psychopathic Billy Clyde Tuggle, Tad was blown off a bridge and presumed dead. Dixie grieved, and so did a disconsolate Brooke, especially after discovering she was pregnant with Tad's child!

Two years later Tad—suffering from amnesia—miraculously returned to Pine Valley, unaware that Brooke had given birth to his son, Jamie. Upon regaining his memory, Tad and Dixie enjoyed a tearful reunion, but their elation was not enough to bring them back together. The news that Dixie had married two different men in his absence came as a shock to Tad. And the revelation that Brooke had borne him a child had a profound impact on Tad, who had come back to town older and wiser. Tad, abandoned when he was seven years old and then adopted by the Martins, wanted to give his son the life he never had—so he proposed marriage to Brooke. They married in May but, by July, Tad was back in Dixie's arms. Realizing that they loved each other more than ever, Tad and Dixie began a secret affair that, when revealed, destroyed Tad's fledgling marriage to Brooke.

Derek Frye and Mimi Reed

February 21, 1994

Police Officer Mimi Reed enjoyed romances with both fellow cop Derek Frye and architect Lucas Barnes and when she became pregnant, she had a perplexing problem: Which man was the father? Furthering her predicament, both men proposed marriage!

When Mimi gave birth to a beautiful baby daughter, Danielle, her dilemma loomed larger. Mimi finally made up her mind when Derek sweetly promised to be both father and husband—no matter who turned out to be the baby's natural father. Touched by the gesture, Mimi said yes! Her joy turned to fear when baby Danielle was kidnapped from Pine Valley Hospital. Everyone suspected Lucas, but the kidnapper turned out to be Grace Keefer, a hospital volunteer, who went off the deep end after the death of her own son. After several tension-filled days, Danielle was finally located. Adding to the joy of her return, test results revealed Derek to be her daddy! Days later, after whirlwind preparations, Derek and Mimi married in a private ceremony at Mimi's loft.

Charlie Brent

and

Cecily Davidson Kelly

December 31, 1995

It was love at first byte when Charlie and Cecily fell in love! The couple had known each other for years, but their relationship was always strictly platonic. When Private Eye Charlie hired Cecily to be his new partner, they spent as much time sniping and bickering as they did working! Neither realized that the sparks flying between them were igniting a burning love!

Lonely Cecily logged onto the Internet and, calling herself "Clueless," began a flirtatious chat with a fellow who dubbed himself "Beyond Clueless." As the electronic love affair continued for months, both Charlie and Cecily remained clueless to the fact that they were actually communicating with each other! When the truth came out, the amazed couple realized that passion could flare just as well in person as it did on-line. The romance of daytime's first cyber-sweethearts culminated in a New Year's Eve wedding as 1995 gave way to 1996.

Luke Spencer and Laura Baldwin's Wedding Album

Never before in the history of daytime soaps has one couple so captivated an entire nation. Luke and Laura! The mere mention of their names bring back fond memories for the tens of millions of viewers lucky enough to witness their unforgettable journey to the altar.

General Hospital

November 16 & 17, 1981

I n the fall of 1978 Luke and Laura came to know each other indirectly: Laura was Luke's unseen enemy. Luke's sister, Bobbie, had recruited her big brother in her quest to break up Laura's marriage to Scotty. Eventually Luke became bored with his sister's vengeance plots and set up shop as manager of the Campus Disco—for Frank Smith's mob! Luke finally met the young woman who'd been the object of his dirty tricks in the campus coffeeshop. Laura hardly noticed Luke, who was enamored with her beauty. But their lives would take surprising twists and turns when Laura asked Luke for a job at the disco.

Luke and Laura's summer on the run came to an end when Laura watched in horror as Luke was shot in the chest at the statue of the Left-Handed Boy. Fortunately, a bulletproof vest saved his life.

While the Cassadines plotted to freeze the world in their underground island enclave, Luke and Laura flirted with danger—and each other— in their hidden tropical hideaway.

"Hey, World! Lucas Lorenzo Spencer, king of the single life, is getting married today!" On the morning of his wedding, Luke expressed his joy by shouting from the balcony of his apartment (below, left).

Viewers were treated to on-screen romance, drama, and intrigue when *General Hospital* went on location to the home of a prominent doctor in the exclusive Hancock Park section of west Los Angeles for the wedding of Luke and Laura. Hundreds of crew members, extras, and onlookers brought an atypical sense of excitement to the normally quiet neighborhood (below).

Bobbie Spencer and Tiffany Hill led the parade of bridesmaids down the red carpet. Moments before, the bridesmaids showed up at the wedding in high style in an antique Rolls-Royce (left).

Luke, along with his best man Robert Scorpio, eagerly awaited the arrival of the beautiful bride (above). The pensive and emotionally charged couple listened as the mayor began the long-awaited wedding ceremony (below).

The wedding party erupted in applause when the mayor pronounced that Luke and Laura were man and wife! (above) "A curse on you, Laura and Luke. A curse on you both!" (below). Skulking in the background during the wedding ceremony, a vengeful Helena Cassadine (played by General Hospital fan Elizabeth Taylor) offered some ominous words of warning to the bride and groom. Helena had ample reason to despise Luke and Laura since Luke was responsible for the death of her diabolical husband, Mikkos, who died trying to hold the world hostage with a high-tech weather machine.

Luke was grateful to his fashion designer friend, Delfina, who lent her stylish hand to each detail of the autumn wedding (left). At the wedding reception, Luke and Laura scooted under a man-made trellis during a square dance led by the friendly country folks from Beechers Corners. After the ceremony the bride and groom retreated to the fabled town for their honeymoon (below).

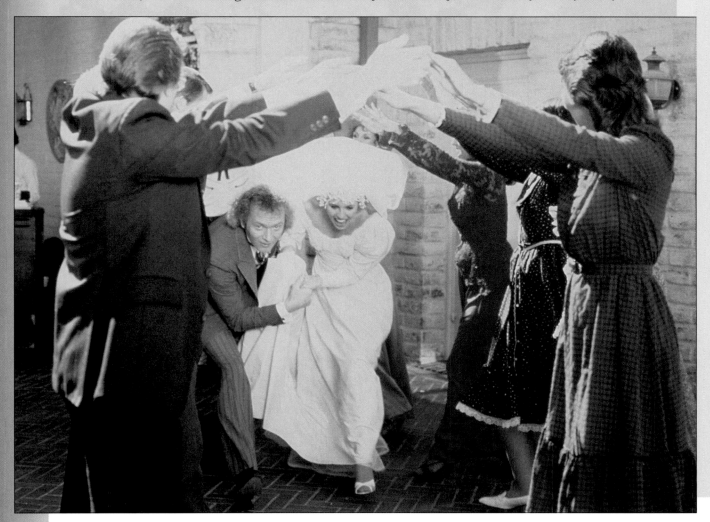

With Port Charles' most eligible women poised below, Laura prepared to toss her bouquet from the balcony of the mayor's mansion (top and bottom). Laura's ex-husband, Scotty, crashed the wedding to bring extra excitement to an otherwise elegant affair. Scotty posed a threat to Laura's happiness when he squirmed his way into the

crowd in time to snatch the bride's bouquet! The fabulous day ended with some unexpected fireworks when Luke took out his pent-up anger at the gate-crashing Scotty Baldwin. Luke pummeled his longtime rival (center), then dusted himself off and whisked Laura away for their honeymoon at the Whitaker farm in Beechers Corners.

"Just married!" (left) Luke and Laura's week of honeymoon bliss was unceremoniously interrupted by a call from Helena Cassadine insisting on a meeting with Luke. Unaware that it was Helena who cursed them at their wedding, Luke agreed to return to Port Charles for an audience with the Cassadine matriarch.

The newlyweds shared a homespun honeymoon in the quaint farm community of Beechers Corners. Their dear friends the Whitakers turned their homestead over to Luke and Laura, who quickly found themselves overmatched when it came to feeding the chickens and milking Bessie the cow. Between chores the Spencers had plenty of time to make hay! (below)

Behind the Scenes

ore than 16 million Americans stopped in their tracks to witness the two-day extravaganza, making the wedding of Luke and Laura the most-watched event in daytime soap history. With "Luke and Laura" fever sweeping the nation, it came as no surprise that this long-awaited wedding received a 52 share of the Nielsen viewing audience. *General Hospital*'s former Executive Producer Gloria Monty, pulled out all stops to ensure that viewers would be treated to an affair to remember!

Along with several other weary "guests," Tristan Rogers grabbed a quick nap during a break in the long taping day (above). Executive Producer Gloria Monty goes over some last-minute notes with Norma Connolly (Ruby) and Denise Alexander (Lesley) (right). As actors Anthony Geary and Genie Francis bask in the glory of Luke and Laura's special day, Gloria Monty (in the background) calls out some instructions to the technical crew (below).

In 1981, Luke and Laura would soon be drawn together by an unforgettable summer of adventure. Together they set sail for an exotic island to crack the secret of the Ice Princess and save the world from the evil Cassadine brothers who had threatened to freeze the world with their weather control machine.

Back home in Port Charles, Luke astounded himself by asking Laura to marry him. When Laura answered him with an enthusiastic yes, the duo hurriedly planned their November wedding. The lovers hoped to have a private ceremony, but all of Port Charles simply wouldn't have it. They wanted a lavish celebration for the couple who helped save the world from destruction, so Luke and Laura reluctantly agreed to hold "the wedding to end all weddings."

Executive Producer Gloria Monty inspects the multitiered wedding cake, which was as real as the autumn leaves dotting the landscape. Bushels of autumn leaves were trucked cross-country to give the wedding a real New York State feel (above). Between takes, Genie Francis (Laura) rested her weary feet on a lighting dolly (right).

"You're still the most beautiful bride I've ever seen!" *Luke and Laura Spencer brought their legendary magic back to Port Charles in 1993 for a new series of exciting adventures. After over a decade in hiding, the popular pair returned to Port Charles with a splash! Parachuting into a swimming pool during an outdoor wedding, Luke grabbed the bride's veil and placed it on the head of his loving wife.*

LUKE AND LAURA'S
WEDDING VOWS

MAYOR

*Today is a day of joyous celebration. And with love in our hearts,
we are here to witness the exchange of marriage vows between
Lucas Lorenzo Spencer and Laura Webber Baldwin.*

*We are gathered here to celebrate the marriage of two people, but we're doing more than
that. We are celebrating life itself. The young people before us, through their love for one
another, remind us what it is that makes life precious to all of us. Love. Loyalty. Courage.
Together in the face of extreme danger to themselves, they overcame powerful forces that
sought to destroy Port Charles and its people. Even the entire world.*

*We call Luke and Laura heroes. That they are indeed. But more importantly,
they are the children of our community. We love them. We care about them.
We admire and respect them. I know I speak for every one of you when I say,
Luke and Laura, it is with great admiration and affection that we share
with you today, this, your wedding day.*

*Dear friends, we have gathered together in the sight of God to join this man
and this woman in holy matrimony. It is an estate commended and honorable
among all men. Therefore, it is not to be entered into unadvisedly or lightly,
but reverently, soberly, and in full knowledge of one another. Into this loving state,
these two persons present come now to be joined. I require and charge you both
that if either of you knows any impediment why you may not be lawfully
joined together in matrimony, you do now so say, for no marriage can be
considered truly lawful if it is not entered into in full disclosure and with an
open heart. And if there be any present who can show just cause why these
two may not be lawfully joined together, let him now speak or else hereafter
forever hold his peace.*

*Lucas Lorenzo Spencer, will you take Laura Webber Baldwin to be your
lawful wedded wife? Will you love her, comfort her, honor and keep her,
in sickness and in health, forsaking all others, cleave only onto her
as long as you both shall live?*

LUKE

I will.

MAYOR

*Laura Webber Baldwin, will you take Lucas Lorenzo Spencer to be your
lawful wedded husband? Will you love him, comfort him, honor and keep him,
in sickness and in health, forsaking all others, cleave only onto him
so long as you both shall live?*

LAURA

I will.

MAYOR

The ring please. Take Laura's hand. Repeat after me. I, Lucas Lorenzo Spencer . . .
(He repeats.)

MAYOR

Take thee, Laura Webber Baldwin . . .
(He repeats.)

LUKE

Take thee, Laura Webber Baldwin, to be my wedded wife. To have and to hold, from this day forward, for better, for worse. For richer, for poorer. In sickness and in health. To love and to cherish, till death do us part.

MAYOR

And thereto . . .

LUKE

And thereto unto thee I pledge my troth.

MAYOR

Laura? Now Laura, repeat after me. I, Laura Webber Baldwin . . .

(She repeats.)

LAURA

Take thee, Lucas Lorenzo Spencer, to be my lawful wedded husband. To have and to hold, from this day forward, for better, for worse. For richer, for poorer. In sickness and in health. To love and to cherish, until death do us part. And thereto I pledge thee my troth.

MAYOR

Forasmuch as Luke and Laura have consented together in holy wedlock and have witnessed the same before God and this company and thereto have given and pledged their troth each to the other and have declared the same by giving and receiving a ring and by joining hands, by the power invested in me by the authority of the State of New York, I pronounce that they are husband and wife. You may kiss the bride.

(They kiss.)

Bobbie Spencer's Wedding Album

Bobbie Spencer is a crackerjack surgical nurse, a super mom to her son, Lucas, and a friend to many at General Hospital. However, when it comes to love, Bobbie has seen more heartache and been romanced by more handsome men than just about any other woman in Port Charles.

Former teenage hooker Barbara Jean "Bobbie" Spencer first culti-vated a taste for handsome men when she locked horns with teenager Laura Webber over the affections of law student Scotty Baldwin. Though Laura won the battle, a scheming Bobbie was determined to not let go of her first-ever lover. She faked a preg-nancy and called upon her streetwise brother, Luke, to help her in an ultimately unsuccessful plot to break up Scotty and Laura.

With support from her Aunt Ruby, Bobbie underwent a remarkable metamor-phosis and pledged to end her cruel schem-ing. The new, improved Bobbie next became engaged to mob flunky Roy DiLucca. Before they could marry, he was gunned down while undertaking a suicide mission for the mob.

Bobbie Spencer Brock Meyer Jones Cassadine

Next, Bobbie got involved in a hospital romance with dashing Dr. Noah Drake. Unable to get the playboy doctor to commit to their relationship, Bobbie feigned blind-

For a time in early 1979, it appeared as if Bobbie had won Scotty Baldwin away from Laura Webber by claiming to be pregnant with his child. To ensure that her scheme worked, Bobbie produced a falsified pregnancy test. Ultimately the scam was exposed, and Scotty married Laura.

Frustrated by the fact that Dr. Noah Drake couldn't say "I love you," Bobbie resorted to her old, wicked ways and faked blindness to gain his affection. Although Noah admitted his love in a moment of panic, he later recanted his confession (above). Bobbie met tough-as-nails investor D. L. Brock and the pair struck up an immediate rapport. In their first meeting, Bobbie poured out her heart to Brock, confessing that she felt "put down" by the snooty people of Port Charles. "Stick with me, kid. I'm from the same side of the tracks that you are," Brock assured her. On January 3, 1983, they tied the knot in a civil ceremony in the office of the mayor of Port Charles, Lee Baldwin. Afterward, Bobbie cringed when her groom offered a champagne toast to his bride. "To Bobbie, who will make the best wife and mother ever!" he proclaimed, unaware that Bobbie was keeping a secret—she could never have children! (below)

ness. Again, her scheme failed when Noah finally confessed that he didn't share Bobbie's feelings of love.

In the wake of her broken romance with Dr. Noah Drake, Bobbie jumped into a stormy relationship with crafty real estate developer D. L. Brock. Against her better judgment, Bobbie made the ill-fated decision to marry Brock in late 1983. Their brief happiness came to an end when this wife-beating scoundrel was murdered. Bobbie was accused of pulling the trigger, but her attorney, Jake Meyer, got the charges dropped—then became her next husband.

Bobbie and Jake's 1986 marriage suffered when Jake slept with Lucy Coe, who became pregnant with his child. Though Bobbie forgave Jake's indiscretion, she never

Love, Honor and Cherish

let Lucy off the hook! Later Bobbie suffered the ultimate insult when Jake declared that he would rather minister to South American flood victims than spend time with her. Soon after Jake's departure, Bobbie licked her wounds and began a short, ill-fated interlude with her first love, Scotty Baldwin.

In 1989 Bobbie swore off men and adopted Cheryl Stansbury's son, Lucas. She became what she never thought she would: a mother. That same year Bobbie's deep friendship with Dr. Tony Jones blossomed into something more—love. Together with his daughter, B. J., and Lucas, the Joneses formed a tight-knit family unit.

In 1993 Bobbie's marriage to Tony was put to the test when she became infatuated with suave Damian Smith, unaware that he was

Jake and Bobbie's Wedding Vows

BOBBIE

Jake and I want to share our happiness with all of our friends as we pledge to spend the rest of our lives together. I promise to honor and obey Jake—when he is right. And to respect him always, right or wrong. And to love him no matter what lies ahead. I promise I will follow Jake wherever he goes. I will follow his call because he's my husband and my helpmate. Because he loves me and he wants what's best for me.

JAKE

I take thee Bobbie Spencer as my lawful wedded wife. I love you. And I will be your best friend, your lover, and care for you as long as we both shall live.

BOBBIE

And I take you Jake to be my lawful wedded husband. I love you. And I will be your best friend and your lover. And I will care for you and protect you for as long as we both shall live.

Bobbie and Jake first got together as friends sharing a house—a brownstone they now wanted to make their home by pledging a commitment to each other. When Bobbie refused to go to Uruguay with Jake, he left anyway—without even saying good-bye. Jake's departure crushed Bobbie—but never fear, Scotty Baldwin was there to take care of her!

trying to seduce her as part of a wager he'd made with Bobbie's longtime nemesis, Lucy Coe. When Tony cornered Bobbie and Damian in a passionate embrace in the hospital stairwell, he was devastated. This, coupled with B. J.'s tragic death in a school bus accident, shattered Tony and Bobbie's marriage.

Though she and Tony decided to stay together for the sake of their child, over a year passed before they would share the same bed. As she and Tony sought to mend their fractured union, Bobbie fought off a strong attraction to her colleague Dr. Alan Quartermaine.

Friends for years, Tony and Bobbie were both leery of deepening their relationship. Burned by their ill-fated marriages to Jake and Lucy, neither wanted to admit what everyone else already knew—they had fallen in love!

Just as Bobbie and Tony appeared to get their marriage back on track, young nursing student Carly Roberts swept into town and used her feminine wiles to lure Tony into her bed. Carly, who unbeknownst to anyone was the child that Bobbie had given up for adoption back when she was a prostitute, seduced Tony. To her horror, Bobbie caught Tony and Carly together and promptly filed for divorce. On the rebound, she became romantically involved with her brother Luke's arch-enemy, Stefan Cassadine. Stefan smoothly charmed Bobbie, who married him in a whirlwind ceremony at his Gothic mansion, Wyndemere. It was a decision Bobbie would quickly come to regret. The ink had barely dried on their marriage license before she realized the depths of her husband's deception. Once again the much-married Bobbie obtained a divorce.

Will Bobbie ever find lasting love? As she ponders her fate, Nurse Spencer Brock Meyer Jones Cassadine can always take a fond look back at the men, the memories, and the mayhem in her always interesting love life.

Erica Kane's Wedding Album

For nearly three decades, we've followed Erica Kane through her never-ending search for love and affection. One of Erica's greatest fears is the terrible thought that she might be unlovable, a feeling she's had since the day her father, famed film director Eric Kane, walked out on her mother when Erica was just a little girl.

After all these years, Erica never ceases to surprise us. You never know what she's going to do next! But whatever it is, you can be sure it will involve the opposite sex. To enjoy life to the fullest, Erica needs a man by her side. The inimitable Erica Kane has sailed through men and marriages to get what she wants. In most cases, Erica's farfetched schemes made her husbands want to strangle her, but her impulsiveness was part of the reason these men agreed to take the plunge with the daytime dynamo. Will Erica ever be ready to hang up her bridal veil? Judging from her illustrious track record, not a chance!

• To ensnare husband number one, Jeff Martin, Erica heaped false praise and adoration upon the up-and-coming young doctor. He wanted a stay-at-home wife, while she wanted a modeling career in New York. When Erica got an abortion behind Jeff's back, he called a halt to their marriage.

• In snagging husband number two, Erica used a conveniently timed pregnancy to win high school heartthrob Phil Brent away from her longtime rival Tara Martin. But soon after the marriage, Erica suffered a miscarriage and a nervous breakdown that forced her to be committed.

• When she couldn't get her mother's best friend, Nick Davis, to commit to marriage, Erica tried to get even by wooing her next husband, good guy Tom Cudahy. Tom wanted a quartet of kids running around the house, so he was stunned to discover his new wife was taking birth control pills behind his back.

• Movie financier Adam Chandler wooed Erica with the promise that he would make her star of the silver screen. He whisked her to the altar for a hurried ceremony, with friends and family banging on the door to try to stop it from taking place.

• Though their wedding ceremony was not legal, Erica considers Mike Roy to have been her husband nonetheless. The handsome writer showed Erica she was capable of love, but their time together was short because tragically, Mike, was presumed dead.

• Politician Travis Montgomery became the next man to walk down the aisle with Erica after she gave birth to his daughter. His desperate deceptions cost him the woman he loved. Erica remarried Travis for the sake of their child, but her affair with his brother, Jackson, destroyed the union.

- Erica stunned the world when she married Adam Chandler for the second time in 1992. There's only one reason she would submit to tying the knot with this tyrant—blackmail. Erica nearly fainted when Adam revealed that they had never been legally divorced. To keep the shocking scandal out of the press and away from her highly sensitive daughter, Bianca, Erica consented to remarry Adam publically—then proceeded to make his life a living hell. After months of marital war, Adam realized that he could never win back Erica's heart. So he did the noble thing and set her free.

- Married man Dimitri Marick relentlessly pursued Erica in 1993. Though she cared for him deeply, Erica steadfastly refused to become a mistress again. Dimitri continued the chase, eventually wearing down her resistance. After overcoming many obstacles, Dimitri and Erica became man and wife—again and again.

Erica and Tom Cudahy

September 6, 1978

To get over her disastrous romance with Nick Davis, Erica took a job at Pine Valley's newest restaurant, The Goalpost, where she took up with her boss, former football quarterback Tom Cudahy. Hoping to make Nick jealous, Erica rushed Tom into marriage, but when Nick called on her wedding day, she prayed he would propose! Instead, he offered an apology for not being able to attend the wedding. Heartbroken, Erica forged ahead with the ceremony, but her mother, Mona, could easily see that she still loved Nick. Moments before entering the church, Mona warned that she would "Stop the wedding in the middle of the ceremony if I have to. I will not let you marry that wonderful Tom Cudahy if you don't love him." At the last second, Mona kept mum and the ceremony went on as planned. Father Tierney, assisted by Father Currin, officiated at the traditional Catholic service uniting Erica and Tom in holy matrimony.

TOM AND ERICA'S WEDDING VOWS

A Roman Catholic Service

FATHER TIERNEY

(Reads the greeting)

*Father, when you created mankind you willed that man and wife should be one.
Bind Tom and Erica in the loving union of marriage; and make their love fruitful so that
they may be witness to Your divine love in the world. We ask this through our Lord.*
(To the congregation) *Please be seated.*

FATHER CURRIN

(Delivers gospel)

A reading from the first book of Corinthians . . . (Reads) *Love is always patient and kind;
it is never jealous or conceited; it is never rude or selfish; it does not take offense and is not
resentful. Love takes no pleasure in other people's sins but delights in the truth; it is always
ready to excuse, to trust, to hope, and to endure whatever comes . . . Love does not end.*

FATHER TIERNEY

(Delivers homily)

*John the Baptist once remarked, "The bride is only for the bridegroom and yet the bridegroom's friend who stands
there is glad." Now John the Baptist was actually referring to the church, but I think that statement does sum up
why we are all here today. We are glad for Tom and Erica. And happy to be able to share their wedding day with
them. It's no secret that this marriage was a little late in coming together today. There was a problem—but due to
Tom and Erica's effort it was overcome. And that same effort, I trust, will be transferred to their married life also.
For only if you are willing to work at marriage can it succeed. And that work must continue the rest of your
lives. . . . Marriage is, in my opinion, one of the most beautiful sacraments of our church. But it is a sacrament.
Therefore, it must not be entered into unadvisedly or lightly . . . and if anyone here can show why Tom and Erica
should not be joined together, let them speak now or forever hold their peace. All stand. My dear friends, you have
come together in this church so that the Lord may seal and strengthen your love in the presence of the church's
minister and this community. Christ abundantly blesses this love. He has already consecrated you in baptism and
now he enriches you and strengthens you by a special sacrament so that you may assume the duties of marriage in
mutual and lasting fidelity. And so, in the presence of the church, I ask you to state your intentions . . . Tom and
Erica, have you come here freely and without reservation to give yourselves to each other in marriage?*

ERICA

I have.

TOM

I have.

FATHER TIERNEY

*Will you love and honor each
other as man and wife for the
rest of your lives?*

ERICA

I will.

TOM

I will.

FATHER TIERNEY

*Will you accept children lovingly from
God, and bring them up according to
the law of Christ and His church?*

TOM
I will.

ERICA
I will.

FATHER TIERNEY
*Since it is your intention to enter into marriage, join your right hands
and declare your consent before God and His church.*

TOM
*I, Tom, take you, Erica, to be my wife. I promise to be true to you in good times and in bad,
in sickness and in health. I will love you and honor you all the days of my life.*

ERICA
*I, Erica, take you, Tom, to be my husband. I promise to be true to you in
good times and in bad, in sickness and in health.*

FATHER TIERNEY
I will love you and honor you—

ERICA
I will love you and honor you all the days of my life.

FATHER TIERNEY
*We're halfway there. What God has joined, men must not divide. Amen. Lord, bless these rings which
we bless in Your name. Grant that those who wear them may always have a deep faith in each other.
May they do Your will and always live together in peace, good will, and love.
We ask this through Christ our Lord. Amen.*

TOM
*Erica, take this ring as a sign of my love and fidelity. In the name of the Father, and of the Son,
and of the Holy Spirit.*

ERICA
*Tom, take this ring as a sign of my love and fidelity. In the name of the Father, and of the Son,
and of the Holy Spirit.*

FATHER TIERNEY
*Please join hands and kneel. My dear friends, let us ask God for His continued blessing upon
Tom and Erica. Holy Father, creator of the universe, maker of man and woman in Your own likeness,
source of blessing for married life, we humbly pray to You for this woman who today is united with her
husband in this sacrament of marriage. May Your fullest blessing come upon her and her husband and
enrich Your Church with their children. Lord, may they both praise You when they are happy and turn
to You in their sorrows. May they be glad that You help them in their work and know that You are
with them in their need. May they pray to You in the Community of the church, and be Your witness
in the world. May they reach old age in the company of their friends, and come at last to the kingdom of
heaven. We ask this through Christ our Lord. Amen. May Almighty God, with His word of blessing,
unite your hearts in the never-ending bond of pure love. Amen.
Tom and Erica, you are now husband and wife.*

SHARE A ROMANTIC RENDEZVOUS IN ST. CROIX, U.S. VIRGIN ISLANDS

Erica and Tom shared one of daytime TV's most romantic honeymoons on St. Croix. Turquoise waters and white-sand beaches color the island with a vivid setting that's been a favorite of honeymooners for decades. Even though it's an American territory, it's pure Caribbean—lush palm trees swaying in the gentle breezes, friendly, laid-back islanders, a pastoral landscape of gently rolling hills, and sugar mills.

What to do: Honeymoon on St. Croix and you'll spend a lot of time in the water. Every imaginable sport is available, including snorkeling, scuba diving, deep-sea fishing, windsurfing, plus sailing and kayaking. (For land lovers, there's also first-rate golf, tennis, and horseback riding.) After sampling some of the island's gorgeous beaches, such as Cane Bay and Davis Bay, take your sweetheart to nearby Buck Island Reef. An 850-acre national park with sensational beaches and terrific underwater snorkeling trails teeming with tropical fish, this island is also a popular place with hikers and picnickers. When it's time to spend some of those wedding-gift checks at the duty-free stores, head to Christiansted and Frederiksted, the island's two waterfront towns. Check out the jewelry, china, perfume, and leather. Each of you are allowed to spend up to $1,200 on merchandise without paying duty.

Erica and Tom in St. Croix.

Romantic rendezvous: Tiptoe through the ginger thomas, the island's native flower, at St. George Botanical Gardens in Estate St. George. A former nineteenth-century homestead for sugarcane plantation workers, the seventeen-acre gardens include more than 800 species of trees and plants and its own eco-rain forest.

Stepping out at night: While evenings are generally quiet, you can have a boogie night dancing to calypso, reggae, or a steel band at numerous hotels.

For more information: Call the United States Virgin Islands Tourism Information at (800) 372-USVI.

Erica and Adam Chandler

March 8, 1984

When Erica decided to become an actress, she wanted an Oscar. But she wound up with an *Adam*. Here was a man every bit as crafty and cunning as she was. Adam lied and schemed to get what he wanted, and what he wanted was Erica. However, she was already involved in a tempestuous romance with writer Mike Roy. Determined to split them up, ruthless Adam arranged for Mike to take a tempting new job in Tibet. With Mr. Roy out of town, Adam pulled out all the stops to court Erica in an extravagant fashion. Heartbroken over Mike's apparent rejection, Erica impulsively married happy Mr. Chandler on the rebound.

Erica and Adam, Wedding 2

December 13, 1991

To force Erica to marry him again publically, Adam crafted an article declaring that her daughter, Bianca, was illegitimate. He threatened to fax it directly to the *National Intruder* if Erica did not consent to marry him immediately. Totally trapped, Erica agreed. At Opal's suggestion, she hired a fake minister so the warp-speed marriage would be invalid.

Erica and Mike Roy

October 16, 1984

Erica's greatest love might very well have been world-traveling writer Mike Roy, who never tried to change her flighty and egocentric ways. Mike loved Erica just the way she was, though he never allowed her to get away with an ounce of nonsense. With Mike, Erica found out she was capable of love, but sadly, their time together was short because Mike apparently died in a shooting. However, in 1998, he made an amazing return to Pine Valley, bringing with him a new chapter in Erica's oft-turbulent love life.

Erica and Travis Montgomery

February 16, 1988

The moment she laid eyes on him, Erica knew she wanted to make aspiring Senator Travis Montgomery the next in her long line of husbands. She even arranged to meet the charismatic millionaire as if by accident. Though they began a torrid romance, Travis was more committed to his political ambitions than he was to his

budding romance with Erica. Confounding the romance for Erica was an unplanned but welcomed pregnancy. Erica was faced with a dilemma since career-driven Travis had made it abundantly clear that children were not a part of his master plan. After much deliberation, Erica nervously broke the news to Travis—who was elated! He proposed on the spot, and Erica made elaborate plans to become Mrs. Travis Montgomery.

Erica loved Travis enough to give him a beautiful daughter, Bianca. After a harrowing pregnancy in which she nearly died from toxemia, Erica became Mrs. Travis Montgomery. Their marriage fell apart when Travis's business failed. Desperate to secure some quick money, Travis secretly plotted his own kidnapping. But his plan backfired, and baby Bianca was kidnapped instead. Discovering the charade, Erica divorced him. In stepped Travis's brother, Jackson, who had been impatiently waiting for Erica to be free.

WORDS OF LOVE
ERICA TO JEREMY MOMENTS AFTER HER MARRIAGE TO TRAVIS

ERICA

I finally learned what you tried so hard to teach me. My happiness is in my own hands. Now that I know it, I plan to make this marriage last. I won't let the ghosts of the past destroy it.

MARK DALTON'S TOAST TO HIS SISTER ERICA'S NEW MARRIAGE

Please raise your glasses to Erica and Travis. They have already seen enough adversity to last a lifetime. May their life together with their new baby be filled with love and happiness. To Erica and Travis!

Erica and Travis's Second Marriage

May 21, 1990

Travis was a first for Erica. Not her first husband, not her first divorce. He was the first man she (legally) married *twice*. Erica remarried Travis because she wanted her daughter, Bianca, to have a stable family life. This was one of the most unselfish things Erica has ever done. If only she hadn't fallen for his brother, Jack! Erica's relationship with Travis was impassioned; with brother Jack, impulsive. The Reverend Thompson reunited Erica and Travis two and a half years after their first

wedding. Though the bride and groom wrote their own special vows in which they pledged that their love would "endure forever," the marriage quickly collapsed. Erica and Travis were stunned when Jackson Montgomery arrived sans invitation just before the start of their second wedding ceremony. Days earlier, Erica had turned down Travis's brother's proposal, but he simply would

not take no for an answer. In a last-minute huddle in the church vestibule, Jack pleaded with his lady love to fly away with him to Paris, but she gently turned him down in favor of an ill-fated remarriage to Travis.

Travis and Erica's Wedding Vows

REVEREND THOMPSON

Who gives this woman to be married to this man?

ERIC KANE

Her mother and I do.

REVEREND THOMPSON

Travis and Erica have written their own vows.

TRAVIS

I, Travis, take you, Erica, to be my partner in life, my best friend. I promise to love and cherish you from this day forward, to be as good a father as I know how to our daughter, Bianca, and most of all to give thanks daily for the gift of knowledge, or, as the Apostle Paul said, "These three remain: faith, hope, and love; and the greatest of these is love." Erica, my love for you is eternal.

ERICA

I, Erica, take you, Travis, to be my wedded husband, to live with you in the security of our family, to make a home for ourselves and our child, and to be faithful to you for as long as I live. Travis, my love and commitment to you will never end.

REVEREND THOMPSON

The rings, please. The wedding ring is the outward and visible sign of an inward and spiritual grace, signifying to all the uniting of this man and woman in holy matrimony, through the Church of Jesus Christ our Lord. Let us pray. Bless, O Lord, the giving of these rings, that they who wear them may abide in Thy peace, and continue in Thy favor; through Jesus Christ our Lord. Amen.

TRAVIS

In token and pledge of our constant faith and abiding love, with this ring, I thee wed.

REVEREND THOMPSON

In the name of the Father, and of the Son, and of the Holy Spirit. Amen.

ERICA

With this ring, I take you to be my husband. I promise to share with you my life, the responsibilities of our home, the fruits of our labor, and all our sorrows and joys. I promise to build with you through our love a oneness of mind and spirit which shall endure forever. In the name of the Father, and of the Son, and of the Holy Spirit. Amen.

REVEREND THOMPSON

Forasmuch as Travis and Erica have consented together in holy wedlock, and have witnessed the same before God and this company, and thereto have pledged their faith each to the other, and have declared the same by joining hands and by giving and receiving rings; I pronounce that they are husband and wife together, in the name of the Father, and of the Son, and of the Holy Spirit. Those whom God hath joined together, let no man put asunder. Amen. Let us pray. God the Father, the Son, and the Holy Spirit bless, preserve, and keep you; the Lord graciously with his favor look upon you, and so fill you with all spiritual benediction and love that you may so live together in this life that in the world to come you may have life everlasting. Amen. You may kiss the bride.

Erica and Dimitri Marick

June 22, 1993

Erica became enchanted with dashing Dimitri Marick when he tried to engineer a hostile takeover of her cosmetics company, Enchantment. Though he romantically pursued her with fierce determination, Erica refused to have an affair until he divorced his wife, Angelique. When they were finally free to marry, Erica and Dimitri did so in pure fairy-tale style in an elaborate wedding that took its cue from Dimitri's Hungarian ancestors. Erica Kane Martin Brent Cudahy Chandler Montgomery

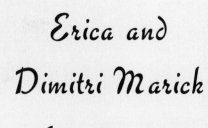

Montgomery added one more surname as she took the plunge once again, wedding Continental charmer Dimitri Marick. The couple tied the knot at Wildwind, Dimitri's Gothic estate, in a ceremony fit for a king and queen. A vision in gold, Erica was attended by her daughters Bianca and Kendall. Edmund Grey served as his brother's best man, and Jackson Montgomery and Opal Cortlandt provided readings. The colors cream and gold were especially prominent throughout the wedding. The three-tier wedding cake featured gold accents and many delicate flowers. The floral bouquets were comprised of peonies, orchids, and roses.

The newlyweds had barely walked up the aisle before they had to deal with Erica's vengeful daughter Kendall. (As a teenager Erica had been raped by actor Richard Fields, and Kendall was the result.) Kendall proceeded to dredge up Erica's painful past, sending her mother over the edge and into an emotional tailspin. When Kendall convinced Erica that Dimitri had raped her, she confronted her husband, and in a fit of hallucinatory rage, she mistook him for the man who raped *her*. In a posttraumatic episode, Erica then grabbed a letter opener and plunged it into Dimitri's chest! Gasping in pain and disbelief, Dimitri slumped to the floor—nearly killed by his very own wife! In the aftermath of the tragedy, Dimitri filed for divorce.

DIMITRI AND ERICA'S WEDDING VOWS

DIMITRI

When we met, I wasn't looking for love. I had lost once too often. I had resigned myself to my life. But someone knew better and that someone let it rain and rain and rain. And thanks to one glorious port in the storm, I looked into your eyes and I found love. We've had more than our share of trouble, but we've overcome and forgiven. Today we are marrying as a family. And our family will not look backward but forward. I vow to do everything in my power to make every day of your life as dazzling as you are. I vow to be your port in every thunderstorm and your partner in all life has to offer. I give you this ring and hope it will be your most prized piece of jewelry. But let the love it represents be your most precious possession.
I love you.

ERICA

I love you more than anyone I've ever loved in my whole life. I always fought hard to protect my heart. But you wouldn't let me take the easy way out. I have been honest with you—after a few false starts—and open with you in a way I didn't think possible. I will concede all the lessons I have learned. I vow to forget my fears and let go with you . . . I vow to bring out the best in you always. I vow to share all my honors and fortunes with you. You not only asked to share your life with mine, you asked for my children's blessings. You want my family to become our family. I want that too. May this ring be a sign that I am choosing to share the rest of my life with you. I know that as your partner, I shall become much more than I am. I love you.

Erica and Dimitri's Second Wedding

December 31, 1994

When they made plans to marry again, Erica and Dimitri hoped that their troubles were behind them at long last. Naughty Kendall had been exiled from Erica's life, and Dimitri finally had forgiven his ex-wife for stabbing him with a letter opener. In celebration of her triumph over adversity, Erica chose a stunning silver-beaded gown for the wedding ceremony. With a helping hand from Erica's daughter, Bianca, Dimitri dazzled his once and future bride by making all the preparations for their second wedding

on New Year's Eve, 1994. In the candlelit Russian Orthodox ceremony, Erica and Dimitri pledged their eternal love.

Their seemingly unbreakable bond was put to the test by Erica's addiction to painkillers. Dimitri divorced his wife after catching her in bed with Dr. Jonathan Kinder. Little did he know that Kinder intentionally staged the tryst.

WORDS OF LOVE
DIMITRI GIVES ERICA THE KEY TO HIS HUNTING LODGE, 1994

DIMITRI

I want to give you the world. This key is a symbol of that part of it that belongs just to us.

ERICA

Thank you.

DIMITRI

I want you to keep this with you, whatever happens. And down the road, whatever trials that we face, you take it and you hold it in your hand like this, tightly, and you remember all that we have to hold on to.

SHARE A ROMANTIC RENDEZVOUS IN BUDAPEST, HUNGARY

Erica and Dimitri fell deeply in love while on a romantic rendezvous in Budapest. An Old World beauty graces this modern metropolis, which is Hungary's capital. Many of the historic sites are conveniently located right along the Danube. Adding to the magical ambiance, eight bridges connect the city's two banks, including the landmark Chain Bridge, in Pest. The city has almost fifty museums devoted to art, history, science, and literature—quirkier museums highlight such subjects as stamps, electricity, and rescue-operation techniques!

When to go: The warmest months are June through August; January is the coldest.

What to do: Explore the elevated sights on Castle Hill, a stunning area in Buda with a fabulous panoramic view of the city and the Danube. It has an intimate ambiance, thanks in part to the fact that no major roadways traverse it. Stop by the Royal Palace, which now houses several major cultural institutions, including the National Gallery, an art museum. Another highlight of Castle Hill is the neo-Gothic Matthias Church, which is surrounded by restored medieval homes on cobblestone streets. Look down from Gellért Hill, a natural reserve and popular strolling place in the middle of the city, for another superb city view.

Romantic rendezvous: For a glittering view of the city, a popular evening stroll for visitors is the Danube Promenade. Or take a boat ride on the Danube to see the sights bathed in light.

Stepping out at night: Music plays a starring role in this cultured town. The opera, housed in a neo-Renaissance palace, is outstanding, as is the Danube Symphony Orchestra, which performs in the neo-baroque Dunas Palace.

For more information: The Hungarian National Tourist Office has a branch in New York. Information also can be obtained on-line at www.goeurope.com

Erica and Dimitri in Budapest.

Susan Lucci on Erica's Husbands:

Jeff Martin: "I remember that we eloped and it was snowing. It was the first time that I ever encountered that plastic snow, and oh, that's terrible stuff. You kind of had to put those feelings about the plastic snow aside and go on with the romance of the scene."

Phil Brent: "The snaring of Phil Brent was a matter of pride for Erica Kane. I don't know that she was in love with Phil, but she had to get him. And then she did."

Tom Cudahy: "This was a tragedy. Tom was the dream man: Handsome, athletic, loving, warm, but Erica wanted her career more than anything else at that time. When Tom found her birth control pills, that was the end."

Adam Chandler: "Adam offered her immortality as a movie star, and that's what she wanted to be. She jumped out of Adam's bed on their wedding night in the Caribbean because he had fooled her into thinking they were going to Hollywood. She hopped on the next plane to Hollywood and that was the end."

Mike Roy: "He was Erica's first great love. They were very different: He was very intellectual and she was not, and still he loved her for what she was."

Travis Montgomery: "He was very romantic, dashing, and he charmed her. Then she saw his brother, Jack, and was conflicted. But Travis is the father of Bianca, and that was a big turning point for Erica, even when she was in love with Jack."

Dimitri Marick: "From the time Erica met Dimitri, she has been in love with him. She really wanted their marriage to work. She was devastated when it didn't."

Adam Chandler's Wedding Album

A brutal, amoral man who will stop at nothing to gain an edge over his competitors, Adam Chandler is driven to accumulate wealth and wives. When it comes to marriage, Adam asks only one question: "What's in it for me?" His rich first wife, Althea, died under mysterious circumstances, leaving her entire fortune to her wily widower. Ever since, this silver fox has manipulated his way through a multitude of marriages, each one more dysfunctional than the next!

Adam and Erica Kane

March 8, 1984

Erica and Adam raised their glasses to a glorious future as man and wife, but it quickly became apparent to the new Mrs. Chandler that Adam did not plan to deliver on his pledge to allow her to star in the film version of her autobiography, *Raising Kane*. Realizing that Erica would never love him, Adam eventually consented to a divorce, but he got the last laugh when he sent his twin brother, Stuart, to the Caribbean to dissolve the marriage. Years later, after being divorced by Natalie and dumped by Brooke, Adam announced to Erica that, because their divorce had never really been finalized, they were still man and wife!

Adam and Brooke English

November 20, 1987

Brooke English holds the singular distinction of being the only woman who ever truly loved Adam without any secret motives. In November 1987 she accepted Adam's proposal but didn't want a grandiose ceremony. It was Brooke's idea to ask a justice of the peace to officiate at a simple wedding held in the offices of *Tempo* magazine. The quickie marriage met with mixed reactions from the friends and family on hand. Brooke's Aunt Phoebe was disgusted. Her ex-husband Tom hid his misgivings, while Adam's daughter Skye was overjoyed.

Not many women could keep Adam Chandler in check. But somehow, strong-willed Brooke and ruthless Adam actually had one of Pine Valley's most perfect marriages for a while. However, everything changed when Brooke discovered that she was not able to give Adam a child. Adam's desire to have a son proved stronger than his love for Brooke, so he secretly seduced the family housekeeper, young Dixie Cooney, and got her pregnant. When Brooke discovered Adam's bed-hopping antics, she gave him the heave-ho. To this day, Adam regrets destroying his marriage to Brooke. Over the years he has made at least four separate pleas for Brooke to marry him again. Each proposal has been met with a negative response from the once-burned bride.

Adam and Dixie Cooney

June 1, 1989

When crafty Adam Chandler discovered that his wife, Brooke, could not conceive a child, he took swift action! Desperate for a male heir to follow in his footsteps, Adam seduced their youthful maid Dixie during an encounter in the Chandler boathouse. The clandestine tryst worked! Dixie became pregnant and Adam secretly plotted to adopt her baby when it was born—without Brooke ever knowing it was his. However, when Brooke discovered what he had done, she divorced him.

Down but never out, Adam quickly changed his tactics. Scrambling to secure his legacy and legitimize his child, Adam persuaded Dixie to marry him. However, his disdain for this homespun ex-housekeeper was so great that he devised a dirty scheme to drive her out of his life. After convincing Dixie that she was losing her mind, Adam had her committed to a mental institution.

Adam and Natalie Hunter
September 3, 1990

Adam married Natalie Hunter for only one reason—to get his greedy paws into her bank account! Battered by a rash of bad business moves, Adam suddenly found himself flat broke. Desperate to regain his fortune, he saw a gold mine in Nurse Natalie, who recently had inherited a fortune from a wealthy patient who died and left her the bulk of his estate. Natalie was grateful to Adam, a financial wizard who offered to manage her portfolio. Unaware of Adam's true motives, Natalie was so impressed by Adam that she agreed to elope with him. Within days the greedy bridegroom began siphoning off his new wife's assets.

Adam and Gloria Marsh
April 28, 1993

Gloria's fantasy wedding came true when Adam arranged for them to be married aboard a beautiful yacht. Feeling overjoyed and blessed, she tied the knot at sea with Pine Valley's charismatic millionaire.

After failing in his first five stabs at marital bliss, Adam set his sights closer to home in 1993 when he seduced his own brother's fiancée! Once the town tramp, Gloria Marsh mended her wicked ways when she fell for kindly Stuart Chandler. Though she adored Stuart's sensitive soul, Gloria yearned for Adam's passionate kisses. Adam, too, was utterly fascinated by this tough, smart woman. He wanted Gloria! At first, Stuart was devastated when Gloria told him that she loved Adam, but in time he persuaded her that she was entitled to happiness, so she should seize it. Fortified by Stuart's forgiveness, Gloria married Adam in a nautically themed ceremony aboard a ship on the high seas in the spring of 1993.

The following year Adam began to suspect that Gloria had renewed her affair with one-time lover Alec McIntyre, so he faked his own kidnapping to test Gloria's loyalty. He wanted to see for himself that Gloria truly loved him, not the handsome young Alec. Gloria discovered Adam's charade on the day she and he were to renew their vows in a lavish ceremony in the Chandler Mansion ballroom. She decided to teach Adam a lesson. With a minister presiding, the assembled guests listened as Adam professed his love to Gloria. Then it was her turn to speak.

"I wouldn't marry Adam Chandler if he were the last man on earth!!" she proclaimed. Jaws dropped as the ceremony—and the marriage—ground to a halt.

Adam and Liza Colby

December 20, 1996

For Adam and Liza, first came marriage, then came love. In an inspired pairing of two of Pine Valley's strongest personalities, Adam and Liza pretended to plan a wedding to make their former loves Brooke and Tad jealous. When Liza discovered that her husband-to-be was secretly reneging on his premarital promise to give her half of WRCW-TV, she outsmarted him! She was supposed to leave Adam at the altar, but Liza tricked Adam into actually going through with the ceremony. A cat-and-mouse game ensued in which Liza tried to seduce Adam, consummate their marriage, then stake her claim to the Chandler fortune. Adam constantly rejected her advances in order to avoid handing over his millions. Meanwhile, something happened that the groom never expected—he found himself growing jealous of young Jake Martin, who was wooing his new bride! Could it be? Could Adam be falling in love with Liza? After countless encounters fraught with sexual tension, they finally gave in to their mutual attraction and shared a sizzling night of passion. Though they were still too pig-headed to admit it, Adam and Liza were in love!

ADAM AND LIZA PLAN THEIR QUICKIE, LOVELESS WEDDING . . .

LIZA
What are we waiting for?

ADAM
Full steam ahead. Tomorrow it is. (They shake hands on the deal.)

LIZA
Well, we're really going to have to haul if we're going to get this wedding together by tomorrow—the day that will live in infamy.

ADAM
A bloodless coup by the bride and groom.
Yeah. The trap is set. Brooke and Tad are ready to take the bait.
By this time tomorrow, you and I will have it all.

LIZA
Who says you can't have everything you want? All right. Chef Jay is a friend of mine at the Elephant Grill. He can do the food. We can have the orchids flown in from Maui, and the music—

ADAM
The music? Why don't you get the Boston Pops, fly them in from Boston? How much is this going to set me back?

LIZA
I'll tell you what. Since I am half owner of WRCW, I will foot the bill. It will be my wedding present. Okay. How about the guests?

ADAM
Well, why don't we invite the whole town, since you're buying?

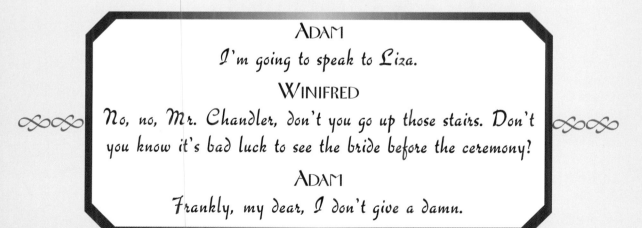

ADAM
I'm going to speak to Liza.

WINIFRED
No, no, Mr. Chandler, don't you go up those stairs. Don't you know it's bad luck to see the bride before the ceremony!

ADAM
Frankly, my dear, I don't give a damn.

ADAM AND LIZA'S WEDDING VOWS
A NEW AGE CEREMONY

SILVANA

Friends and fellow travelers, attend. We are gathered here as midwives to witness the birth of the new. Two souls merging and fusing for their mutual evolution. Two spirits fusing their light to search for their higher selves. In the age of darkness, before we were conscious, we called them bride and groom. The woman came draped in veils, wrapped as a gift. The man opened the gift and took possession. The woman came untouched, like a jar of unguent. The man opened the jar and used it. From this primitive state, deliver us. Grant us the gift of growth. Grant us the vision to see beyond our limits, the courage to break free of outworn bonds—to risk all earthbound comforts as we struggle to achieve security and enlightenment. Like Mother Earth realizing her glory through volcanic fires. Like the wind and the rain—powerful alone, but together a force of transformation.

SILVANA

Adam, will you open your soul to Liza? Will you promise to embrace her light? Will you free yourself from the shackles of the past and forge a new path with your life partner? This is a blending in no way signifying weakness as a single entity, rather reflecting increased energy. (Adam now has the ring and Liza's left hand.)
Will you take this woman as your co-spirit, your lifetime comrade in the quest that has no end?

ADAM
I will.
(He puts the ring on her finger.)

SILVANA

Liza, will you open your soul to Adam? Will you promise to embrace his light?
(Liza takes the ring.)
Will you free yourself from the shackles of the past and forge a new path with your life partner? Will you take this man as your co-spirit, your lifetime comrade in the quest that has no end?

LIZA
I will
(Adam stands in stunned silence as she puts the ring on his finger.)

SILVANA

I now pronounce you united as one. What the cosmos has joined, let nothing part. In the spirit of the mother, sister, Juno, Isis, Aphrodite, I bless this earthly convergence. You may now bestow a token of your contract on the chosen male.
(Liza wraps her arms around Adam, who has now fully comprehended what she's done.)

ADAM
You were supposed to make a break for it! Who the hell do you think you are?

LIZA
I'm your champion, Adam. Mrs. Adam Chandler has a nice ring to it, don't you think?
(The room applauds as Adam stares at Liza in silence.)

Palmer Cortlandt's Wedding Album

Daisy...Donna...Daisy...Cynthia...Natalie...Opal...Palmer Cortlandt's roster of wives reads like a laundry list of lost loves. Born Pete Cooney in Pigeon Hollow, West Virginia, Palmer is a self-made man who overcame his humble beginnings to amass a great fortune—only to lose it again and again. The shrewd, silver-haired tycoon has been equally unlucky in love. When it comes to Palmer's associations with the opposite sex, passion often has forced good sense out the window. Time and time again Palmer and his lover of the moment have refused to let the threat of heartache and humiliation stand in the way of their betrothal.

Palmer and Daisy Murdoch

It has been said that second marriages are the triumph of hope over experience. Older and wiser, Palmer and Daisy saw great promise for their future when they tied the knot for a second time in the spring of 1984. Palmer first married Daisy Murdoch—his housekeeper's daughter—when she was a young girl. After she gave him a daughter, Nina, Daisy felt imprisoned by her overbearing husband. After rebelliously having an extramarital affair, Daisy was banished from Cortlandt Manor by her humiliated husband.

Years later Daisy snuck into Pine Valley to see her daughter. She and Palmer shared many heated battles, but there was no denying the attraction they still felt for each other. Palmer divorced Donna so that he and Daisy could marry again.

Palmer and Cynthia Preston

In 1985 gold-digger Cynthia Preston wriggled her way into Palmer's life. The sexy temptress got his blood boiling, but when it came to marriage, Palmer dragged his feet, causing Cynthia to attack him where it hurt—his libido. "No making love until we're married!" she cooed to a frustrated Palmer, who called on Judge Martel to marry them as soon as possible.

The newly enshrined mistress of the manor exasperated Palmer when she painted his library *pink!* Upon divorcing Cynthia, Palmer swiftly restored the pastel palace to its original, mahogany glory.

Palmer and Donna Beck Tyler

In May 1981 Palmer stunned Pine Valley society by marrying ex-hooker Donna Beck Tyler. In Svengali-like fashion, Palmer relished the opportunity to transform his new wife into a woman of the world. At the same time, Donna wanted very much to have a child of her own, unaware that her new husband was sterile. When she became pregnant several months into their new marriage, Palmer knew the child must have been fathered by Donna's ex-husband, Chuck, during the night they spent trapped in a Swiss cave during an avalanche.

WORDS OF LOVE
PALMER PROPOSES TO DONNA, MAY 1981

DONNA
I've never seen a diamond this size in my whole life.

PALMER
It looks beautiful on you. As though it were made just for these perfect hands.

DONNA
But it's all too much for me. I don't deserve anything this nice.

PALMER
You deserve the whole world at your feet. And I intend to give it to you.
Marry me, Donna—tonight!

Palmer and Natalie Hunter

Palmer fell for Natalie Hunter when she nursed him back to health after a near-fatal gunshot wound. While living at Cortlandt Manor, Natalie engaged in a steamy affair with Palmer's married son, Ross Chandler. However, when Ross

informed Natalie that he loved his wife, Ellen, and wanted to make their marriage work, she turned to Palmer on the rebound and accepted his perpetual proposal of marriage. Ross was understandably flustered when Palmer asked him to be his best man. Still, he accepted the awkward task, and watched in silence as Natalie and Palmer recited their vows.

Palmer and Opal Purdy

Palmer's relationship with tacky Opal Purdy began as a business arrangement when he made her a lucrative offer to break up Dixie and Tad. Opal pulled off the job and picked up her check but didn't want to bid farewell to her benefactor. She decided that Palmer was going to be her next husband. But first she had to get him to notice her!

Although he was unattached, Palmer had no use for the uncouth woman. Strangely enough, it was Palmer's two-time wife, Daisy, who played matchmaker for Pine Valley's oddest couple. Daisy successfully transformed Opal into a sophisticated woman fit for an urbane gentleman like Palmer. Daisy's efforts

paid off when newly glamorous Opal made a grand entrance at the annual University Ball, catching the eye of her intended. Within weeks they were engaged!

Opal nearly canceled her trip to the altar at the last minute when Palmer, at his nephew Will's urging, presented his bride-to-be with a prenuptial agreement. Outraged, Opal called the wedding off, claiming that Palmer didn't trust her. Palmer apologized, and wedding plans were resumed, much to Will's dismay. On the morning of the wedding, Opal freaked when Palmer bucked

tradition and came to see his bride-to-be. Fortunately, he calmed Opal's fears, convincing her to drop her superstitions and get on with their wedding. Petulant Palmer and eccentric Opal's unusual pairing really takes the cake! Oddly enough, only this most offbeat marriage has shown signs of success and longevity.

WORDS OF LOVE
PALMER PROPOSES TO OPAL

PALMER
I have something for you.

OPAL
Oh? Oh, oh, my stars! Is that real?

PALMER
Yes, it's real. Yes, it's real. It's not nearly as precious as you are. Opal, would you do me the great privilege of becoming my wife?

Victoria Lord's Wedding Album

For over three decades, viewers have followed each twist and turn in the incredible romantic saga of Victoria Lord Riley Burke Riley Buchanan Buchanan Carpenter. Through motherhood, multiple personalities, and a multitude of marriages, Viki has proven to be the most classic of soap opera heroines. Behind the kind, thoughtful, and understanding exterior there is strength, toughness, and a resiliency that has seen her through each personal crisis and marriage.

1968   Working at *The Banner* as a reporter, sparks flew when Viki was thrust into a working relationship with the dynamic, "hard-drinking, hard-living" reporter Joe Riley. When her father pushed Viki to end her relationship with Joe, Viki's split personality Niki Smith emerged. Niki was every bit as sexy and flamboyant as any vixen ever to inhabit the city of Llanview.

1969   Despite her illness, Viki agreed to marry Joe. During their wedding ceremony at Llanfair, Viki turned into Niki and ran away with Vince Wolek, before returning to Llanview for treatment.

1970   Although drawn to the compassionate nice-guy Vinnie, Viki finally became Mrs. Joe Riley. While in California, Joe had a car accident and was presumed dead.

1972   Viki, devastated by the loss of her beloved Joe, turned for comfort to the new executive editor of *The Banner*, Steve Burke. Her father, Victor, pushed Viki toward Steve. After many months Viki returned Steve's feelings, and they married on Memorial Day. Suffering from amnesia and a potentially fatal brain aneurism, Joe Riley secretly returned to town. A stunned Viki learned Joe was alive just as he was about to undergo brain surgery. Facing a perplexing dilemma, Viki chose to do her duty and stay with her new husband, Steve, though subconsciously she wanted Joe.

1974   Viki made Joe the happiest man in the world when she told him she was leaving Steve. Viki and Joe made plans to marry. While Viki was in the Caribbean getting her divorce from Steve, Joe learned that Cathy Craig was pregnant with his child. Being an honorable man, Joe asked Cathy to become his wife. A liberated woman, Cathy decided she could not possibly marry Joe—not even for the sake of her child. On September 16 Joe and Viki married in a small Catholic Church in New York City.

1976   On September 12 Viki gave birth to Joe's son, Kevin Lord Riley.

1979   When Joe discovered he was dying from a brain tumor, he hand-picked his successor at *The Banner*, an Arizona newspaper editor named Clint Buchanan. Pregnant with her husband's second child, Viki courageously accepted Joe's untimely passing.

1980   On January 9 Viki gave birth to her late husband Joe's second son, Joey.

1982   Though they were constantly at odds, Viki discovered that her feelings for Clint Buchanan were deeper than she had realized. Viki went to jail when she refused to reveal her sources in a scandalous baby-switching case involving Jenny Vernon and Katrina Karr. While incarcerated, she and Clint decided to marry. Viki and Clint were finally united in marriage at Llanfair after evicting Dorian from the mansion.

1985	When Tina Clayton confronted Viki with the shocking secret that she was her sister, Viki's alter ego, Niki Smith, returned and divorced Clint.
1986	Clint romanced Niki Smith, then shocked Viki into returning by having her find him in bed with Tina. To her delight, Viki found out that she was pregnant and told Clint the wonderful news on the day of their second wedding at Llanfair.
1988	In Arizona, Clint was thrown off his horse. After a long search, he was presumed dead, and Viki and her children mourned his loss. However, he wasn't dead after all—Clint had been transported back in time to the old West, circa 1888. Viki traveled back too, interrupted Clint's wedding to her look-alike ancestor, Ginny, then returned to the future with her husband.
1989	While trapped with Viki in the secret underground city of Eterna, Roger Gordon confessed that they had made love years earlier and she had given birth to his daughter, Megan. While in Eterna, Viki and Roger's old feelings for each other began to resurface. Later Viki was stunned to learn that she had once married Roger.
1992	While Viki resisted her attraction to retired Army General Sloan Carpenter, Dorian showed Clint incriminating photos that made it look as if Viki was having an affair with him. In a huff, Clint moved out of Llanfair, and Viki began to have real feelings for Sloan.
1993	Daughter of the late Victor Lord, Viki has been through just about everything and survived. Of all the *One Life to Live* characters, she is number one in importance, both in terms of story and in the hearts of viewers. Her love for and devotion to her family in their times of need are well known. Because she has suffered through so many emotional trials and tribulations of her own, she would like to help others—people she feels particularly close to—to overcome their own problems and solidify their happiness. She is never one to intrude herself on others' problems, but she is always there and available when those close to her need her.
	Clint filed for divorce from Viki after finding her in bed with Sloan Carpenter at a ski lodge. Deeply in love, Viki accepted Sloan's marriage proposal, but Clint refused to sign the papers ending their marriage.
1994	After Clint agreed to a divorce, Viki married Sloan Carpenter on December 2. Sloan, who suffered from Hodgkin's disease, discovered his illness was out of remission.
1995	Viki mourned the loss of her husband Sloan, who passed away on January 9, 1995.

Viki and Joe Riley

Working side by side, Viki (then played by actress Gillian Spencer) and Joe engaged in a hard-fought rivalry as they competed for stories at *The Banner* newspaper. All the while they harbored a deep attraction for one another. Against her father's wishes, she married the hard-drink-

ing, charismatic reporter. Shortly after the wedding, Joe was presumed dead in a car accident. Overcoming a mass of obstacles, Viki (now played by Erika Slezak) and Joe were finally united. On September 16, 1974, they remarried in a small, quiet ceremony in a Manhattan chapel.

Finally reunited with her beloved Joe, Viki radiated joy on their second wedding day. Joe and Viki rejoiced in their love during a romantic and private reception for two in New York City's Central Park.

Viki and Steve Burke

Devastated by the "death" of her beloved Joe, Viki found comfort in *The Banner*'s new executive editor, Steve Burke. Victor Lord pushed her daughter toward the stable and conservative Steve. Eventually Viki let down her guard and accepted Steve's love.

Viki and Clint Buchanan

Shortly before Joe's death in 1979, he introduced Viki to his successor as editor of *The Banner* newspaper, Clint Buchanan. After Joe's death and the birth of Joey, Viki went back to work at *The Banner* and found love again with her handsome coworker. On November 15, 1982, Viki and Clint were united in matrimony. Clint's brother, Bo, and father, Asa, gave Viki a warm, Texas-style welcome into the Buchanan family fold. On the morning of their second wedding on April 17, 1986, Viki delighted Clint with the incredible news that she was pregnant with his child. They remarried in a sweet ceremony at the family estate, Llanfair.

WORDS OF LOVE
CLINT PROPOSES
MARRIAGE TO VIKI

CLINT

*Just the sight of you drives me crazy.
I mean, like right now, you think you've withdrawn from me,
but this "thing" is still between us. You know, you walk into a
room and I can't concentrate. I can't concentrate on The Banner.
I can't concentrate on a . . . grocery list. I want you.
Can I bring up something, ah, important?*

VIKI

That depends on how important.

CLINT

It's important.

VIKI

Oh. It's that important. Go ahead.

CLINT

Will you marry me?

In 1982 Viki languished in prison after refusing to reveal the name of a confidential source in a news story. The only bright note in her prison stay was a tender proposal from Clint Buchanan, which she readily accepted.

CLINT AND VIKI'S WEDDING VOWS
NOVEMBER 15, 1982

PRIEST

In token and in pledge of the vow between us made.

CLINT

In token and in pledge of the vow between us made.

PRIEST

With this ring, I thee wed.

CLINT

With this ring, I thee wed.

PRIEST

*Repeat after me. In token and
in pledge of the vow between us made.*

VIKI

*In token and in pledge of the
vow between us made.*

PRIEST

With this ring, I thee wed.

VIKI

With this ring, I thee wed.

PRIEST

*Look preciously upon them that they may live
together in faithfulness, in patience, and
that their home may be a haven for
blessing and a place of peace.
Through Jesus Christ, Our Lord. Amen.*

GINNY

*Isn't it strange? We were separated by all
those years, but we found each other. It is
quite extraordinary. I am a rational, logical
woman. Never in my wildest dreams could
I have imagined something like this.*

In 1988 Clint hurtled back through time, landing in the Old West, circa 1888, where he encountered some familiar faces. One of them was Viki's ancestor, Ginny Fletcher. Just as Clint and Ginny were about to marry, Viki tumbled through time and arrived on the scene to stop the ceremony.

Viki and Roger Gordon

Viki was shaken to discover that, as a teenager, she had married Roger Gordon and given birth to his daughter, Megan. Viki blocked out this chapter of her life thanks to her father, Victor Lord, who had hired a hypnotist to erase his daughter's memory.

Victoria Lord Buchanan
and
U.S. General Sloan Hayford Carpenter

request the honor of your presence

at their wedding

at twelve o'clock.

Saint James Church

929 Mill Street

Llanview, Pennsylvania

Viki and Sloan Carpenter

Viki and Sloan Carpenter planned to marry in a bittersweet ceremony at St. James Church, but when Sloan fell gravely ill with Hodgkin's disease, they decided not to postpone their wedding. The couple tied the knot in a bittersweet ceremony held in the Intensive Care Unit of Llanview Hospital.

Asa Buchanan's Wedding Album

Asa Buchanan has never had a problem finding a woman willing to become his wife. Keeping her happy is another matter! The cantankerous billionaire has left a trail of ex-wives in his wake. On at least ten separate occasions, he has earnestly spoken those two simple words: "I do."

Asa and Samantha Vernon

June 24, 1981

Soon after the tall Texas oil baron put down roots in Llanview, he hired young Samantha Vernon to work for him. Sam was enthralled by her boss's power and bigger-than-life charm. Asa was equally impressed by Samantha, but he was more interested in her body than her business acumen.

The groom failed to mention to his bride that his first wife (and mother of his sons), Olympia, was still very much alive! During the grand wedding ceremony, Olympia (whom Asa had held prisoner) showed up at the church but was subdued before she could stop the wedding. When Samantha eventually learned the truth about Asa's bigamy, she dumped him.

Asa and Delila Ralston

February 7, 1983

In 1983 the bitter competition between Asa and his son Bo was at its peak when the men competed for the affection of lovely Delila Ralston. Delila loved Bo Buchanan, but turned to Asa upon discovering the horrible news that Bo was her blood cousin. Soon after Asa uncovered conclusive proof that he was Bo's natural father—and that meant that he and Delila were not related after all.

Asa realized that revealing the secret would send Delila running back into Bo's arms. And Asa wanted Delila for himself! He clearly understood that Delila and Bo were in love, but he selfishly chose to keep them apart. To keep Delila under his thumb and in his bed, Asa convinced her to elope with him. Despite a last-minute appeal from Bo, Delila went ahead with the short-lived marriage.

Delila's beauty and youthful sex appeal often drove Asa crazy with jealousy. Soon after making her wife number three, Asa had a boating accident where he faked his own death to see if his "widow" and "grieving" son Bo were having an affair.

WORDS OF LOVE
DELILA ACCEPTS ASA'S LONG-STANDING PROPOSAL OF MARRIAGE

DELILA

I'd love to marry you. That is, well, if you still want to marry me.

ASA

Good Lord! I mean, I never, I never thought I'd hear . . . Are you serious, Delila?

DELILA

Yeah!

ASA

You just made me the happiest man in the whole world!

Asa and Becky Lee Abbott

July 11, 1983

When Becky Lee became pregnant with Bo Buchanan's child, she thought she would have to be content with single motherhood. Bo loved Delila Ralston and had recently married her. However, when Bo's daddy, Asa, discovered that Becky Lee was carrying Bo's child—Asa's future grandchild—he made a gallant offer to marry her in order to make the child a true Buchanan. With Brad and Jenny Vernon standing up for them, Asa and Becky became man and wife. Eventually their marriage of convenience developed into a tender one of love—but as in all of Asa's unions, it failed to last.

Asa and
Pamela Oliver Stuart
January 20, 1986

The people of Llanview were stunned to discover that Asa, posing as a sea captain named Jeb Stuart, had married a woman named Pamela Oliver years earlier on the faraway island of Malakeva. Asa's double-dealing eventually was discovered by Tina Lord. Armed with this hot news, Tina decided to set Asa up. After telling Pamela that her seafaring husband, Captain "Jeb," was really a Texas oil baron, Tina convinced her to pretend to be on her deathbed—then get Asa to confess his sins and marry her for real!

Giving in to her "dying wish," Asa married Pamela moments before she "died." Imagine ol' Asa's surprise when, seconds after the deathbed ceremony, Pamela leapt up and proclaimed herself to be the new "Mrs. Asa Buchanan!" Very much alive, the feisty bride promptly moved to Llanview and took her rightful place as matriarch of the Buchanan dynasty.

Asa and Renee Devine

November 30, 1988

A feisty ex-madam from Reno, Nevada, wrangled the heart of the crusty billionaire in 1988. Renee, who once ran a brothel in Nevada, had known Asa years earlier. Now, decades later, they picked up where they left off. Renee was so charmed by her handsome millionaire that she retired from running a house of the world's oldest profession and stayed in Llanview to start a new life with Asa.

Asa and Renee's decision to join Cord and Tina at the altar for a dual ceremony added a double note of joy to a landmark family occasion. On the day she became the sixth Mrs. Asa Buchanan, kind-hearted Renee was radiant in a gold peau de soie skirt with matching gold silk chiffon blouse and pillbox hat.

Asa and Blair Daimler

June 16, 1992

Wife number seven turned out to be more than even Asa, a born manipulator, could handle. Blair Daimler wanted money, while Asa desired a glamorous young wife to show off to his wealthy friends. Asa also wanted Blair to give him another son to carry on the Buchanan legacy. Little did he know that his bride was popping birth control pills behind his back. As the marriage fell apart, Blair worked her husband into an angina attack, then withheld his heart pills. When he recovered, the cantankerous billionaire kicked Blair out of his mansion!

Asa and Alex Olanov

March 29, 1996

Asa married outrageous blond bombshell Alex Olanov not once but twice. Their 1994 Egyptian-themed nuptials (see page 85) was a wedding designed to last a lifetime. However, two years later Mr. and Mrs. Buchanan were forced to arrange a second wedding after Alex's not-so-late husband Carlo returned from the dead. Alex flew to San Domenico to obtain a quickie divorce. While Asa remained in Llanview to prepare for his wedding, Alex made love with Carlo in the Caribbean! Returning to Llanview, she tied the knot with Asa, while memories of Carlo invaded her every thought. Later, suspecting his wife's infidelity, Asa shrewdly faked insanity to get back at Alex and Carlo for their deception.

Tina Lord's Wedding Album

Tina Lord is one of soap opera's most celebrated altar addicts. Over the decades, her acute self-absorption and extreme gullibility have driven her into the arms of countless unethical opportunists who were looking for more than love. Only good-guy Cord Roberts has given Tina reason to believe in the sanctity of marriage. Still, "I do" has always served as a prelude to "adieu" for the couple, who have tied the knot no less than three times. Despite her marital failures, Tina never quit her quest to find a husband. Take a peek into her wedding album and relive her matrimonial memories.

Tina and Cord Roberts

Wedding 1

August 12, 1986

Devious Tina Lord (portrayed by actress Andrea Evans) had never met anyone as honest and moral as Cord Roberts. During the summer of 1986, they spent every waking moment together. Cord had it all—except for the one commodity that Tina truly coveted, money. Despite her feelings for Cord, Tina became engaged to marry another man, blue-blooded Richard Abbott. However, Tina's outlook changed dramatically when she discovered a secret that Cord didn't know about himself—he was Clint Buchanan's son!

Her head spinning, Tina kept Richard at bay as she contemplated her next move. Should she string both men along? Should she tie the knot with respectable Richard? Or should she marry a Buchanan who didn't know he was a Buchanan? In rapid time, Tina knew exactly what she must do. She dumped Richard—and eloped with Cord!

Eager to get her mitts on his money, Tina pushed Cord to elope. She knew that one obstacle stood in her way—Cord's mother, Maria.

Tina and Cord

Wedding 2
November 30, 1988

It's hard to picture Romeo without Juliet, Rhett without Scarlett, or Tina without Cord by her side. Despite the divorced couple's stormy history, viewers felt that Cord and Tina belonged together. On November 30, 1988, the captivating couple wrote an exciting new chapter in their lives as they solemnly renewed their vows for the second of three times. The wedding, a dual ceremony with Renee and Asa, went off without a hitch, but the reception was marred by an exploding wedding cake, designed to kill the bride by her enemy, Ursula Blackwell. Instead of Tina, an innocent victim, Steve Holden, was killed by the powerful pastry.

Tina and Cord

Wedding 3

February 13, 1991

By 1991 the institution of marriage was nothing new to Tina (now played by actress Karen Witter) and Cord. Their stormy relationship had weathered two divorces as well as a third attempt to reach the altar, which was disrupted by the mobster Johnny Dee. In the winter of 1991, life was finally going right for this passionate couple. Cord proposed to his now-pregnant bride, who gave birth to Sarah, their second child together, just one week before the wedding. Tina's friends and loved ones—Renee Buchanan, Gabrielle Medina, Julia Medina, Sheila Price, and Jessica Buchanan—wished the bride the best of luck on her third trip to the altar with Cord Roberts. For the nuptials held at the Buchanan Palace Hotel, the bride wore a cream-colored silk, off-the-shoulder wedding gown, with a long train, encrusted with lace and pink silk rosebuds.

WORDS OF LOVE
CORD PROPOSES TO TINA
FOR THE THIRD TIME

CORD

I wake up every morning, brush my teeth, do my sit-ups, and love Tina. From the moment I first saw you back in Texas. To the moment I thought I'd lost you in Argentina. To the moment you brought C. J. into my life. To the moment tonight when I saw your purple high heels missing from the shoe rack in your closet.

TINA

Thank God for those purple heels.

CORD

Some things are worth keeping, aren't they?

TINA

The precious things.

CORD

Like what we have. We're still here. Still together. Still in love.

TINA

Maybe it means no one else wants us.

CORD

*Possible. But speaking for myself here, there's no one else I want.
Tina, have you figured out by now what I'm trying to say?*

TINA

If this is a dream and I wake up, I'll kill myself.

CORD

*It's no dream, Tina. I've made my choice tonight. Now it's your turn:
Will you let me be your husband and the father of your children,
all of your children? Will you marry me, Tina?*

Tina and Max Holden

March 18, 1988

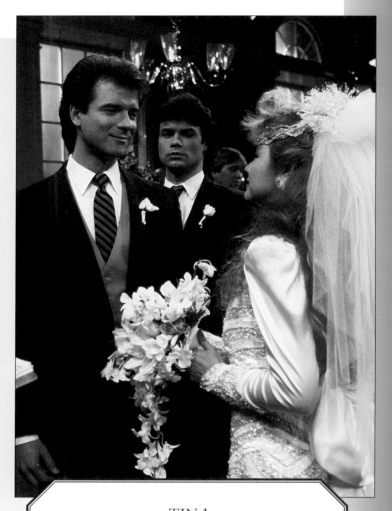

Divorced from Cord, Tina seemed especially conflicted on the day of her wedding to Max Holden. Was she doing the right thing marrying Max while having lingering feelings for her ex-husband, Cord Roberts? Tina told herself that she loved Max with all her heart, but standing at the altar, her mind began to wander back to the man who stood just inches away—Max's best man, Cord. During her vows, she slipped and spoke the wrong groom's name.

Tina and Cain Rogan

February 10, 1994

TINA
I take thee, Cord . . .
(Gasps)
Oh, what I meant, look, what I meant
to say was that I take thee Max.

MAX
No, no, Tina.

TINA
No, Max, please take my hand.
You know what I meant to say.

MAX
You said it. I heard it, we all heard it.
I can't go through with this marriage!

When Cord was presumed dead, Tina enjoyed a steamy relationship with con man Cain Rogan. The sexy pair were virtuosos when it came to finding exotic locales to make love. Among the unusual places they enjoyed themselves were a cage, an abandoned movie theater, and the back of a pickup truck.

Their 1994 wedding, a quiet ceremony held in the Lord Library at Llanfair, was tame in comparison. When they strolled down the aisle to exchange their vows, the bride and groom should have taken a more discerning look at the minister who married them. The couple departed on an extended honeymoon without ever realizing that the clergyman performing the ceremony was actually an actor hired by Cain's vengeful ex-wife, Angela Holliday!

Tina and

David Vickers

January 17, 1995

When Tina (now played by actress Krista Tesreau) returned to Llanview after having ditched Cain, she became enchanted by David Vickers, the handsome young man who shared her passion for life. However, Tina fought to break the bond because David claimed to be her brother—the heir to the Lord family fortune! Still, the attraction between David and Tina was not to be denied. David was in a bind because he knew *he*

wasn't related to Tina, but if he revealed his secret, he'd blow his cover. One night, "brother" and "sister" gave in to their passion. Afterward, David confessed that they weren't related after all and enlisted her in his scheme to "steal" the Lord millions.

Tina ran off to Las Vegas to marry David in a secret ceremony at the Love Me Tender Chapel, presided over by an Elvis impersonator! Suspicious of David's motives, Tina's ex-husband, Cord, hopped on the Buchanan jet, arriving moments too late to stop the wedding.

Photo Credits

All photos and video images are copyright © American Broadcasting Companies, Inc. Photographer credits are as follows:

	bottom: Ann Limongello	187	all: Craig Sjodin	241	Ann Limongello
133	top: Steve Fenn	188	all: Ann Limongello	242	Donna Svennevik
	bottom: Ann Limongello	189	all: Ann Limongello	243	Ann Limongello
134	top: Ann Limongello	190	Ann Limongello	244	all: Ann Limongello
	bottom: Donna Svennevik	191	Ann Limongello	245	ABC, Inc.
135	Robert Milazzo	192	Ann Limongello	246	ABC, Inc.
138	Cathy Blaivas	194	Ann Limongello	247	ABC, Inc.
139	Frank Carroll	195	Ann Limongello	248	ABC, Inc.
140	Craig Sjodin	196	Ann Limongello	249	Steve Fenn
141	Cathy Blaivas	197	Ann Limongello	250	all: Steve Fenn
142	all: Cathy Blaivas	198	Ann Limongello	251	Steve Fenn
143	Craig Sjodin	199	Ann Limongello	252	ABC, Inc.
144	ABC, Inc.	200	Ann Limongello	253	Ann Limongello
145	all: Daniel Watson	201	Erik Hein	254	Ann Limongello
146	top: Craig Sjodin	202	Erik Hein	255	Steve Fenn
	bottom: Daniel Watson	203	Jonathan Exley	257	Ann Limongello
147	Daniel Watson	204	Janet Van Ham	258	Ann Limongello
149	all: Donna Svennevik	205	Craig Sjodin	259	Kimberly Butler
150	Donna Svennevik	206	Cathy Blaivas	260	Ann Limongello
151	Ann Limongello	207	Jim Ober	261	Ann Limongello
152	Ann Limongello	208	Craig Sjodin	262	Scott Humbert
153	all: Ann Limongello	211	all: ABC, Inc.	263	Ann Limongello
154	Ann Limongello	212	ABC, Inc.	264	Ann Limongello
156	Bob D'Amico	213	all: ABC, Inc.	265	Ann Limongello
157	Craig Sjodin	214	ABC, Inc.	266	all: Ann Limongello
158	Cathy Blaivas	215	ABC, Inc.	267	Ann Limongello
159	top: Bob Long	216	ABC, Inc.	268	top: Ann Limongello
	bottom: Ann Limongello	217	ABC, Inc.		bottom: Cathy Blaivas
160	Janet Van Ham	218	Erik Hein	269	top: Robert Milazzo
161	top: Ann Limongello	219	all: Craig Sjodin		bottom: Kimberly Butler
	bottom: Robert Milazzo	221	Craig Sjodin	270	Donna Svennevik
162	Cathy Blaivas	222	Craig Sjodin	271	Ann Limongello
163	Craig Sjodin	223	Ken Schauer	272	Donna Svennevik
165	Ann Limongello	224	Craig Sjodin	274	ABC, Inc.
166	Erik Hein	225	Craig Sjodin	275	ABC, Inc.
168	Ann Limongello	226	Jim Warren	276	Erik Hein
170	Ann Limongello	228	ABC, Inc.	277	top: Erik Hein
171	Ann Limongello	229	ABC, Inc.		bottom: Bob D'Amico
174	Donna Svennevik	230	Ann Limongello	278	all: Erik Hein
175	Steve Fenn	231	Al Rosenberg	279	top: Erik Hein
176	Udo Schreiber		"Daytime TV"		bottom: Bob D'Amico
177	Frank Micelotta	232	Ann Limongello	280	all: Eric Hein
178	Craig Sjodin	233	Ann Limongello	281	center: Erik Hein
179	all: Jerry Fitzgerald	234	Ann Limongello		bottom: ABC, Inc.
180	Jerry Fitzgerald	235	Ann Limongello	282	all: Erik Hein
181	Erik Hein	236	Ann Limongello	283	Erik Hein
182	all: Erik Hein	237	Donna Svennevik	284	Craig Sjodin
183	Steve Fenn	238	Steve Fenn	286	Bob D'Amico
185	Craig Sjodin	239	Ann Limongello	288	top: Timothy White
186	all: Craig Sjodin	240	Ann Limongello		bottom: ABC, Inc.

289	all: ABC, Inc.	308	Donna Svennevik	328	Ann Limongello
290	Craig Sjodin	309	Andrew Eccles	330	Danny Feld
291	Craig Sjodin	311	top: Bob Sacha	331	all: Ann Limongello
293	Andrew Eccles		bottom: Ann Limongello	333	all: Ann Limongello
294	Steve Fenn	312	Kimberly Butler	335	Ann Limongello
295	Steve Fenn	313	all: Ann Limongello	337	Ann Limongello
297	Steve Fenn	314	Ann Limongello	338	top: Steve Fenn
298	Joe McNally	315	Jim Antonucci		bottom: Ann Limongello
300	Andrew Eccles	319	top: Cathy Blaivas	340	Don Carson
301	all: Ann Limongello		bottom: Ann Limongello	341	Ann Limongello
303	all: Ann Limongello	320	Ann Limongello	342	Cathy Blaivas
304	Ann Limongello	321	top: Cathy Blaivas	343	Cathy Blaivas
305	Ann Limongello		bottom: Ann Limongello	344	Ann Limongello
306	top: Frank Micelotta	322	all: Ann Limongello	345	all: Ann Limongello
	bottom: Ann Limongello	326	all: ABC. Inc.		
307	Ann Limongello	327	all: ABC, Inc.		

Index